MONEY
CHANGES
EVERYTHING

Also edited by Jenny Offill and Elissa Schappell

The Friend Who Got Away

MONEY
CHANGES
EVERYTHING

Twenty-two Writers Tackle the Last Taboo

with Tales of Sudden Windfalls,

Staggering Debts, and

Other Surprising Turns of Fortune

Edited by
Jenny Offill and
Elissa Schappell

DOUBLEDAY
New York London Toronto Sydney Auckland

PUBLISHED BY DOUBLEDAY

Published in the United States by Doubleday, an imprint of The
Doubleday Broadway Publishing Group, a division of Random
House, Inc., New York.
www.doubleday.com

Book design by Donna Sinisgalli

Library of Congress Cataloging-in-Publication Data
Money changes everything : twenty-two writers tackle the last
    taboo with tales of sudden windfalls, staggering debts, and other
    surprising turns of fortune / edited by Jenny Offill and Elissa
    Schappell. — 1st ed.
        p. cm.
    Includes bibliographical references.
    1. Money—United States—Fiction. 2. Money in literature.
3. Money—Psychological aspects. I. Offill, Jenny, 1968–
II. Schappell, Elissa.

PN56.M547M64 2006
810.8'03553—dc22

                                                      2006016845

ISBN-13: 978-0-385-51669-3
ISBN-10: 0-385-51669-X

PRINTED IN THE UNITED STATES OF AMERICA

10 9 8 7 6 5 4 3 2 1

First Edition

To Deb Futter, Joy Harris, and Sally Wofford-
Girand, to whom we are greatly indebted

The rule is not to talk about money with people
who have much more or much less than you.

—Katherine Whitehorn

Contents

Jenny Offill and Elissa Schappell

Americans live in a culture of confession. We talk freely about whom we've slept with, what we're addicted to, how crazy our families are, and why we take a rainbow of antidepressants. But even in this tell-all age, there is one topic that remains decidedly taboo.

Ask a friend how she spends her time in the bedroom and chances are you'll get a breezy answer about tantric games or the perils of certain sex toys; ask her how she spends her money and you're likely to be met with an awkward silence. It's one thing to confide your latest romantic disaster or family drama to a friend, quite another to let her see your disgraceful credit report. In fact, 47 percent of Americans say they'd rather disclose their weight or age than the amount of money in their bank account.

It's no surprise. Who wants to talk about a spouse who blows the family nest egg on the ponies or a divorce settlement that has you digging in the couch for the kids' lunch money? Who wants to confess that they hide their credit card bills or that they're crying poor even though they never need to work another day in their life? Who wants to come clean about the fact that money has made them do things they're ashamed of?

Such money stories are hard to tell because they feel incredibly revealing. To shine a light on how much we make, how much we spend, how much we owe, and how much we've got secretly socked away is to give others a potent glimpse into the values we live by. Because of this, admitting to money troubles can often feel like admitting to a weakness of character. To find yourself broke is to face an ever-widening spiral of self-recrimination. If only I hadn't bought that leather coat or taken that vacation, you think. If only I'd worked harder, or planned better ... If only I wasn't so careless, so lazy, so weak ...

We may know logically that our checking account balance is not a true indicator of our worth, but an ATM receipt that deems us "insufficient" can still register like a character judgment. Given the emotional stakes, it's no wonder most of us clam up when it comes to discussing money woes. It can be humbling to admit that such an important part of life has slipped out of our control.

This desire to seem prosperous even when one is barely getting by leads many Americans to completely ignore the reality of their financial situations. Instead, we try to live up to the "champagne and caviar" celebrity culture that is endlessly touted on television and in magazines, leasing fancy cars and jetting off on lavish vacations. And since we live in the land of mega-malls, no-money-down credit, and twenty-four-hour ATMs, it's easier than ever to get in over our heads.

Economists report that middle-class families are now carrying record levels of credit card debt, going without health insurance, and filing for bankruptcy at several times the rate of the early 1980s.

Turns out those McMansions and shiny SUVs have us mortgaged up to our eyeballs, but until the wolf is truly at the door, you won't find many of us admitting it.

Some of us are quietly shaking in our boots, though. Debt is a legacy that gets passed down through families, and even those of us who aren't in the red yet worry that we may inherit our parents' pathologies about money. Jonathan Dee describes how incurring a huge debt he thought would break up his relationship cast him back to the final days of his parents' crumbling marriage. "The real agent of decay in our lives was always, and unmistakably, money. It did the one thing it knew how to do—it ran out—and with it, gradually, went our ability to stand being around one another."

Money frays the family ties of the rich, too, especially when each subsequent generation finds there's a little less of it. The shame of having to admit to newly straitened circumstances can be unbearable for families such as Ruth Konigsberg's who continue to play at being rich long after the money is gone. It takes the shock of having to auction off the family's antiques at Sotheby's to finally bring home to her how far they have fallen.

Conversely, in this topsy-turvy world, deceit about money can take the form of those with money passing for poor, pretending to be worse off than they really are. For the slumming artist who brags about his fifth-floor walk-up and ramen noodle dinners, the fear of being "outed" can be just as strong as it is for those whose finances truly are a mess.

Some attempt to mask their solvency in order not to seem like a dilettante or a trust fund baby. Claire Dederer, whose grandfather built her family's fortune on fur, kept the "stash" her generous father gave her a secret (until now). Here, she writes of struggling with warring feelings of entitlement to the money and resentment about the sense of "inauthenticity" it provokes. What does it mean, she wonders, when "your financial worth is unmoored from your actual achievement"?

In our closemouthed society, there are a few exceptions to this "don't ask, don't tell" approach. It is still de rigueur for artistic types to wear their poverty like a badge of pride or to one-up each other with tales of the outlandish jobs they've done for money. In "Dirty Work," Lydia Millet tells how she left her feminist ideals at the door and took a job editing smut at *Hustler* magazine just out of college. And Brett Martin exposes himself as the least successful drug dealer Northampton, Massachusetts, has ever seen.

Yet in some ways, the biggest surprise when it comes to Americans' reticence about money is that we don't even share our tales of good fortune with one another. This may be because our gain is often another's loss. In the case of the humorist Henry Alford, the gain was scooping up an incredible bit of Manhattan real estate for a song, the loss, well, here's the first line of the essay: "I've never killed anyone before. But I once felt like I had."

Even money stories that involve windfalls or sudden boons tend to be kept secret out of guilt or fear that others will be envious of us. Marian Fontana, who lost her firefighter husband on 9/11, writes movingly of the difficulties of dealing with an unwanted windfall that comes from tragedy. Chris Offutt explores the uneasiness he felt when his family unexpectedly became one of the richest in a dirt-poor Appalachian town, and Daniel Handler, who made some serious coin as Lemony Snicket writing a series of novels for children titled A Series of Unfortunate Events, describes how he used the money from writing his essay for this volume to buy a $1,200 bottle of wine, and the effect this grand gesture had on his less well-off friends.

The truth is that money is often a divisive influence in our lives. We keep our bank balances secret because we worry that being candid about our finances will expose us to judgment or ridicule—or worse, to accusations of greed or immorality. And this worry is not unfounded. At times, money serves as a cruel mirror, casting a surprising and unflattering reflection back at us, a picture of someone we never thought we were, or of someone we hoped never to be. No one wants to admit to fighting a relative tooth and nail over an inheritance, especially when, as Meera Nair recalls all too well, the effects of pitting family members against one another create rifts that never heal and leave everyone poorer in spirit.

"For richer or poorer" is the standard wedding vow, but for many couples money becomes a source of constant tension. Indeed, in America, more marriages break up over finances than over any other issue. Sometimes a marriage, especially a coltish, wobbly-legged one, can't bear the pressure money puts on it, as Walter Kirn acknowledges in "Treasure Me." From his Mormon adolescence, to dealing with gold-digging hussies and a haughty former girlfriend, to marrying and divorcing a much younger woman, Kirn tallies up just how much it costs to have sex.

It should come as no surprise that having children only adds a final straw to the overworked, underpaid camel's back. The way spouses view money and the security it can buy a family can be grounds for fierce battles, as Fred Leebron and his wife, Kathryn Rhett, reveal in their paired essays.

Even unmarried couples sometimes find that money can make or break them. For the heiress Isabel Rose, the dance of courtship often stumbles because men who don't have as much money as she does grumble about being "kept," and men who do act petulant if they think their lavish gifts don't impress her.

Rose is proud of her storied background and unapologetic about her wealth, but for more neurotic rich folk an entire cottage industry has sprung up to help them get over their good fortune. Shrinks have coined the term "affluenza" to describe the angst and aimlessness that arise from being so wealthy you don't have to work for a living. And amazingly, even being filthy rich doesn't seem to give people a true sense of freedom and security. *Barron's* magazine recently reported that the majority of wealthy Americans think they would need to be worth exactly twice as much as they already are in order to feel truly content with their situation. As Andy Behrman, an entrepreneur who has made and lost millions over the years during manic earning and spending sprees, writes, "I remember thinking that if I ever accumulated $50 million in the bank, I could die happily with no material possessions."

No wonder the market for shrinks who specialize in the problems of the very rich is booming. Yet despite their insistence that affluenza can be a genuine hardship, therapists are finding it a hard sell to make others feel sorry for their clients. Most people can sympathize with the pain and struggle of the less fortunate, but the anxieties that attend being "too rich" are much harder to imagine.

We like to complain about rich people driving up real estate prices and tooling around in ostentatious automobiles (Who needs a Humvee in Philadelphia?), but very few of us are really willing to listen to them explain the difficulties of their situation. And so this culture of silence cuts both ways, not only toward those who are one paycheck from being kicked to the curb but also toward those who gaze down at them from their swank penthouses.

But why, in this day and age, does such secrecy still surround the issue of money? Once sensitive topics such as race and sexual orientation are now casually debated on talk shows and campuses, but an honest discussion about how money or the lack thereof informs people's lives is still the exception.

Perhaps this is because America's bedrock mythology is that it is the land of opportunity, a place where all people, no matter the color of their skin, or their gender, or how lowly born they are, can succeed if only they work hard enough. Call it the Great American Pipe Dream. And yet race and class do matter, as Steven Rinehart makes clear in his essay about a convenience store robbery he pulled when he was in his teens. The cost of such a crime for a middle-class white boy like himself turns out to be quite different from the price his African-American cell mate has to pay.

For the radical activist lawyer Tony Serra, it was just these sorts of inequities in the criminal justice system that led him to take an informal vow of poverty in order to allow himself the freedom to take mostly pro bono cases. He has since defended groups such as the Black Panthers, the Symbionese Liberation Army, and Earth First! and continues to fight passionately for the rights of the disenfranchised.

It is a rare person who can ignore the siren call of consumer culture as Tony Serra has. But for the rest of us mere mortals, is there any way to become less enslaved by money and our ideas about it? Part of the answer may be to take another look at that bedrock American mythology. As a culture, we have been sold the idea that we live in a meritocracy, free from the hidebound class conventions of the Old World. In America, only the self-made man or woman represents the vaunted ideal. Anyone else is suspect, either too lazy to be successful or too privileged to identify with.

But very few of us fall into that narrow faultless category of those who have more than enough money but earned every penny of it, damn it. Instead, most of us are either too poor or too rich to approach the topic of money without shame or guilt, and it is these uncomfortable emotions that keep us from openly discussing the powerful ways that it shapes our lives. We are grateful to have found twenty-two talented writers willing to buck this trend of silence. Some of their stories are harrowing, some moving, others comic, but all attest to the truth of the title: money changes everything.

MONEY
CHANGES
EVERYTHING

The Guy Next Door

Henry Alford

I've never killed anyone before. But I once felt like I had. This man and I did not, at first blush, have much in common. I was a pot-smoking, Joni Mitchell–listening thirty-one-year-old gay man; he was a profane, eighty-year-old former longshoreman named John Maguire whose nickname was Mugsy. In the two years that I'd been living in the apartment contiguous to his, we'd never shared more words than the occasional grunt-based hello in the hallway.

And then I made the phone call that changed both our lives.

"Mr. Maguire?"

"Yeah." His voice was brusque and Bronxy.

"It's Henry Alford. I live across the hall in 4E?"

"Uh-huh."

"Do you know about the auction being held on Friday? For the three apartments in the building, including yours?"

"No. I'm not a member of the co-op board, so they don't tell me anything."

"Your landlord, Mr. Z——, is about $13,000 in arrears," I explained. "So the co-op board is holding a public auction of his three apartments on Friday. You and the other tenants have what are known as statutory rights, so you can't be kicked out and the rent can't be raised no matter who owns the apartments."

"I know all about it. I've been down to the attorney general's office."

"Good, so you know your rights," I said, a small amount of relief helping to bolster my mounting anxiety about my next statement. "Well, anyway, I'm thinking about, uh, making a bid on your apartment."

As soon as the words came out of my mouth, I wanted to soften or reshape them. It was no secret that John had had two heart attacks. I added, "As a, as a—as a sort of long-term investment, of course."

"You can do what you want."

"Great. But I've never been in your apartment, and I wonder if I could look at it sometime." The evening before, I'd walked out on our mutual fire escape and tried to peek in through his windows, to no avail.

"Okay," he said.

"Well, I was wondering if I could look at it, say, right now."

"Let me put my pants on," he said, and hung up the phone.

About ninety seconds later, I heard John open his door and then knock softly on mine—an act that requires merely leaning forward, as the two doors are thirty-five inches apart. I greeted him and shut the door behind me. A wiry and fastidious man, John projected equal amounts of boyishness and scowling, a sour angel. I stood stone-still in his doorway, cowed. Although in the weeks previous the prospect of inexpensively doubling the size of my apartment had filled me with a sensation that I can only describe as tingly, that tingle now fled me. No, this was not the wonderfully grabby, slightly narcissistic feeling that looking at real estate usu ally engenders—the one where empty rooms symbolize solutions to your problems, the one where hobbies get their own dedicated spaces and children get their own bedrooms and novels gush from printers like lobsters from an aquarium during a Mob hit. This was much more like an IRS audit.

"Come on," John said, waving me into the living room.

We grimly and quickly toured the premises. His apartment, I could see, was almost identical to mine. We both had six hundred railroad-style square feet overlooking a lovely, tree-shaded street in Greenwich Village; each was worth about $130,000, a price that would have been higher were the apartments not fourth-floor walk-ups. John's place was immaculate. It had a sweet, slightly soapy smell.

"I'm surprised it took the co-op board so long to catch on to Mr. Z———," John said when we'd returned to the kitchen. "He's no good and he'll never be good! He has the building next door, too. You ever been in there? It's a dump!"

"I've never been in there."

"It's a dump!"

I thanked John for the tour and left.

Two days later, I realized I'd forgotten to ask him an important question, so I called again. I asked him how he was doing, and he said, "Alrighty."

"Uh, some of the people who are bidding on your apartment are wondering what you're paying for rent," I said. "Would you be uncomfortable . . ."

"It's $81.23."

"Eighty-one twenty-three a month?" I asked, surprised it was this low. The maintenance on the apartment was $332 a month, so a rent of $81.23 meant that whoever bought the apartment would be $250.77 out of pocket a month.

"That's right. Anybody buying this is gonna get stuck."

"Right," I said, laughing nervously. "How long have you been living there?"

"Fifty years."

"Wow. You're a . . ."

"I'm a fixture. I'm a goddamn fixture."

I needed to figure out how much to wager at the auction, so that night I sat down and did the actuarial work. Two hundred and fifty dollars and seventy-seven cents a month was about $3,000 a year. So if John lived another five years, I'd be spending $15,000. If he lived ten years, I'd be spending $30,000. If he lived twenty years, I'd be spending $60,000.

I decided twenty years was a good, conservative figure to work with; after all, it wasn't as if John were some female goatherd in the Urals subsisting on a diet of yogurt. Subtracting $60,000 from the apartment's $130,000 value left me with $70,000. Then I subtracted another $25,000 for cost-of-living increases and the hassle of being your next door neighbor's landlord. That left $45,000. That was my ceiling for bidding.

The auction took place a few days later. The setup was much

more casual than I'd imagined: a spindly, middle-aged auctioneer stood at a card table he'd set up under the rotunda of the Supreme Court of the State of New York; four of us bidders and our companions huddled round, clutching our checkbooks. Office workers and other passersby drifted past us, unmindful of the tiny acts of manifest destiny taking place just feet away.

Each of the three apartments underwent a short volley of bidding. Because the apartments were being sold with rights-bearing tenants in them, and because there was no formal process by which potential buyers not living in the building could meet or learn the age and medical status of these tenants, the auction attracted only one outside speculator. In the end, all three apartments were bought by people already living in the building.

I felt like I was taking part in insider trading—a dark, sweet, criminal feeling made only more so when I got the apartment for $17,000.

When I saw John in the hallway the next day, I told him that I'd bought his apartment. His face betrayed no reaction. We agreed that he would slip his rent check under my door the first of each month. John explained that Mr. Z—— had four of his rent checks that he hadn't cashed. John said, "Oh, he's no good. He's a louse." The part of my brain that I had been labeling "I Am a Yuppie Interloper" was slightly relieved by this statement; I knew I'd be a better landlord than Mr. Z——.

But the following day as I was leaving the building, I ran into a fellow resident I'll call Tina. Tina said she'd heard about the auction, and was glad that Teresa in 2E and I had been able to buy our own apartments, but was dismayed that Jere in 1E had bought Mrs.

Englehardt's apartment, because now Jere—a building developer by trade—would be waiting for the frail, ninety-something Mrs. Englehardt "to drop dead."

I corrected Tina, telling her that I had not bought my own apartment—I'd bought John's. She laughed nervously.

Eager to undercut the awkwardness, I started rambling, telling Tina that I didn't know much about John and asking her if he'd ever been married. She said he hadn't. She said the only family she was aware of was a brother who lived in the city.

Later that night, I ran into Tina again, this time in the vestibule of the building. She was picking up a brass doorknob that had fallen off the inside door. "If we get new brass knobs, I'm gonna keep the old ones and hit Jere over the head with them," she told me, referring to the man who was waiting for the old woman to drop dead. "I'm not kidding: he better watch it."

I wondered if I should, too.

But to my friends, the fact that I'd bought an apartment that housed a man who'd had two heart attacks was the stuff of comedy. More than once did I hear the line "Getting enough heavy cream in your coffee, Mugsy?"

My early days of landlordship were marked by a certain suspensefulness. One afternoon about a month after the auction, I heard a beeping sound in the hallway; the battery of our floor's smoke alarm was dying. Not having the right size to replace it with, I decided simply to take the smoke detector down, bring it into my apartment, and remove the dying battery.

When I awoke the next morning and saw the smoke detector on my kitchen table, I got a chill. What if John had died in the night and the cops had found the smoke detector in my apartment? That wouldn't have looked too good for me.

But the biggest change that resulted from buying John's apartment was that I became much more conscious of the fact that if the space between our doors was only thirty-five inches, the walls between us weren't even five inches. I heard John through these walls far more frequently than I had in the past. Usually these sounds were unidentifiable bumps or scrapes, but sometimes they were John muttering or yelling to himself. I knew that John liked a drop of whiskey from time to time, and sometimes in the evening, presumably after some liquid refreshment, he would sing softly. One muffled ditty I heard repeatedly sounded like:

Someone runner sleef Angola.
Doctor leaving town his molar.
She was gentle from I lingered.
Now he is a big brown cow.

More mindful now of John's existence, I suddenly realized that, like me, he almost never had anyone to his apartment. His one friend was a lady named Loretta, who, accompanied by her yippy little shih tzu, would sidle up to the intercom at our building's entrance, buzz John, and then broadcast screamingly loud conversations with him.

"John!" I heard her yell one afternoon. "I have some meat for you!"

"What?!"

"MEAT!"

"Okay."

"Come and get it. I'm not coming up."

"For what?"

"The meat! I have meat!"

I could sense that there was a lot of love in this relationship, but I could also sense that this love had congealed or hardened over the years, perhaps as a result of a misunderstanding or a too-long car trip.

The chief noise by which John and I could detect each other's presence was the opening and closing of our front doors. If I was getting ready to go outside and suddenly heard John's door open, I would sometimes wait thirty seconds so I wouldn't have to talk to him in the hallway; this landlord figured that the more relaxed my tenant felt around me, the more he might start lodging complaints about his heating or plumbing.

But actually John had very few gripes at the beginning, and our encounters in the hallway were mostly charmed. One day, trailing him down the stairs by a floor, I saw him suddenly reverse direction and come back up the stairs. Just as he passed me, he smiled tightly and said, "Forgot my teeth."

We weren't sure, though, whether to acknowledge each other when we passed on the street. The first three or four times, we betrayed no recognition of each other. Then, one balmy August afternoon, I saw him—turned out in his usual plaid pants, porkpie hat, and cardigan sweater, with a rolled-up *New York Post* under his arm—walking Loretta's dog down West Fourth Street. Sensing an easy opportunity for conversation, I walked over to them. Beholding the dog's pink barrette and rhinestone-studded collar, I asked John what her name was. He looked down at the sidewalk in embarrassment and told me: "Muffin."

———

About five months after the auction, water from the apartment above John's started dripping through his bathroom ceiling. John was incensed. He knocked on my door one afternoon and hustled me over to his apartment to show me how the rust-colored water was oozing into his bathroom lighting fixture; in showing it to me, he called Roberta, the woman upstairs, "that bitch" four times.

"Thirty-seven years I'm living here, and nothing like this ever happened to me!" he said. I realized then that when he'd told me before that he'd been living in the building for fifty years, he'd probably been trying to scare me off. I called Roberta, who promised to fix the leak. All seemed well until the following week, when it started again and John called her at 4:00 a.m. and yelled at her.

"John, you should probably let me handle those kinds of calls," I told him.

"I can talk for myself!"

"Right. But calling at 4:00 a.m.?"

"That bitch is gonna electrocute me!"

I apologized to him and promised to get a handyman in; John thanked me.

Time passed. John's next problem was a much less troublesome one concerning his bathtub, whose handles leaked water. This time, softly knocking on my door with a knock that was as much a scratch as a knock, he asked me to come over and take a look. I went. As I stood in his tiny kitchen, John smiled and reached for my right hand; holding it, he guided me into the bathroom. I watched, my hand still in his, as he turned on the water and showed me how it burbled through the handles.

There was absolutely nothing sexual about the way John touched me, and yet I was surprised he'd do it because I was fairly certain that he knew I was gay. No, the hand-holding felt avuncular. And, somehow, like something more, too. I imagined that John knew how few people there were in my life, so maybe the hand-holding was like a concentrated dose of friendliness, a kind of bodily hello meant to rebuff our mutual isolation. That we hadn't exactly paved the way to this moment didn't seem to matter. Sometimes you reach into the dark and hold the hand you find there.

I noticed something with the bathtub leak, as well as with a subsequent leak from the kitchen sink: I actually enjoyed dealing with these problems on John's behalf. It had started when I followed him up the four flights of stairs one day. John, out of breath, stopped and told me to pass him. "These stairs are getting to be too much for me," he said. Uncertain how to react to the rawness of this confession, I wondered if John was hinting that he'd like me to try to buy him out of his apartment. But then remembering that he'd once told me, "I'm not going anywhere," I rejected this idea. "Yeah, they're getting to me, too," I said.

Seconds later I entered my apartment feeling like an asshole for having been so glib; the man, after all, had had two heart attacks. The only antidote, I quickly decided, was to take action. I called a plumber to look at John's kitchen sink leak, as I had promised to do three days earlier.

I needed to make a cake for a friend's birthday that day, so while I waited for the plumber to come, I pulled out some supplies and started baking. Just as I began whipping some eggs, it occurred to me that having the power—and, yes, perhaps the money—to bring a plumber-shaped ray of sunshine into John's life felt really good. Maybe I didn't HAVE to be an evil yuppie who relished the sight of his neighbor's deterioration, abetting it by letting the leak from a kitchen sink turn into a juggernaut of Chinese water torture. I could be something else—a take-charge relief worker; Mother Hale with a whisk.

John's problems got worse. The apartment directly below his had housed Mrs. Englehardt, the ninety-something woman who'd now moved to a nursing home after Jere bought her place. Mrs. Englehardt had been the building's other longtime resident; that her and John's situations were parallel was only underscored by the fact that they lived on top of each other. Shortly after her departure, the new owner started renovating the apartment. This was the loudest and most disruptive renovation I'd ever witnessed; daily we heard floorboards being crunched by a machine that I imagined as a cross between a chipper and an angry pachyderm. The sound was earsplitting. It was all too easy, as this crunching went on, to imagine the scenario; you got the sense that the hideous cruncher-beast had ejected, or devoured, the old woman down below and was now busily devouring her apartment. Soon the beast would eat its way through John's floor and devour his apartment, too.

One day, when the whole building was shaking with vibrations, John knocked frantically on my door. His face looked drained of all blood. He brought me over to his place and showed me large cracks that had been formed in his kitchen walls by the renovation. "This apartment, when I move out of it, it's gonna be a shithouse!" he gasped.

I went downstairs and talked to the construction crew, telling them that they'd put large cracks in John's walls; they apologized and said they'd come take a look in about an hour. I relayed this information to John, who looked unmoved. I promised to have any damages repaired as soon as the renovation was finished. I wasn't sure what else I could do for him, though. I couldn't stop the renovation, as much as I would have liked to, and I probably couldn't make the workers proceed with any more gentleness or care.

Over a period of days, this powerlessness made me slightly crazy and was leavened only when I formed the quasi-Christian opinion that I should "do unto John" as I would have him do unto me. After all, I told myself, he's you in fifty years.

This mind shift helped. But the renovation continued to body forth horrors. One day, walking upstairs, I noticed that the hallway rug, from the renovated apartment all the way to the building's front door, was grayed with the chalky residue of pulverized plaster. My mind flashed on the final line of a Joan Aiken short story, a chilling line of dialogue that runs, simply, "Bone manure."

"Henry! Henry!"

John was knocking on my door one morning at nine. Two dust-covered workers from downstairs were in his apartment, wanting to cut the floor near John's stove. He didn't want them to do it. I asked them why they needed to; they explained they were leveling the walls of the downstairs apartment.

"It's your apartment," John said to me, eyeing the two workers as one might human-shaped turds. "I live here, but I'm not gonna forever."

I allowed as how I didn't know whether or not cutting the floor was actually necessary. John huffed, "They're cutting up my floor!"

I got bossy with the workers and tried to impress upon them the daily trauma they were causing John. They said they'd talk to their boss and disappeared downstairs. John said to me, "Thank you, brother."

Then I told him that if the workers' boss said they needed to cut the floor, John should let them. He started yelling angrily, wondering why the brunt of the renovation was falling on him. I tried to offer succor. "I'm eighty-one years old," he told me. "I'm not going to live here forever!"

"Why not?" I shot back. "I hope you do. It's a good deal for you. I hope you stay for a long time."

"Well, if I win the lottery, then I'm outta here!"

"What are your chances of winning the lottery?"

"I'm only here because the rent is so cheap."

I told him I was sorry about the noise and damages, but that if he'd bear up for just another week or two, the workers would be finished, and then I'd get them to fix John's cracks and other problems.

"I don't give a shit," he said. "I won't be here long."

In the months after the renovation, our hellos in the hallway were far more resonant and prone to sympathy, like those of neighboring farmers after a devastating winter. We swapped the occasional story from the tabloids that had amused us. We called the four-flight climb "Everest" and agreed that it should be oxygen assisted. We shared bewilderment about recycling.

One morning I awoke to some bumping sounds coming from John's apartment. I stood up, and then I heard voices coming from his place, too. Opening my front door, I saw a big sash of yellow police tape stretched across his doorway, and then an EMT guy stepped out into the hall. John had passed away in the night.

I didn't go to his funeral. I wanted to pay my respects, but every time I thought about John's relatives asking me who I was and my saying, "I lived next door to him," it was all too easy to imagine their slightly horrified response.

At a certain age, staying alive is mostly a question of your will to live. And hadn't I, in buying John's apartment and then hovering over it from only three feet away for two years, eroded that will? Hadn't I created a situation in which John and I both knew—despite my protestations—that my life would be better as soon as he died? I wished, in retrospect, that I had ridden herd on the renovation downstairs, or that, during it, I'd badgered John into staying in a hotel for a month at my expense.

I also felt negligent in not being the person to find John dead. Loretta had tried buzzing him that morning and, getting no response, had alerted his brother, who came over and found him. Why hadn't it been me? I was inches away.

Concurrent with John's last days, I'd published a comic essay about the manner in which I wanted to die—how I wanted to leave behind a highly complicated will so as to induce the greatest amount of grievous busywork and intercontinental faxing. The essay was all joke, a mountain of joke, and yet beneath the har-har-har, I can now see, was my subconscious dread and anxiety about John's imminent demise. When it finally happened, it hit me in the face. The guilt was one thing. But there was something else, too. When you see the man next to you die alone, you can't help but experience a touch of there-but-for-the-grace-of-God-go-I.

Though I've had several long-term couplings in my adult life, including one that lasted ten years, I've never lived with anyone. If I go down alone, it's not like I wasn't warned.

My sadness sapped me of resolve and kept me from taking possession of John's apartment for almost three months after it became available to me.

When I finally did join the two apartments—I removed a shared, sealed closet door—I spent a slightly eerie afternoon paw-ing through the few items and knickknacks that John's brother had left behind. There was a tiny pile of old Lotto tickets. A calendar with days marked for when John should take his heart medication. A bottle of Winnie-the-Pooh bubble bath. In his closet, I found a black cardigan sweater. Sometimes I wear it.

Nouveau Poor

Ruth Konigsberg

Sotheby's is no place to be on a hot July afternoon. I have lied to my boss about having a doctor's appointment and ridden an emphysemic bus up First Avenue to get here, and I'm sweating through my clothes. Sitting in the back of a windowless auction room, I fan myself with a paper paddle. I'm not here to buy; I'm here to sell. Across the aisle from me, I take particular note of a man wearing Bermudas and a golf shirt with a visor on his head. I guess I'd thought Sotheby's was like the Vatican: no shorts allowed.

I am twenty-six years old and my family is broke. Angry-creditors-calling-the-house broke. Auction-off-the-heirlooms broke. Not only are we in debt, but neither my mother nor my father has any retirement savings, or, for that matter, any income to speak of. Six years earlier, upon their divorce, my father decamped from our apartment on the Upper East Side to the $600-a-month top floor of a two-family house in a working-class section of Norwalk, Connecticut. The only possessions he took were those that could fit into a rental car. He was a city planner, a former Fulbright scholar, with undergraduate and master's degrees from an Ivy League college, but he had been laid off during the recession in the 1970s and was unemployed for most of my childhood. In order to pay for our private school tuitions, both of my parents gradually sold off the investments they had inherited. Even though my father had no office to go to, he would leave our apartment every morning anyway. Occasionally, a classmate or teacher would mention having seen him wandering the neighborhood, and I'd say that I didn't know what he did for a living; perhaps he was in the CIA—a little fantasy that my brothers and I had cooked up one day.

When I was twenty, my mother asked my father for a separation, leaving her alone in an apartment that she couldn't afford to keep but didn't want to sell. She had grown up in a duplex in Manhattan and was a singer who'd gone to a Seven Sisters college and then had become a chorus soprano with a light opera company before she stopped to raise three kids. In the absence of real financial stability, the apartment became her mental safety net. "Where would I go?" she asked when I suggested she sell. Later I would decide, with a certain amount of bitterness, that this tendency to become paralyzed by financial downturns was a family trait, the result of thinking that money would always be around when you needed it, because it had always been around.

The divorce was a long time coming, and although it was probably for the best, it also led to some transactions that, in retrospect, were more than a little imprudent. By this point, any family money that my father had was gone. As per the agreement drawn up by the lawyers, my mother had to buy out my father's half of the apartment, which she was able to do only by completely emp-

tying her bank account and then obtaining a loan from my grandmother. I was in college at the time, at the University of Pennsyl-
vania, and suddenly found myself having to apply for student loans
and work-study jobs. The summer my father left, my mother helped
me fill out the financial aid forms, blaming our lateness in apply-
ing on the sudden changes brought on by the divorce. That fall, I
headed back to school with a new awareness of the capriciousness
of wealth and an ever-growing anxiety about money.

The sale begins, and I follow along in my auction catalog.
I don't have much affection for the things we are selling—in fact,
part of me is glad never to see them again. I've taken the Sotheby's
appraiser at her word that they should bring in at least $50,000.

A PAIR OF PORTUGUESE ROCOCO BEECH WOOD ARMCHAIRS, mid-
eighteenth century, $2,000–$3,000.

The first lot. For all the time that these chairs sat in the front
hallway of our apartment, I don't recall anyone ever sitting on them.
They belonged to my grandmother's parents, who had gotten married in 1908 and purchased them while on an extended, around-
the-world honeymoon that lasted five years. The wood is so old that
it's infested with tiny, three-hundred-year-old wormholes. I try not
to read too much into this.

I was out of college and living at home while looking for a job
when I discovered that my mother, like many women following a
divorce, had gotten into some considerable debt—not, mind you, by
spending extravagantly, but in order to cover her basic living expenses. Her only asset was the apartment, a prewar "classic seven":
three bedrooms, dining room, living room, kitchen, and maid's
room. Today, I'm guessing that the apartment would fetch somewhere in the neighborhood of $2 million, but that moment in the

history of New York City's real estate—the early 1990s—happened to be a terrible time to sell. The market had recently crashed, leaving my mother a prisoner of her co-op. So my two brothers, both of whom were in law school, and I accompanied my mother down to the Fourteenth Street offices of Budget and Credit Counseling Services (I'd found them through the Yellow Pages), where they recommended we get a home equity loan to pay off the debt. As we hurried out, I spotted standing on the floor of the waiting room a large Lucite box of cut-up credit cards with an open slot at the top, like the containers of used buttons near the exit of the Metropolitan Museum of Art. Back on the street, heading for the subway, we ran into a young man who lived on my hall my freshman year in college. I remember feeling intensely ashamed and also protective of my mother, as if we'd been caught checking her into a rehab center.

It was only several years later, after falling in love and remarrying, that my mother finally put the apartment on the market. After a couple of price reductions, she got an offer for $625,000. Before the sale officially concluded, she gave one of my brothers the power of attorney. Then she flew to Europe with her new husband and left us to handle her affairs. I was both relieved that things were finally being resolved and annoyed at the way that she'd sidestepped the messy details.

That's when I discovered, while picking up her mail one day, that she had incurred even more debt. Among the bills: anesthesiologist and surgeon fees for putting a metal pin in her elbow after she fell and broke it while jogging. (Her health insurance plan, the cheapest one offered by Blue Cross, only covered the cost of the hospital stay itself.) The first time my mother got into debt, I had felt scared—for her future, and for mine. But this time I was incensed, for by that point I'd become a compulsively frugal young adult who split the $945 rent on an East Village walk-up with my boyfriend, rode a bike to work to save on the subway fare, and bought my lingerie at a place called National Wholesale Liquidators on lower Broadway. If I was able to learn how to live within my means, why couldn't she? My mother faxed me from Europe to explain that incurring more debt was a necessary investment in her relationship with her new husband, and in a way she was right—they are still happily married. Besides, I figured, we still had the furniture and rugs, which should help cover this latest setback.

The Portuguese beech wood armchairs go for $2,000, and I feel somewhat reassured.

A CLASSICAL CARVED MAHOGANY GAMES TABLE, circa 1825, probably Philadelphia, $2,000–$3,000.

Now things are starting to slip. The table only gets $1,300. Suddenly I feel proprietary about the stuff and whip my head around to see who the buyer is, thinking to myself, It had better not be the fat man in the visor, when I should actually be grateful that the man in the visor is here at all. I don't expect much sympathy for lamenting What Was Lost. Like Miss Havisham in her tattered yellowed wedding gown, the downwardly mobile are often both arrogant and delusional, an unwinning combination.

Briefly, then: My great-great-great-grandfather on my mother's side was William Wilson Corcoran, the son of an Irish immigrant who started a bank called Corcoran and Riggs in Washington, D.C., which, among other things, became the main depository for the U.S. government and financed the invention of the telegraph by Samuel Morse. In 1848, W. W. Corcoran floated $16 million in U.S. bonds to fund the Mexican War, a risky move that brought him great profit. "For the better part of a decade between the 1840s and

1850s, he was the chief intermediary between Wall Street and Washington," a historian named Henry Cohen wrote in his book *Business and Politics in America from the Age of Jackson to the Civil War*. In 1869, W. W. founded, built, and endowed the Corcoran Gallery of Art for the purpose of "encouraging American genius"— and to house his personal art collection. (This is the same museum that drew the ire of the art world when it canceled an NEA-sponsored Robert Mapplethorpe exhibition in 1989 under pressure from Senator Jesse Helms.) Corcoran's wealth wasn't near the magnitude of John D. Rockefeller's or Andrew Carnegie's, but his descendants lived very well.

That is, until my parents.

My mother and father both chose their professions based on their passions, but they would be the last generation in my family to have that luxury. They met at a cocktail party and quickly discovered that they had similar backgrounds. When my mother told my father that she had to leave the party early because she had opera tickets, he announced that he would join her. At the time of their marriage in 1961, I don't think either of them gave a thought to money. It's not that they were particularly extravagant or fanciful. In fact, they were rather selfless, preferring to spend whatever they did have on their children's education rather than on themselves. It was just that both seemed to have a profound disinterest in understanding where money came from. By the time my brothers and I realized that we would have to teach them that lesson, it was too late.

AN ITALIAN NEOCLASSICAL WALNUT INLAID PETITE COMMODE, $1,200–$1,800.

Another lot from my great-grandparents George and Rosamund Corcoran, who indulged their taste for Italian furniture while living

in a palazzo on the Grand Canal in Venice. George was W. W. Corcoran's grandson. His parents had both died when he was young, leaving him to be raised by his wealthy grandfather. The orphan George
wanted to be a doctor, but for some reason W. W. Corcoran frowned
on the idea, so he developed a passion for polo and speculating in the
stock market. When W. W. died in 1888, George, at twenty-four, was
his oldest direct male descendant and his primary heir. Later, after
he'd gotten married and had two children, George abided by his
grandfather's wishes and legally changed his entire family's name
from Eustis to Corcoran, which was otherwise in danger of becoming extinct.

And so, at the age of six, my grandmother, born Lucinda Mor-
gan Corcoran Eustis, became Lucinda Eustis Corcoran. In 1929, the
newly named Corcorans moved in to 1001 Park Avenue, a brand-new
building on the corner of Eighty-fourth Street in New York City.
George and Rosamund had purchased the apartment, which occu-
pied the entire fourth floor, from blueprints: five bedrooms, three
maid's rooms, dining room, living room, library, foyer, pantry, and
kitchen. George had also just bought a house in Lawrence, Long
Island, with money he'd made from the stock of a company called
Owens Bottle. He called the place Bottle Cottage, but it quickly
became known as Cottle Bottage.

That fall, my grandmother started ninth grade. In October,
the stock market crashed. George, who had been trading the Corcoran fortune on margin, was wiped out. Luckily, Rosamund had
some inherited money of her own and was able to keep the family
afloat, but George, once the swashbuckling bon vivant, was demor-
alized and sank into a depression. His only respite was to take my
grandmother and her friends to the Bronx Zoo, where, he said, the
animals made him feel better.

I have no way of knowing, had the Crash not happened, whether any of that money might eventually have found its way to me. Certainly other wealthy families were able to rebound from the Depression. But lacking an income-producing business, or even a profession to fall back on, George had neither the means nor the wherewithal to rebuild the family fortune.

In 1932, my grandmother dropped out of high school and spent most of the year going to debutante balls in hand-me-down dresses courtesy of her mother's friends. Then she got hired as a salesgirl at Saks, for which she was paid $18 a week, including Saturdays. As the Depression wore on, her father concluded that her only hope was to find a husband. In 1934, when she was eighteen, she met my grandfather, a doctor ten years her senior from an upper-middle-class family, and married him in the living room at 1001 Park. Shortly after the wedding, her parents were forced to forfeit the apartment to their bank and moved in with Rosamund's wealthy and single sister, Susie. "Nearly everything was gone," Rosamund later recalled in her typewritten memoirs. "I still hang on to a few reminders of Venice . . . a few bits of furniture are worthy of Parke-Bernet sales, though I hope that they won't be sent there."

The bidding for the small chest of drawers gets to $1,200, and then stops. This is not going as we had planned. The extra windfall is turning out to be a drop in the bucket. Come on, I say to myself, trying to will the price higher. When it doesn't budge, I take a deep breath and start to think about making a deadline at work. That, at least, is something I can control.

AN EMPIRE MAHOGANY AND ORMOLU-MOUNTED FAUTEUIL, second quarter nineteenth century, $2,000–$3,000.

My parents were launched into newlywed life with family

money, which they used to buy the apartment on the Upper East Side and live in the manner in which they had been brought up. After my father was laid off, he freelanced on some city-planning projects for a while, and then resorted to looking for jobs, unsuccessfully, through help-wanted ads in the Sunday newspaper, while my mother started working as a part-time secretary.

Meanwhile, although my parents never spoke to us directly about it, the financial strain was growing more obvious. Our tableware was a strange combination of fancy wedding china supplemented by plates from the five-and-ten store Lamston. As kids, my brothers were both athletes who quickly wore holes in the knees of their jeans. Instead of buying them new pants, my mother ironed on layers of patches like denim mille-feuilles. Like most children, we didn't really comprehend where money came from, but we could tell when it wasn't there. One year, all I got for my birthday was a Fonzie coloring book; another year, a charm bracelet previously owned by my mother. The only conceivable way to interpret this, in my twelve-year-old mind, was that she didn't care enough to get me something I wanted.

By the time I reached high school, the apartment was showing major signs of wear and tear. One day our clothes washer overflowed, but instead of getting a new one, we started bringing our laundry down to the basement to use the coin-operated machines alongside the superintendent's wife. Our kitchen tiles got so warped that my mother pulled them up and painted the concrete floor herself, leaving rigid whorls of tile glue still visible underneath. If my classmates noticed, they didn't comment. One of my closest friends lived in the Dakota on Central Park West—her brother's bedroom contained a miniature basketball court and had appeared in a glossy shelter magazine. Her family, the B———s, ate in restaurants every night, and I was delighted to join them. During one spring break, they took me with them to Aspen, where I learned how to ski. My family never ate dinner out or took family trips other than visiting our grandparents in New England. I loved spending time with the B——s and made a good guest, as I was both grateful for their generosity and cowed by their largesse.

A COLONIAL VICTORIAN SUITE OF PADAUK WOOD MOTHER-OF-PEARL AND BRASS-INLAID SEATING FURNITURE, third quarter nineteenth century, $2,500–$3,500.

My mother cherished this matching set of couch and chairs. They had originally come from Zanzibar, where her father, the son of an ivory trader and diplomat, had been born in 1904. At the auction, they fetch a paltry $1,500.

My mother liked having old family things in the house; I think they cheered her up by reminding her of her origins. ("Look," she would say, turning over one corner of the large Persian carpet in the living room to show me its underside whenever I complained how threadbare it was. "Hand-loomed. Look at how many knots there are.") I, in turn, blamed the presence of family furniture for allowing her to ignore our situation. The more value with which she endowed it, the less urgent the problem seemed.

And so my brothers and I were sent to boarding school, even though it cost as much as college, because that's what everyone in my family had always done. When I was fifteen years old, my mother signed me up for cotillions that cost $100 but didn't buy me anything to wear. To one such dance, at the Pierre hotel, I arrived in a T-shirt dress and rubber Chinese slippers, an outfit so inappropriate that I spent much of the evening hiding in the ladies' room watching other teenage girls bustle in and out wearing floor-length gowns. Adolescence had bestowed upon me the usual antennae for differences in class and status, but my senses were heightened further by my rarefied environment. I began to feel deeply embarrassed as my father's clothes got rattier and rattier and my mother started making tissue boxes and bags out of French fabric to sell, a skill she picked up while working for a church tag sale. For a while, she had several seamstresses manning industrial-strength sewing machines in our kitchen. Though I used to have friends over all the time, once our apartment became a sweatshop, I made a point of playing at their homes instead.

Predictably, my parents' marriage buckled under the pressure. When my mother asked my father for money, I would instinctively hold my breath. Sometimes he had some cash on him, perhaps from a temporary gig or the sale of a stock; sometimes he didn't. They would fight for days every year around tax time. My father always waited until the very last minute to file, which drove my mother crazy. This desire to put off the difficult made every occasion for spending money an unfriendly deadline. One winter, he waited until December 24 to bring home a Christmas tree. When he came in the door that night dragging a meager fir behind him, my brothers joked that perhaps he had stolen it from the front yard of the brownstone next door, and as soon as they said it, I could no longer feel certain he hadn't.

A SET OF NINE QUEEN ANNE–STYLE DINING CHAIRS, $4,000–6,000.

If our dining room set is valued so high, why are they starting the bidding at only $1,500? And why are they having this auction in late July? *Don't they know that all the rich people leave the city for the summer?!* After Sotheby's 10 percent commission on the hammer price (this on top of a 15 percent buyer's premium; they skim from both ends) and a $75 handling charge and a 1 percent charge for "risk of loss," whatever that is, we aren't even getting $150 a chair. I could have gotten that much myself if I had just dragged them over to the flea market on Sixth Avenue and Twenty-sixth Street, where I buy my furniture. And I would have, if need be.

By my mid-twenties, in what I can say was a pretty direct reaction to my parents' example, I had embraced financial prudence with the vehemence of a convert. I read *Making the Most of Your Money* by Jane Bryant Quinn, and *One Up on Wall Street* by Peter Lynch, and spent an entire weekend poring over *BusinessWeek*'s annual guide to mutual funds to decide how I should invest my tiny 401(k). I took the Nine Steps to Financial Freedom, and yes, by God, I had the Courage to Be Rich.

This was all well and good, but I was not without my own blind impulses. In my dating life, I was both attracted to men with family wealth and fearful of the lack of ambition I knew it could instill in its recipients. My boyfriend N., whom I had gone to boarding school with and started dating after college, hadn't grown up rich, and in that I felt a kinship. But after his parents divorced, his mother married a member of the Mellon family who promised to pay any and all tuition bills for his step-grandchildren, and I won't pretend that didn't make the very sweet but somewhat listless N. more attractive as a potential life partner. In the end, though, it wasn't enough that he had a safety net, because if I had learned anything from my parents, it was that there *were* no safety nets. I needed him to have the kind of drive to succeed that my father seemed to lack, and N. simply wasn't hungry enough. And so after three years together, I broke it off.

This of course threw me into my own little financial tailspin, mostly involving real estate, as I bounced around from illegal sub-let to illegal sublet. I dreamed of buying an apartment but de-spaired over how I would ever save enough money for a down payment. Slowly, after several years of scraping by, I finally got a toehold. I took a decent-paying job and started putting aside $1,000 a month. I saved a nice chunk, cobbled together some gifts from my mother, grandmother, brother, and sister-in-law, and in 2001 bought a one-bedroom apartment in Chelsea for $300,000. Then I got en-gaged and sold the one-bedroom, got married, had a baby, got a bet-ter job, bought a bigger apartment, and so on.

My brothers have followed similar trajectories: careers, invest-ments, home ownership, family. We have all taken a path that is conventional, stable even, and that's the main reason we like it, though at times I wonder if stability is its only selling point. I envy the risk takers, the people buoyed by wealthy parents or those who have otherwise found the psychic strength to chuck it all to follow their dreams of becoming an actor, a painter, a writer. Someday, I think to myself, I'll be able to do that. If I can just save enough money.

As for my mother, she is back on her feet and doing well, liv-ing a stable yet still interesting life with her husband, whom she cherishes. We've all come out of it just fine. But I worry that by staying in New York City, where, as everyone knows, to have the normal things in life—a place to live, a child, a car, a dog—is to hemorrhage money, I'll wind up always feeling like the poorest kid in the class.

FEDERAL-STYLE MAHOGANY-INLAID SERPENTINE-FRONTED SIDE-BOARD, $2,000–$3,000.

The last of our lots. It goes for a mere $1,800. I started adding up the total haul, and it is nauseatingly low—$12,150 before commission. After all the years I'd heard about the couch and the rug and the sideboard and the chairs, the truth was finally, glaringly obvious: they were hardly worth anything at all.

"That's the thing about family heirlooms," my mother says to me later over the phone. "They only really have value to the family."

My Inheritance

Meera Nair

Several years ago, a man named Mr. Lal Bihari, in the Indian state of Uttar Pradesh, petitioned the government to proclaim him alive. His uncle had bribed bureaucrats to list him in various official records as legally dead so that he could appropriate Mr. Bihari's share of the family's ancestral farmlands. Expunged from legal reckoning, rendered deceased in the eyes of the government, Mr. Bihari found himself unable to accomplish simple tasks—like getting a bank loan.

Mr. Bihari was not the type of man to let his so-called demise go unchallenged. He started a lobbying group called the Association of Dead People, registered in his village of Azamgarh. This august body soon attracted hundreds of others who had suffered similar losses at the hands of venal relatives. Accompanied by his fellow living dead, Mr. Bihari marched in raucous parades. He and his association held a mock funeral for themselves in Lucknow, the state's capital. He tried to get arrested, ran for office, and sued people in an attempt to get the powers that be to acknowledge what had been taken from him.

When I first read about Mr. Bihari, I clipped the article and put it in a file I keep of strange and wonderful news stories that come out of India. The circumstances themselves didn't surprise me. After all, there are one billion of my countrymen crammed into an area about four and a half times the size of Texas. It is easy to see where the longing for land, any land, comes from. Add corruption and bribery into the mix, and Mr. Bihari's plight, though unusual, is still only an extreme variation on a theme. Everything is for sale in India, if you know which official to bribe for it.

What pulls me back to the news story, though, is the photograph that accompanies it. In it, Mr. Bihari, dressed in a long-sleeved striped shirt, sits on a cot opposite one of the relatives who helped rob him of his official existence. Mr. Bihari is smiling at him. I have looked at his expression again and again, trying to puzzle out the emotions behind it. It affects me in ways that I struggle to understand, that smile. Does it signal forgiveness? Or something more complicated?

My great-grandfather lay in a coma for five years. When I was a child, going to see him was an unavoidable part of my summer vacation. To visit him, we had to travel for days by train and bus to get to my family's ancestral home, a farm in a tiny village in Kerala. The trip was long and miserable, but I knew protesting was futile—in our family we did our duty, we met expectations.

It is late afternoon by the time we arrive at his house and step gingerly over the raised threshold of the door into the dark well of the room. The trees outside the many windows are loud with birds, yet only one window stands open because his wife is afraid he'll catch cold.

She waves me in and I approach silently. My great-grandfather lies flat on his back on the canopied bed, a huge man with a bald head that looks too big even for his substantial body. I avoid looking at his mouth hanging open in his fleshy, shining face. Even now, I sometimes have nightmares in which he opens his eyes and stares at me.

There is a full-length portrait hanging in the corridor outside his room. In it, he stands soldier-straight in a Western-style suit, his chin raised pugnaciously, ferocious eyes staring into the distance under his *sola topee,* the kind of pith helmet the British favored.

Before he fell ill, he was a district agricultural officer, a bureaucrat aware of his power and unashamed to use it. He owned acres and acres of land, mansions and stores in town, and farmlands and plantations of mangoes and coconuts on its outskirts. He was known for his terrible temper, a man who thought nothing of slapping his subordinates for the slightest misdemeanor. His sons grew up terrified of him and of the switch he used to keep behind his rocking chair at all times. Everything I've heard about him makes me glad not to have known him when he was well.

His wife, a short woman with white hair that fluffs about her face, crushes me into her billowy chest, then releases me. She fusses with his sheets and wipes his face with a wet rag, pattering nonstop like a saleswoman pressing her wares.

"Look who's here. Our Bhanu's granddaughter—you remember her? She got the first rank in her class—ten out of ten in English composition." She turns to me. "Why don't you recite something to him—How about Wordsworth? You know 'Daffodils'?" She pats my shoulder in encouragement, but I can't bring myself to perform. Then she asks me to look for flies. Her manner as she relinquishes the whisk to me clearly indicates that this is a privilege, a reward for having made the pilgrimage. I walk around the bed inspecting my great-grandfather's feet and palms, which lie open, pink, plump, and unresisting as any baby's against the flies that dare to alight on him. My great-grandmother watches to make sure I do it right.

Every day since he'd fallen ill, she'd performed such duties without complaint. When medicine, both Western and ayurvedic, failed to revive him, she brought in exorcists, astrologers, and magicians; masseurs who soaked her husband's body in herbal oils; and priests who lit huge blazing fires in the courtyard and chanted mantras to the unresponsive gods through the night. She only left his side to bring him his meals—liquidized rice with tomatoes or tender coconut water that she dripped drop by drop down his throat. By the time breakfast was done, it was time for lunch.

When my great-grandfather died, his wife of fifty-four years discovered that he had changed his mind about his bequest to his family. Her sons produced a new document, an annotated, meticulous will with her husband's signature ratifying every page. Every yard of land he owned, every store, every mansion, every plantation, was divided up among them. The only thing his wife and her only daughter, my grandmother, received was a share each in the house that he had died in, where two of her sons still lived.

Until the will was read, my great-grandmother must have presumed that everything he owned would be hers to distribute among her children. She had lived in the house all her life, given birth to her children and helped bring her grandchildren into the world under its roof. She didn't have anywhere else to go. Her share in the house would at least let her live there until she died, but her daughter would have to defer her inheritance until her brothers felt like selling the house.

What made our situation doubly scandalous was that my family is part of the Nair community. We were, not so long ago, one of the few matrilineal societies on the planet. And although the matrilineal system was abolished in 1976, its effects and traditions still linger. In our community, the right of inheritance passes from the mother to her children and their children. Before new laws of Hindu succession decreed that property be equally divided among all children, the women got the lion's share of all family wealth. If the will hadn't been changed, my great-grandmother would have passed much of her inheritance on to her daughter, who would have passed it on to my mother and her sisters, and eventually some portion might have fallen to me.

The will my granduncles created is undeniably legal, authorized by a lawyer, a drinking buddy of theirs. Because of our family's prominence, most of the residents in that very small town knew that my great-grandfather had lain as one dead for many years and could not have produced that will. Yet the town's only notary stamped and signed it. There was nothing the women in my family, the suddenly dispossessed, could do.

And yet my grandmother laughs fondly whenever she speaks of her youngest brother, the one the rest of us believe masterminded the new will. "He used to kick me in my stomach whenever I carried him. He was two years old, and I was nine months pregnant with your mother at the time," she tells me.

My grandmother is eighty-two now, and she's been looking out for her brothers all her life, even after she married and moved

fifty miles away to her husband's farm. Even after we install a telephone at the farm, they arrive unannounced from her hometown,
a convulsion of large, bald men heaving out of the car, and yell,
"Edathi!" in unison from the courtyard, as if they can't wait to see
their big sister until they are decently inside the house. They come
bearing gifts—sticky-sweet *jilebis*, expensive grapes, news of the
world outside the farm. My serene grandmother, who normally
professes a profound indifference to the workings of the kitchen,
rushes to the cook and starts firing off instructions about lunch. A
lifelong vegetarian, she dispatches farmhands to chase down and
slay chickens. She has a perfect memory for every brother's favorite
dish from their childhood, and it falls to my mother or one of her
sisters to persuade the by now thoroughly disgruntled cook to make
at least some of them.

Her brothers spend the day eating and drinking, shaking out
handkerchiefs big as tea towels to mop their sweating foreheads,
competing with one another to entertain us. The youngest one was
once the brother my mother always wanted. He taught her to whis-
tle, to fight and use a slingshot, and to climb fences and steal mangoes from the baskets passing vendors carried on their heads. The
middle one wiggles his hairy ears back and forth to make my young
cousins scream with delight. They are collectively charming and
worldly, born raconteurs who mesmerize us with their stories. My
frail, pretty grandmother grows pink with laughter as she listens.
She is girlish in their presence, beside herself, squeezing any grand-
child within reach too tight in her happiness. Her giddiness drives
my mother and her sisters insane.

The moment the men leave, quiet, like the aftermath of a
thunderstorm, returns to the bright, whitewashed rooms, and my
mother flees upstairs to her bedroom with her two younger sisters

at her heels. There, out of my grandmother's earshot, all hell breaks loose.

"They have smiles on their faces and poison in their hearts, but she'll never see that," my mother, ever dramatic, rails through clenched teeth. If I so much as giggle, she turns on me.

"And you, I saw you laughing like a fool at their jokes. Just like her. And they were not even so funny." I had noticed her laughing once or twice, too, but I know better than to say anything.

In private, my mother and aunts forget the lessons in humility and respect that they have always dinned into me and my cousins. They lampoon my grandmother—exaggerating the way she shakes her head at a brother in mock exasperation, as if at a naughty but beloved child, and parodying the silly diminutive she calls them. Their mouths twist in rancor.

"How can she? How can she?" the sisters question one another, collapsed in the same bed, prostrate from anger. They search one another's impressions of the day, dissect every sentence, and weigh every expression, wanting answers, seeking even more ways to be outraged.

My cousins and I all have heard the facts—the stolen fortune, the cheating, the litany of what could have been. It is a mountain we have climbed before. The story comes up without fail every time the family gets together. We arrive from cities scattered across the country, full of news of our different lives, yet end up listening to our mothers repeat our history, the narrative in all its twists and turns, as reliable and as unavoidable as rain in the monsoons.

Our mothers take it upon themselves to keep the memory of our misfortunes alive and immediate, to keep the pain from passing. They don't allow us to question the facts, which are immutable, chiseled in stone long ago at some point in our family's journey from fabulous wealth to ordinariness. They need this legend, this loss; it welds my mother and her sisters together. One night, lying on the cool floor, I listen to them talk about the old house, the one they don't visit anymore. My mother and her sisters fall asleep one by one, then snort awake to continue the conversation without a break. In the dark, their voices are similar, their yearnings interchangeable; they are all my mother and loved as such. I am jealous of their closeness.

When my father has a stroke that leaves him partially paralyzed and unemployed, my parents come back to my grandmother's village. My father has retired early, and they hope to cobble together a new life on the farm, but his medical expenses soon wear our savings down to terrifying lows. My aunts are experiencing hardships as well. One of my cousins cannot get into a good college because he needs thousands of rupees to pay the "donations" they demand. It is in times like this of financial crisis that the wails of "if only" and "what if" grow louder. My mother weeps at the injustice that has been perpetuated on us, nineteen, twenty years after the fact. She blames our broken luck, our privations, on her uncles. Her sisters, I hear from my cousins, do the same. I am astonished and a little frightened at the tenacity of their memory and the resentment that keeps it alive.

And yet they rarely express their feelings in front of my grandmother. When my mother, in her place as the eldest daughter, brings it up one night, she is circumspect, tiptoeing around the topic of how she and her sisters feel. "Perhaps it would be better if the uncles didn't come around as much," she says, "though no one wishes to dwell on the past."

"Yes, it was not right what they did," my grandmother says.

"May God grant them good sense. I'll tell them to stop coming, if that is what you and your sisters want." She agrees and agrees; she can't stop agreeing. What she wants is for the conversation to be over.

My mother is halfway to the kitchen when my grandmother calls her back. "Radha-Sudha-Indira!" she says. My mother is Indira. Her sisters are Radha and Sudha. My grandmother has never been able to say any one daughter's name alone—the three names spill out together, no matter which one she is calling to her side. She tells her she wants her daughters to be like the three stones of the hearth after she dies. It is something I have heard her wish for before. Her language is often lyrical, full of metaphor, the only thing about her that tends toward extravagance. "You can't balance a pot if any one of the stones is missing," she explains. My mother strikes her forehead with her hand. "Ayyo! Do be quiet, Mother," she says.

My granduncle was one of my father's best friends when they were in college. Once, he convinced my father to come to a family wedding with him. My father fell in love at the celebration. The girl was beautiful, with curly, waist-length hair. The first time he saw her she was holding a tray full of flowers to welcome the bride. "I warned him—that's my niece and don't you dare so much as think about her," my granduncle always says when he comes to this part of the story. It is one I never tire of hearing. He was the reason my parents met and married each other. He had a hand in my existence, I tell my mother. But she wants to forget all these connections.

Whenever my granduncles visit, my mother and her sisters wait to see what happens. They hover. They eavesdrop. I know what my mother and her sisters want. I've heard it often enough. They want my grandmother to toss her brothers on their rear, order them to never darken our doors again. For them, only melodrama on a Bollywood scale will suffice—shamefaced departures, triumphant laughter, recrimination and its satisfying aftermath, the four men fallen at their sister's feet cringing for forgiveness. Instead, my grandmother offers them tea and cake, unconditional absolution. When her brothers finally pile back into the car and leave, my grandmother stands at the doorstep, hands raised in blessing, just like her mother used to, until the taillights disappear.

Sometimes, as I watch them drive away, I wonder which one practiced my great-grandfather's signature until he got it right. How did they decide, as they sat upstairs drinking in their mother's house all those years ago, that their sister wasn't worth giving anything to?

My grandmother has few pleasures. She loves music. On one of our annual visits home, my father gives her a transistor radio. She carries it everywhere with her, cradled in the crook of her arm; the faint strain of tinny music that accompanies her presence indicates her whereabouts in the house. My grandmother gives herself up to the transistor, to the music that pours forth at all times. Bending low to catch its whisperings, or switching dreamily from station to station on the dial, she leaves the farm and its persistent demands, her makeshift marriage, the silent disapproval of her daughters. The music creates a cocoon around her, which the rest of the family hesitates to shatter, where she can be most herself. Once I come upon her sitting alone, the vegetables half-chopped on her cutting board, tears streaming down her face, the transistor radio murmuring beside her. When she opens her eyes, she looks remote and exhausted, an ancient changeling. I stammer an excuse and rush off, embarrassed, as if I have transgressed upon her undressed. I worry about the incident for days, search for signs of further transformation in her face. I spy on her from behind my newspaper when she rests in the afternoons, but she stays the same—reassuringly benign, as loving and ineffectual as ever.

When I was thirteen, I accompanied my grandmother back to her old house to visit her mother, who was living with her sons. I was the one my grandfather had entrusted with the bus fare; I was the one he put in charge. As someone who had grown up in cities and was a veteran traveler and a confident conversationalist, I was more capable at getting around. At least I think that was the implication. On the way to her house, my grandmother pointed out her convent school, the hall where she had attended concerts. As a young girl, she had seen her favorite singer perform there, and his sublime voice had brought her to tears. When we reached her house, she took me to her old room, with its glass-fronted cupboards filled with the books of her youth. She tiptoed around, speaking in whispers as if she were in a stranger's room or a museum.

She would have had a life of occasional concerts and of friends she had gone to school with, if she had the house her father had written off to her brothers. She would have had a place to call her own, property that would have helped her hold her head up high among her husband's relatives. This is what I thought as we made our way back to the farm. After her mother died, she never went back.

My grandmother's yearnings have been belied before. Her father arranged her marriage to a man who had just landed a job as an accountant in the Navy in Bombay. She believed that she was marrying a man about to become a cosmopolitan, someone she would make a home with in the biggest city in the country, somewhere unfamiliar, unlike anything she had ever known. Their life to come must have looked like an adventure.

But he resigned his commission in the Navy just weeks before they were to be married. His parents, who had lost one son to Bombay already, didn't want their eldest son to leave, and he was an obedient son.

He studied to become a schoolteacher but went home every weekend, wife and children in tow, to help on the family farm. After a life spent in village schools, he returned to the farm and became a farmer. No one expected my grandmother to do anything but follow him, live his life.

Her husband understood the land and its needs well enough to make money from farming but had no interest in anything else. An excellent student who had once played tennis and studied the violin, she had lived most of her life in her husband's ancestral home in the village, among uneducated farmhands. In the beginning, she had to share her house with her sisters-in-law, to suffer their taunts for her refined ways and citified clothes—the short puffed blouses and flimsy chiffon saris she brought as part of her trousseau, all fashionable and completely unsuitable. But my grandmother made herself over. She became a wife, a daughter-in-law, a despised sister-in-law. She became someone who never traveled unaccompanied, not even the four miles to the market in the next village. After forty years of living in her husband's village, she still thought of it as an alien country and called its inhabitants "these people." It was when the sisters-in-law moved out, when the house finally became her own, that her brothers started coming over. This was the most defiant of her acts, this semblance of a complete fam-

ily that she created without asking permission and that she fero-
ciously held on to once she had it.

Nowadays there is nothing my grandmother wants, nothing she asks for. Her daughters have to divine her wishes to act
upon them, making sure she eats on time, takes her pills, has a glass
of water always within reach. It is only recently, rendered almost
immobile, constantly in pain from osteoporosis, that she will ask
me to fetch her transistor from the other room.

Even when she was in her sixties, my grandfather was the one
who took her shopping twice a year for new clothes. He'd point out
the soft cotton saris he wanted the salesman to display, always
choosing the same colors—baby blue, cream, pale pink, the ones
my grandmother said were her favorites. When he had his money
out to pay, he'd turn to her. "Bhanu, would you like to say anything?" he'd ask, and she'd shake her head, acquiescent as ever.

In 2002, a year after her husband died, my grandmother
executed her will. After her demise, her daughters would get the
farm and the surrounding land. The house would go to my mother,
the only one without one to call her own. The will is a model of fair
distribution, beyond complaint. At least that is what my mother
and her sisters think in the beginning.

But one night, my aunts argue over the will, each accusing the
other of scheming to take over more than the allotted acreage. At
issue is a long, narrow French-loaf-shaped piece of property hem-
ming Aunt Radha's property. Thirty-seven feet altogether, to be exact. It has five coconut palms growing any which way on it, making
it impossible to decide whom they belonged to. Aunt Sudha thinks
that the land and the trees should be hers. Land supervisors are

brought in, measurements taken and disputed. Brutal, irredeemable things are said until the sisters stop talking altogether. The quarrel strains credibility, and at first I do not believe it is serious.

But when I visit India, the two of them come separately to see me. On our usual evening walks along the fields, each one sobs, heartbroken, women in their fifties with grown sons and daughters. They miss each other. Who would think this could happen to us? To this family, after all we have lost over the years? They say this as if they have no control over their desires, their egos, their dreams for their children. They are obsessed with this new outrage, this latest so-called landgrab. My grandmother says nothing to them, even though I beg her—she seems unable to summon the resources for another fight. I wonder if she is in shock, deeply disappointed that her daughters have not heeded the one lesson she tried to teach them all these years, the importance of forgiveness.

Instead, they are stuck in the flypaper of their natures, unable to rise above the hurt and the pain of the words that they have recklessly flung about, unable to see what really matters. They blame each other and dredge up petty arguments and childhood incidents as if they were portents predicting this exact break, this spendthrift pouring away of their love.

Listening to their stories, I am so angry that I cannot breathe. They are confused, taken aback when I lecture them, rip their arguments apart, condemn their behavior. I am ashamed of them for the first time in my life, I say, and I am laughing in relief as I say it, refusing to see it their way, reckless in my disrespect for my elders. I am not, I decide, going to allow thirty-seven feet of land to divide us. I am not my mother's daughter.

My grandmother will die soon. She waits for her time to come. My mother waits with her, the two women alone in the echoing rooms. My aunts visit them sometimes, but never together. I don't know if my harsh words got through to them, but I did hear that my aunts called each other recently. They had very little to say beyond Happy New Year, but three sentences is a conversation, I tell myself. It's a beginning at least. I am waiting for the day when all of us, aunts, cousins, grandmothers, and grandchildren, will get together again, scarred, a little unsure of our reception, but smiling at each other like our lives depended on it.

Safe

I was seven and had a leather purse full of silver dollars, both of which, the purse and the coins, I considered valuable. I wanted them stored in the bank. At the time, the bank had an imposing landmark status in my map of the world, in part because it shared the same red brick as the public school, the two most substantial buildings in our town. I went to the Catholic school and did a lot of fund-raising in the form of selling candy bars, Christmas stamps, and fruitcakes, and my favorite spot for doing business was outside the bank, on Friday afternoons, because that was payday. Workingmen came to deposit their checks and left the bank with a little cash for the weekend. Today, that ritual is nearly gone, its rhythms broken, except for the elderly and the poor, who still visit banks and pack into lines, waiting for tellers. But back then, I'd set my box of candy on the sidewalk and greet customers, holding the door for them like a bellhop. Friends of mine with an entirely different outlook on life tried to sell their candy at the grocery store. I figured that outside the supermarket people might lie or make excuses, claiming to be broke, but not at the bank, for reasons that seemed obvious to me: this was the headquarters of money.

Most of the men were feeling flush and optimistic, flush because they were getting paid and would soon have money in their pockets, optimistic because the workweek was over and they could forget what they had done for the money. On their way in, I'd ask if they wanted to buy a candy bar, and they'd dip a nod and smile and say with a jaunty promissory confidence that I should catch them on the way out. And I did. I sold candy bars like a fiend. Year after year, I won the plastic Virgin Marys and crucifixes and laminated holy cards, all the holy gewgaws that were given away as gifts to the most enterprising saleskids at school. I liked the whole arrangement. On those Friday afternoons and early evenings, I always wore my salt-and-pepper corduroy pants and saddle shoes and green cardigan, a school uniform that I believed made me as recognizable to the world as a priest in his soutane, and I remember feeling righteous, like an acolyte doing God's work, or the Church's. Money touched all the people in town, quaintly humanizing them, and I enjoyed standing outside the bank, at the center of civic life. This was my early education into the idea of money.

My hand will always remember the density of those silver dollars, the dead weight as I tumbled them back and forth, the dull clink as the coins touched. The nature of that weight offered a lesson in value, too; you knew by a sense of the coin's unique inner gravity that the silver was pure, that it wasn't an alloy. Holding the coin in your palm, you could feel the primitive allure of the metal itself. Years later, I would pay for college by fixing washing machines and dryers. I was a repairman for a company that installed coin-operated machines in apartment buildings and Laundromats.

We had collectors in the field who worked set routes, hitting laundry rooms all over the city, emptying the coin boxes into canvas sacks. Late in the afternoon, they returned to the shop and delivered the dirty bags to the counting room, a dingy, windowless, fortified cement vault in back of the repair shop. Inside was a conveyor belt and a slotted metal chute and a machine for sorting the coins. A woman named Laurel did all the counting. She was thin and pale and her hair was limp, and she wore black-rimmed glasses and a flowered smock that seemed a peculiarly sad flourish in that colorless place. She was a drudge in the operation, and unconsciously I equated her plain looks with honesty, her weak sexual presence with a lack of guile. Every afternoon, thousands of dollars' worth of coins slid across her tray. The metallic droning of the coins was mind-numbing, and yet this woman, hearing the slightest deviation in that monotony, would toggle a switch and stop the belt, poke through the money in the chute, and pluck out the one pure silver coin—a Mercury dime, or a Washington quarter that predated copper-nickel composition—and replace it with one of her own. Thus in a matter of seconds she would make between 100 and 1,000 percent on her investment. One day she demonstrated all this to me, and I never thought of her the same afterward. The racket of those rattling coins was hellish in the confinement of her concrete bunker, but this pallid, dreary woman had a keen ear for that one thing, the soft, dull sound of silver as it thunked against metal, and she would eventually amass a small fortune in rare and valuable coins.

My silver dollars felt like a fortune, but they were also playthings, a collection, assembled and protected and given value by an abiding faith, a loyalty to them. Somehow I knew that I would never spend them, never convert them into baseball cards or Slurpees or rides at the Evergreen State Fair. They weren't about acquisition. I didn't view them as vehicles for my desire. They held their own fascination, but only if I kept them out of circulation. As they lost currency, an element of worthlessness thus entered into my idea of money, an aesthetic dimension. I understood that their value increased the more they sank into the past, and because of this the coins had some of the quality of treasure.

At that age, I lost things, I broke them or outgrew them, my interests changed, but I guarded those seven silver dollars jealously. I couldn't throw them or use them to improvise scenarios of valor or heroism; and I couldn't include anyone else in my play, as I did with my guns and balls. I kept the coins in a leather purse that was shaped like a boot, a souvenir from a junket my parents had taken to Puerto Vallarta; the boot zipped shut, and MEXICO was printed across the sole. I hid the purse in the bottom drawer of my dresser, stuffed beneath clothes I no longer wore, but then there was a moment in which I decided it was time to put the whole thing—the boot-shaped purse and silver dollars both—in the bank.

The only times I'd actually been inside the bank were in the company of my father, who, among other things, taught business finance. In back of the bank was the vault, the door a polished-steel slab with a spoked wheel such as you would find at the helm of a ship, and inside the vault was my father's safe-deposit box. He kept important papers in the box, insurance policies and a few stock certificates that must have had sentimental value, either as early or as important trades he'd made in his career, because normally a man like my father would have held the issues in their street name. Also in the box he kept a penknife and an ornate silver watch and fob, a beautiful set stored in a case lined with crushed green velvet. It had belonged to my grandfather, a man I'd never met. My father would set the watch on the table inside the vault and let me play with it while he shuffled through his papers, always telling me that his father had given it to him and that he, in turn, would pass it on to me, when the time was right. Imagining that long continuity and the juncture when the watch and fob would be mine was thrilling. The vault in back of the bank was my father's sanctum sanctorum. He knew this world; he was affable and relaxed in it, friendly with the tellers and the president alike. He addressed everyone by name, flirted and joked, walked briskly and with confidence, taking command of the space. His own father had been a bookie and a figure of the underground. More than once my father had seen him viciously beat other men over money, and I could tell that it had terrified my dad, seeing his father so violent in the conduct of business. As a young boy, he would visit the local precinct, with my grandmother, to bail his father out of jail. Because they were on the take, the police had to make a show of arresting my grandfather periodically, and on those occasions my father would come to the station, only to find his dad laughing and joking and playing cards with the cops who'd arrested him. My father's early education in money must have given him a glimpse of something savage and hollow in the heart of the system.

The power of that insight took the form of shame, as it does for so many of the sons of immigrants, and so it made sense to me that my father's public self glowed in the company of people who did their business legitimately. His passion for securities—and common stock, particularly—is where he ultimately acquired his citizenship; in the bank, or on the phone with a broker, or in class teaching others about finance, he acted like a man with the rights and privileges of a native, a status his own father had never fully attained. Funny, charming, at ease—he became these things the

minute he walked through the bank door. He loved the buildings
that housed the institutions of money, banks among them, the way
a spiritual yearning finds embodiment and feels supported in a
church. The enormous trust implied by the whole system was palpable to him, perhaps because he knew the fragility of it firsthand,
how beneath the flirtation and joking, the first names and hand-
shakes, these essential civil arrangements between people, it could
always devolve into brutal beatings. He would often tell me that
money had no inherent worth, that it only had value because people agreed that it did. For him, money was one vast conversation,
and he liked to keep the level of discourse high.

People who knew him in his capacity as a money whiz have
told me that he was a genius, and there's no question that he was a
smart man. Whether he was explaining why cigarettes were price
inelastic or describing the dissonant notion behind fairly standard
ideas of diversification (that you're actually seeking an utter lack of
correlation as a form of harmony), you felt the force and elegance
of his mind—and at our house, this kind of stuff was table talk.

And so what happened with my silver dollars and my shoe
purse is a mystery, a moment that I've returned to again and again
over the years, always drawing a confused blank as I try to re-cre-
ate the day. The whole thing had the character of a lesson, of something more than a simple transaction. My father and I drove to the
bank and stood in line and waited for a teller. When it was our turn,
I reached up and stuck my shoe on the counter, which was about
level with my chin. My father had instructed me at lunch that I
would do all the talking, and we even rehearsed the lines, so I said
to the woman that I wanted to put my purse and silver dollars in
the bank. Even to this day, I can see myself standing there; I know
the hour, the weather outside as seen through the bank's high win-

dows, the slight feeling of confusion, the hesitance as I wondered if my words were making sense, the coldness at my temples where a faint feeling of doubt registered. My father exchanged a glance with the teller, and I looked back, over my shoulder, at the vault, and when he asked me if I was sure, I said yes. The teller did her work and then handed me back my empty shoe and a green savings book. At this point I was so flustered that I couldn't summon the courage to tell her what I was thinking—that the shoe was part of it, that I wanted that in the bank, too.

Naturally, when I went to retrieve the silver dollars, they were gone, and yet I was shocked when I was handed, instead, seven dollar bills. I felt rooked. All the alchemy of imagination that had brought me to the bank, that had enlarged the idea of those silver dollars, was undone.

What has remained curious to me over the years is why my father didn't see what was happening and intervene. He was the adult, and he had all the savvy, while in some ways my idea of the bank was based on banks in old Westerns. For me, it was a place where people stored money and where robbers could grab it, if clever enough or brutal enough. I imagined that a bank held money in a way that wasn't all that different from the way I hid the shoe purse in the bottom drawer of my dresser. The bank was the physical place, it was the vault with the polished steel door, it was the safe-deposit box in which I'd keep my silver dollars beside the watch and fob that would one day be mine, when the time was right. Most of all, the bank was where my father and I spent some of our best days, the rare place where I saw him happy and at home, his private and taciturn and increasingly violent self set aside in favor of the public man who was upright and worthy and could stride across the carpet to shake the president's hand. I suppose ultimately that's what I was investing in when I decided to put my silver dollars in the bank, that future with my father.

But the last time I saw him, the great brilliance, and the passion that made it so infectious and forceful, had deteriorated. He no longer spoke to any of his seven children, and he rarely left his apartment. He was a physical mess, fat, wheezing, unable to lift himself from his chair without tremendous exertion. I was probably no better-off—reeling from a long-dead relationship that was still desperately dying, smoking too much, clueless as to career and money, and so on. Now and then I could see the old fire in my father's eyes, and with the urgency of some thought roiling inside him, he would struggle forward, but he seemed trapped in his body, wholly bound by his physical decline. And now his mind was just permanently strange. He kept referring to the mystics, as if in fact these mystics were in the room with us. "As the mystics tell us," he would say, "All is well. All is well."

At the end of the night he took me to a closet and gave me a box of red pens and asked if I wanted his old safe. It was beige, about the size of a book box, and weighed at least seventy-five pounds. I took it, I said yes, just because the night had been so awful, and I somehow thought it would be ungracious to refuse this gift. I carried it down the hall and sat on it, winded, while I waited for the elevator. It was one of those nights in Seattle when the wind downtown was strong enough to blow flowerpots off the decks of high-rises and the traffic signals danced a crazed tarantella over the intersections. The safe had the dead-weight feel of an anchor. It took me forever to get the two or three blocks home. I wondered if passing cops would think I was a thief. Every fifty feet or so I set the safe on the sidewalk and sat on it, resting. By the time I got back to my place, I was too wet and miserable and exhausted to carry it up the stairs, and I had no use for it anyway. I left the safe in the alley behind my building, beneath a cedar, and it stayed there for a long time. No one took it because it was empty and it was heavy. And then one day I looked out my window and it was gone.

Desperate Creatures

Felicia Sullivan

At night, my mother left me alone with Manny, who hid out in the bedroom listening to eight-track tapes of Neil Diamond and Carole King. He ignored the strange men who knocked on the door at all hours, asking if my mother or father was home. Recently, we had installed a sliding bar lock in addition to the three dead bolts and chain locks. We were a family obsessed with man-made security. I yelled that no one was home, that I was alone but the phone was right here next to me, that the police would be here any minute. Laughing, they told me their names, which were never their real names, and they shouted, "Trust me, your parents know who we are and how much they owe us," as they descended the stairs.

It had been three years since Manny moved in, dragging his paint buckets and two nylon suitcases up six flights of stairs. A week after he arrived, he decided to repaint all the walls. My mother and I left the apartment and rode the train downtown to a nondescript office building where we sat on uncomfortable plastic chairs waiting for our last name to be called. Hours passed, how many we didn't know. The overhead clock remained fixed at noon or midnight, depending on how you looked at it.

My mother squeezed my hand tight. "Show me sad," she said.

"I am sad," I said. Our name was called.

"Good. Keep that face for another fifteen minutes."

A fat black woman with wiry hair and spectacles that hung from a braided string reviewed my mother's application for welfare. "It says here you went to college," she said.

"For a year." My mother paused. "And then I had my daughter."

After a few more questions and a stretch of silence, the counselor leaned over and sighed. "You're kidding me, right? You're *white.*"

"What does that mean?" my mother asked, her knees bouncing. I tried to make the saddest face.

"That means get a job. Any job. Or come back to me when you have a few more kids."

"So what you're telling me is that we won't be getting any money," my mother said. "Not even food stamps."

The counselor met my mother's eyes, then she called out the next person's name. "Johnson, Awilda Johnson."

That night Manny said, "I know some people. Some Italians on Thirty-ninth Street." I could hear him talking to my mother through the Sheetrock walls. "They're your people. They'll lend you the money with a good rate."

"I don't know," my mother said, uneasy. The bed squeaked.

"Let me tell you what I know," Manny said. "Javier doesn't like not being paid."

I could hear cutting. I could hear my mother blowing her nose.

"Here," Manny said, "take the Afrin."

A week later Javier dropped by. In the doorway stood two men in down jackets, silent, arms folded into their chests. My mother gave Javier a small, thick envelope. He kissed her on both cheeks and left.

When they closed the door, Manny asked about the Italians. How much had she borrowed, at what rate?

"Don't ask me what I had to do," my mother said.

When I was eleven, my mother was fired from yet another diner. Money had mysteriously disappeared again. Save the owners, she had been the only one entrusted with keys. "Who else could it be?" they all said. The police were never called, charges never filed; the owners knew about my mother by then, about her friends, so they let her go quietly with a few weeks' pay and tips. How quickly that money vanished along with the contents of our refrigerator and the 18-karat gold studs I'd bought with the windfall.

Not long after that, Javier was replaced with George, who dropped glassine bags into my mother's coat pocket and always coughed before he spoke. A man of few words, he whistled, nodding his head in approval when he heard my mother had scored a job as a deli manager. Through all of this, Manny ghosted in the background, reminding my mother that they had to keep working. Their house, their bodies, were a machine that had to keep moving. So Manny painted and drywalled houses all over Brooklyn, and my mother rose in the early hours, when it was still dark, and with a quick bump of coke willed the makeup on and moved her body out the door.

In those days, George came by at least once a week. He never touched my mother, never kissed her cheeks.

On the weekends, my mother and I always rode the subway into the city. Resting my head on her lap, I stretched my legs long over the seats. The rattling car, rustling newspapers, and crackling voice announcing each stop soothed us. At Lexington Avenue, we wove our way through the crowds; my head craned every which way just to see everything. Against the towering buildings and magnificently paned glass, I felt incredibly small. To me, Manhattan was horrifying, grand. Tourists planted themselves in the center of the sidewalk, accordion maps opened wide, charting which way to go. My mother and I headed west to Park Avenue, to the delicatessen where she worked as head manager.

One Saturday morning, when we arrived at the deli, I told my mother, "We're home."

She threw open the metal gate. "Not *home*, Lisa," she said, puzzled. "This is *work*."

I thought about the times I had gorged on pints of Frusen Glädje there, that decadent and ridiculously expensive Swedish ice cream, and how at the end of the day I'd feel giddy, buzzed, slightly sick. In our freezer at home, there was a lone flavored Popsicle, covered in burn. Filling our skeletal refrigerator seemed like the work.

After my mother keyed in the alarm code, I bolted inside and marveled over the pristine parquet floors, the revolving display of potato chips, pork rinds, and Cracker Jacks that were suspended by metal clips near the front of the store. Boxes of Nerds, stacks of watermelon gum lined the racks by the register, boxes of pasta and tissue paper sat on the shelves, perfectly arranged. In the back of the store, cans of Coke, Tab, and Pepsi gleamed through the clear refrigerator doors.

"We could live here," I said.

"This isn't our home," she said. "Come help me in the kitchen."

In the back, my mother and I lifted heavy buffet trays. Adjusting food temperatures, she warned me about how hot or cold food must be in order to serve it. Smoke plumed around us. My arms blistered from the metal and the heat.

"But that chicken's burned," I said, pointing to the caked-on barbecue sauce.

"How it *looks* doesn't matter," she said. "Following the rules matters. What the Board of Health says matters." My mother looked proud uttering the words "Board of Health"; how official they must have sounded to her. I could tell it pleased her that she knew something other than how to balance seven plates on one arm. She'd resolved to be more than a waitress smiling through clenched teeth for tips. When you entered our living room, you couldn't miss her certification in food management, in a gold frame, on the coffee table. Her name was written in elegant cursive. And if you moved it to one side, you would see two smaller frames. Pictures of me.

While I worked the register, ringing up items, my mother wrapped roast beef on rye and tuna melts in plastic. When she loaded the last of the prepared sandwiches on a tray, she leaned back on the counter, pulled down a pack of Kent 100s from the overhead cigarette rack, and puffed away on a cigarette. From a register rich with bills, I doled out change and tore off receipts as my mother's boss, Muhammad, watched approvingly.

"Hello, pretty girl!" he bellowed, carrying bags of nuts, dried cranberries, apricots, figs, and licorice. He presented me with the plastic bags as gifts, scattered the bounty on top of the counter. Eyeing my bag of Fritos, he shook his head and smiled, revealing two gold teeth among all the white. "Pretty girl shouldn't be eating chips if you want to grow up strong, healthy like your mother," he said.

My mother's face grew dark. "Don't worry about what she eats."

Muhammad winked at me. "Of course, of course," he said.

Saturday mornings, my mother and her boss would review the weekly ledger. Because of her waitress background, my mother took to numbers easily, and Muhammad taught her basic accounting: debits and credits, margins and net profits. How to balance a budget, how to make numbers foot.

"Someday I'll make you partner," he said to her as they discussed the day's late deliveries. "When I own *fifty* delis. And I will own them."

"Fifty delis," my mother mused.

I beamed, chewing on licorice. Muhammad smoothed my hair. "Your mother is a smart woman. She knows the business. Watch her," he said.

And when I asked if I, too, could work in the deli, Muhammad laughed and said, "Of course. Who else knows the register so well?"

When he left for the day, satisfied with the work we'd done, my mother held me close. "One day we won't need his money," she whispered. "We'll have our own."

For lunch, we'd always fix ourselves sandwiches—salami, cheddar cheese, and turkey piled ridiculously high between two slices of

white bread and mountains of iceberg lettuce and juicy tomatoes—
and sitting on stools in front of the register, food spilled out the corners of our mouths. After lunch, my mother would map out the
specials for the week while I bagged orders. "You see my girl, that's
my girl," she'd say to customers "Eleven years old and look how
good she handles money. Better than me."

I loved it there. There were no empty fridges, no pinching
pennies for cold cuts or lox. And the overhead fluorescent lights
glowed in a way that reminded me of sunlight, so even when it
stormed outside, inside it was calm and warm. At the deli, I took all
my tasks seriously. Methodically, I stacked soup cans on the shelves;
I took comfort in aligning these cans just right so that their labels
faced front, uniform and neat. I stickered boxes of sanitary napkins,
Pampers, Dixie cups, and tubes of aluminum foil. While my mother
planned the weekly menu, I shook bags of Skittles and peanut
M&M's like maracas, pretending I was Carmen Miranda with a
fruit hat towering over my head. Evenings, I helped my mother
clean the employees' bathroom, filling it with freshly cut carna-
tions and air freshener. It had an endless supply of soft tissue, just
like a home should have—not like ours, with its dingy yellow toilet, overflowing garbage can, and mushrooming tiles.

The deli also housed an upstairs office with a desk, an overhead lamp, a few file cabinets, and a floor safe. It was a dim, closet-
sized room, much like the size of a monk's cell. Posters of soup cans,
cereal boxes, and 1940s Vargas girls covered the walls. Before my
mother closed for the night, she'd fiddle with the combination and
deposit the day's cash and receipts. Drowsy, I'd wrap my arms around
her waist while she shut off all the lights, locked all the doors. For
a while now, my mother had quietly been fixing the books. Hand-
written invoices were simple to doctor, and Muhammad hardly

missed a few twenties here or there. And because he had given my mother keys to the store, she knew the combinations to all the safes. She was a woman that could be trusted, he thought. When I saw her forge signatures, heard the dollar bills crumple in her hands, heard her laughing in the bedroom with Manny, I wanted to say something, I wanted to interrupt. But whenever I opened my mouth, no sound came out. My mother was not a woman to be scolded or reproached.

One night when we arrived home from the deli, Manny was at the door waiting for us. "Two men, your connection, came to my job in Bensonhurst," he barked as soon as my mother stepped inside.

"Now they're *my* connection," she said, resting her purse on the table. I slipped quietly into the other room and pretended to fall asleep on the couch.

"They cleared the fucking place out. Came in that black Cadillac. Took the paints, the brushes, the ladders, took it all. *Collateral*, the motherfuckers called it. I had to send Luis to Benjamin Moore for more paint."

My mother drummed her fingers on the chair. "A month," she said. "We're only behind a fucking month."

Manny went on about the two men. "We like Rosie," they said. "We knew her when she was this high," they said, lowering their hands to their knees. "Like one of our own," they said. "We can't keep letting this slide," they said. "One month turns into two. You know how it is."

"We need your job, Rosie," Manny said. The volume dial on the television was turned up. They watched *Dynasty* on Wednesday nights. "Remember what they did to César after six months, his children in that trunk? His wife half in the shower, half in the kitchen."

"I know," my mother said. "Don't you fucking think I know?"

In my room, I built a fortress under my bedsheets with my stuffed animals—the bears, the bunnies, and the plush whale—and Big Michelle, my life-sized plastic doll. One of her blue eyes had fallen out. Under the covers, I clung to my family. I drew them closer.

My mother knelt down on the carpet and clutched my shoulders. Tonight, she announced, I would be in charge.

"Where are you going?" I asked.

"Out with a friend. Norma. Make sure you lock all the doors," she said.

I shuffled my feet in place. "It's a school night. You have work tomorrow."

My mother leaned back, sat cross-legged on the carpet. "I know what day of the week it is," she snapped. "All of a sudden you're my mother. I answer to you now—is this the game we're playing?"

"I hate being alone."

"Manny'll be back tonight," she said, rising. "From Atlantic City."

"He does this all the time. Disappears."

"You think you know everything, don't you?"

I watched her chest rise and fall. My mother couldn't stop moving, even for a second. I could hear her teeth grinding, jaw clicking and locking. When I looked at her, all I needed to do was replace the eye color, darken the skin a few shades, kink the hair, and she would be the image of her sister, Maria, who was either twitching or nodding off, depending on what kind of day she had, what kind of money she could get her hands on. I remembered a night waking to Maria's hands in my pajama pockets, her breath raspy and short. And then the figure in the doorway and my mother's cool voice—"You take one dime from her and see where your fingers end up." Years later I would hear a story about how one day my mother saw her sister on the other side of the street. Calmly, she crossed, walked up to her sister, and lunged for her throat with one hand. She choked her, practically shaking the change out of her pockets. It took three men to pry my mother's hand from her sister's neck.

And now the discos, the hair piled high, and the quick sniffs. Fists clenched, I wanted to shout out: "You should know better!"

"And those men that keep coming over? Asking for you, for Manny? What kind of mother leaves her daughter alone?" I said.

She pinched my arm hard until I fell to my knees, whimpering.

"Try finding better," she said and stormed out to meet her friend.

Hours later, I woke up. All the lights were on in the apartment. I crouched down low and crawled out of my room. Glass table lamps glowed bright, ceiling lights and 60-watt bulbs illuminated the interior, giving off the impression of daylight. The front door was wide open—all the locks freed, the windows unbolted. I moved from room to room. Nothing was missing; everything was in its place. Except for a note that read, "We liked watching your daughter sleep." Barefoot, I ran into the hall and downstairs to the ground floor. It was so cold. Standing in front of my landlords' door, I wondered whether I should knock, if I would be interrupting their sound sleep. If it was rude. But I soft-knuckled the door, and a tall woman in a black pageboy wig opened it. She climbed the flights, hunted through each room, in the closets, under the beds, and assured me in a calm motherly voice, "No one's here. You can come back in."

I lay in bed and stared up at the ceiling. The landlord lingered over my forehead, her lips moist and slightly puckered, then suddenly she retreated.

When the sun came up through the trees, Manny arrived home. I poured cereal into a bowl while he reached inside the refrigerator and got himself a glass of buttermilk. His eyes were bloodshot, and from his shirt pocket he unearthed a bottle of Afrin. After a few sniffs, he hacked, cleared his throat, and stared at the loaf of white bread on the table. I continued to eat.

"Where is she?" Manny asked. He held a slice of bread in his hand and pressed down on it with his fingers.

"With Norma."

"All night?"

I nodded.

He sighed, tore the bread into miniature pieces. "She has work today." In a smaller voice he said, "They've been warning her. About being late. About not coming to work at all."

"Did you come home last night? Early?" I asked.

"That wasn't me," he said, and paused. "Was someone here?" His voice was hoarse, tinged with fear. "In the *house*?"

"I was here," I said. Rising from the chair, I went over to the sink, turned on the tap, and furiously scrubbed my bowl with a Brillo pad. Lathered it up with soapy hot water. My fingers pruned from the soaking. But it felt good, necessary.

I felt Manny's eyes on my back.

"You don't need to go at it that hard," he said. "You can use a sponge."

"I know."

It was then that we heard the fumbling of keys, the easy slip of metal into the front door. We froze. Without looking at either of us, my mother clipped past, leaving Manny and me with the smell of stale cigarettes and powdered musk in her wake.

Manny folded and unfolded his hands. His wiry hair was flecked with paint. "I have a drywall in Canarsie today. I can drop you on the way."

I turned up the faucet to drown out his voice with water.

"I'll go on my own," I said.

Just as Manny had predicted, my mother lost her job at the deli. They were closing down, Muhammad said. Maybe they would reopen in New Jersey, they didn't know. Manny shook his head and said they really fired her because she was always late, but they were too scared to tell her. The night after she was let go, I awoke to find her in my room.

"Wake up, wake up," she said, shaking me from sleep. Rubbing my eyes, I reached on the nightstand for my eyeglasses. For a few moments, my mother appeared as a soothing blur of black hair framing white. But as she came into focus, she looked haggard, unstable. Her teeth were chattering and a cluster of pimples dotted her chin.

"What's wrong?" I asked.

"We have to go," she said. "Put on your clothes."

"Go where? It's the middle of the night." I was scared that she had lost it, that she had finally gone crazy. Because she *looked* crazy.

"We're meeting Norma for a thing. A thing. At the retirement home where she works. But we've got to go now."

When I didn't say anything, didn't move, my mother stripped

the blankets off my bed. "I need you to keep watch for us. We need this money. Don't you understand how much I owe?"

"Not me," I said in a small voice.

"Who else if not you?"

I slid to the floor and drew my knees up close, allowing what she'd said to sink in. I still couldn't believe our sprees at the deli were over. There would be no more gorging on cold cuts and ice cream. No more arranging of the endless rows of treats. After all the months my mother spent in training, I'd really thought things would be different. Why couldn't she have taken her role as manager seriously?

"I'm not going anywhere!" I said, inching myself up. I made a break for the bathroom and hid behind the locked door.

My mother pounded on the door so hard I thought the hinges would break. "Get your ass out here this minute! Wait until you get out of the bathroom. See what I'll do to you."

I knew my mother could kill anyone, including me, if she wanted to. Once, she'd clamped down hard on my nose, tugging— playing noogies, she called it—until my shirt was covered with drops of my blood and I had to lean my head back and breathe through a wad of toilet paper.

Another time she'd hugged me so hard it seemed she was trying to bury me in her. I could feel her ribs against my face and hear her jaw clicking from the spearmint gum she chewed. She held my head against her chest so tightly I couldn't move. And I realized then that my mother could put me on pause, hold my breath if she wanted to. I waved my arms, shouted into her smock that I couldn't breathe. It was only then she let me go.

She was outside the door now, banging on it. I sat in the tub and clung to the plastic shower curtain with the dancing ducks while she cursed, threatened, and begged. I knew she could break down the door if she wanted to.

My mother disappeared for a week and we accepted this. Manny and I went about our respective days as if nothing had happened, watching her space on the couch grow cold, the blankets she crocheted tossed aside. Bits of yarn coming undone. One morning outside school, Manny claimed that this was a good thing, her being gone. "Let her cool off," he said, his hands gripping the steering wheel of the station wagon he drove. "Get her head together."

"I'm late for homeroom," I told Manny and headed inside.

The first time I met Manny at my mother's diner, his face was covered in bruises the color of ocher. Later I would learn they came from men displeased with his unresolved gambling debts. Over breakfast, he gave me a sack filled with pennies and said, "Here, this is for you." At the door of the restaurant, he stood waving, paint speckles on his hairy arms. My mother smiled. She leaned over the counter, her own bruises finally healed after leaving Danny, a man who, for almost four years, considered her his personal punching bag. "That man's going to take us away from Danny, from Maria, the drugs, all of it," she said.

When they married a few months later at City Hall, I wasn't invited.

Barely a year later, my mother had whittled down to nothing, all sallow skin and bone. She pushed food around her plate as if it sickened her to look at it. She'd started to hide vials in her pocketbook, behind the toilet bowl, in the sugar canisters, in my pillowcase—stashing cocaine everywhere. She had become a woman who made a great deal of money but couldn't explain how she spent it, a woman whose hands trembled, who grew her pinkie nails long, who sought sanctuary in locked bathrooms.

I despised Manny. I loathed his fleshy lips, his brittle mustache, how he spit when he talked. How he reeked of paint and household cleaning products mixed with body odor. His damn T-shirt that read: "Menachem Painting—We Do the Best for You." And this is what I hated about him most: he gave my mother her first lines of cocaine.

A week before my twelfth birthday, I woke to the smell of buttermilk pancakes and brown butter. From my bedroom, I could hear the sounds of frying—the crackling hiss from the skillets. I tiptoed into the kitchen to find my mother cooking me an elaborate breakfast. Sugared blueberries, raspberries, and diced bananas spilled out of small glass bowls. Fried sausage links and hotcakes topped with rich maple syrup covered my plate. The abundance of food irked me. We'd been living on thirty-nine-cent packets of Oodles of Noodles for two weeks.

"What's all this?" I asked.

"What does it look like? Breakfast. Eat before it gets cold."

"Where are my Lucky Charms?"

"In the garbage," she said, whistling. "Cereal was yesterday. Today we have pancakes."

My mother sat down and watched me eat. She smoked Kent 100s down to the filter, and when I was done, she collected the dishes and piled them up in the sink.

"Get dressed," she said. "I have your gift."

In my room, double knotting my shoelaces, I wondered what my mother wanted from me.

Outside, we passed windows displaying narcissus bulbs blooming wildly. A carousel of twinkling lights and large-scale Nativity figures decorated lawns. Gutter puddles glimmered with ice that hadn't completely frozen. The snow was coming down in sheets and I felt the crunch underfoot.

"Where are we going?" I asked.

"Into the city," she replied curtly. But first we stopped in front of an abandoned house on Thirty-ninth Street. Vacant warehouses, dilapidated cars with windows bashed in, sidewalks and storefronts covered in graffiti—"Sharky was here"—glass shards from smashed beer bottles, marked the street. The only sound was a Villabatc bakery delivery truck petering its way to the crowded thoroughfare of Thirteenth Avenue. The street appeared blighted, with its gray buildings and dead weeds. We paused in front of one of the two houses on the street. My mother told me to wait outside, that she would only be a minute.

Planks of wood were hammered onto curtained windows. My mother entered through a front door that was missing a knob. I stood in front of the house, shivering and scared, rubbing my hands together. I balled my hands up inside my coat while I waited. It was hailing. After an hour, my mother materialized, glassy-eyed, jittery.

"Let's go," she said, tugging my arm, "we don't have time."

At the token booth, I asked, "What's in the city?"

She was cryptic in her response. "Your gift. I'll tell you on the train."

We boarded the last car of the B train and sat huddled in a two-seater by the conductor's booth. "We're going back to the deli," she said.

I started to shake my head. My mother grabbed me by the chin and said, "Listen to me." Her eyes were so black. The car was empty except for two women barking at each other in Cantonese, arranging their red plastic bags about their feet.

"I'm listening," I whispered.

"All you need to do is talk for ten minutes. You can do that, right? I know *you* can talk. I'll just be in the office collecting what's *mine*..." And then my mother's voice trailed off. Talking to herself, she seemed foreign, distant. "They told me they were closing down, they were going bankrupt, but they lied to me. Hired someone else. A woman they could get over on. Could *fuck* with. They think they can win over me, but I'll show them." My mother's face was tight. She pounded her thighs with her fists. "And so what if I played with the books a little bit? So what?" Angry that she had been caught stealing, again.

"They owe me," she said. "They took my money from me. They took my job from me."

I wondered why my mother couldn't just let it go, why she always had to hold on to her anger.

"We'll be home before you know it."

When we came out of the subway, my mother said, "Keep Muhammad busy for ten minutes, okay?"

"What am I supposed to talk to him about? He doesn't even know me," I said.

"Make up something. Tell him about school. For *Chrissake*, do I have to do all the work here?"

I could tell I was pushing her. She could explode at any minute, and she would blame me for ruining her plan, for messing up everything.

Inside the deli, the overhead light fixtures were too bright, which made the white floors and walls look medicinal. Ammonia and bleach hung heavily in the air. The floors were still damp from a mopping. Muhammad regarded my mother with suspicion, but softened when he saw me. He laid a hand on my head; his fingers were warm and moist, smelling of stale cigarette smoke and cinnamon.

"Little girl, one day you're going to grow big." He chuckled, fluffing my hair.

"She's big enough," my mother said, a toothpick lodged in her teeth. I felt as if I were being passed between them, an object for them to pet, to coddle. She massaged my shoulder, grinning. "I'll only be a minute."

My mother said she had come to collect the rest of her things and get her final paycheck from the office. As soon as she disappeared, I started to talk. I told Muhammad about my clarinet, Harry Penelope, and how I could finally play the *Star Wars* score in addition to the national anthem. "Can I play for you?" I asked him, chattering on when he didn't answer. There was a sense of urgency for my mouth to keep moving, for my words to cover up the goings-on upstairs. As I prattled on, I noticed Muhammad eyeing the office door, silently timing my mother. His brows knitted, his jaw tensed.

"Just a second," he said, walking toward the office.

I scanned the store searching for diversions. A stack of candy that I could accidentally knock over, display cases I could bump against, *anything*—but everything was tucked away, in its place, pristine and clean. I was torn between wanting to stall Muhammad and wanting to expose my mother to him. But I knew if I did what she'd told me to, I'd have a fistful of birthday bills to revel in at the end of the day.

Suddenly my mother surfaced, holding up a pair of sneakers, speaking in my stead. "I looked everywhere for them. Imagine these getting lost. I found them in one of the file drawers," she said, doe-eyed and breathless.

Muhammad took my mother's hand in his and said, "I'm sorry for how things turned out. Try to understand these things happen."

"Think nothing of it. I got what I came for," my mother said, and beckoned for me. "Come on, Lisa, it's getting late. We have to go."

And with a wave we left, and a few blocks down my mother peeled five twenties from her bag, which overflowed with cash. "Happy birthday," she said. In the middle of the street, she danced, swiveled her hips, snapping her fingers to an imaginary beat.

She shoved her head into her black bag and inhaled.

I held the bills in my hand. I was rich! The weight of this crime—that my mother could get arrested, that I could get sent to a home—fell by the wayside. All that remained was the money, the great sums of it, and the fact that my mother had gotten away with it again.

As we made our way to the subway, I peered at all the store-front windows. The crowded, shabby displays of mannequins modeling garish heels, pocketbooks hanging from their arms like pendulums, the torn bean can labels peeking out from bodega windows—all of this overwhelmed me. Everything appeared used, sickly. Not like the gleaming deli we had just robbed. I brought my hand up to my chest. I couldn't breathe. It was only when I let go, a few $10 bills fluttering away, that I joined my hand with my mother's. I reached out for the money, but my mother pulled me back. Didn't I know there would always be more? she asked.

How quickly money goes, how it flies out of your hands before you remember whether you held all twenties or tens. My fortune was spent within a few weeks on sheets of Lisa Frank stickers, feasts in diners, and a midnight blue jumpsuit with silver stars all over it. For weeks I wore the jumpsuit to school, pranced around homeroom, raced down the hall as bits of glitter trailed behind me. "*Que linda,*" everyone said, fingering the soft cotton. It felt good to be envied.

And after it was all gone, all spent on items folded neatly into drawers or protected in albums with plastic or consumed until my fingers were licked clean, it occurred to me that this was what it felt like to have less than when I started. The excitement of that day had dissolved quietly, swiftly, as my mother lay comatose on the couch, staring at nothing, getting lost in it, while Manny buzzed about the house, making a list of people to call. Again and again, he'd run out to the pay phone down the street, frantically trying to drum up some business. The phone company had shut off our phone because the bill wasn't paid. I'd lock myself in my bedroom and lie on the bed, petting all my pretty new things. But as each day passed, these things, which were only things, began to grow old, and their luster faded.

Eight months later, Manny strapped cardboard boxes filled with our possessions, the whole of our lives, onto the top of his station wagon. He crammed them into the backseat of the car, filling any space he could find. We were moving to Long Island, starting over, my mother said. But twenty minutes into our trip, as we barreled down the Brooklyn-Queens Expressway, she let out a scream. The cords on top of the car had loosened, and boxes tumbled down on either side, spilling their contents. Among the mismatched socks, records, and costume jewelry that poured out, I watched my beautiful blue jumpsuit with the silver stars fly up into the air. It soared amid the traffic before settling to the ground. I wanted to swing open the car door and run after it, but it was already down the road, sliding back toward Brooklyn. Cars swerved, but there were no accidents. We veered toward a shoulder and recovered what we could. Manny tied what was left on top of the car and we set off again. As we sped farther away, our old home behind us, a new one ahead, I could barely make out the jumpsuit anymore. It had been reduced to nothing more than a glinting speck on the road.

A Dollar a Tear

Marian Fontana

Checks began arriving at my apartment within a week of the Twin Towers' collapse. Also pictures from children, burning towers drawn in crayon, sad faces in the windows. Quarters, dimes, and dollars were taped sloppily to the bottom of their letters. There were endless sympathy cards, too, many from people in small towns I had never heard of, in states I had never been to, checks carefully placed inside the envelopes. The New York City Fire Department forwarded me so much mail I learned my FedEx deliveryman's name, where he grew up, and what he liked to watch on TV. I opened each envelope slowly, touched by the kindness of strangers and saddened by a windfall I could never enjoy without my husband.

Dave had always told me that he was worth more dead than alive. Every fireman knew it was the truth. I hated when he talked like that and would often plug my ears like a five-year-old, humming until he stopped. We both knew his job had risks, but neither of us could have imagined his violent death on September 11, our eighth wedding anniversary.

In the days that followed, friends, family, neighbors, and the world, it seemed, wrapped their arms around my shoulders as I waited and wept. More and more checks arrived. I threw them into a drawer of my desk, hiding them under stacks of mail like they were porn. I didn't want anyone to know of my secret wealth. I just wanted everything back the way it was before.

On my first birthday without Dave, I got drunk. My sister threw me a birthday party at a local bar where my friends bought me an endless supply of too-sweet margaritas and I lit my cigarette from my birthday candles. I tried not to remember the party Dave had given me the year before, when he rolled up our rug in the living room to make a dance floor. The fire truck double-parked in front of our apartment, and firefighters danced with my giggling friends, filling the living room with the smell of stale smoke and sweat. Most of them died along with Dave.

When I woke up the next morning in my six-year-old son's bunk bed, the painting of a rainbow he had taped to the top bunk was spinning in circles. It took me a moment to realize where I was, to remember that Aidan had slept at my parents' and that Brigid, the widow I was closest to, was snoring lightly in my bedroom. I stared at Aidan's stuffed animals lined up against the wall, his "kingdom" he called it, and I suddenly missed him with a deep, infinite emptiness. Last week I'd tried to remove a few of the animals on his bunk to keep him from falling out of his bed at night, but he had panicked, his eyes mapped with worry. His therapist told me it was normal for grieving children to cling tightly to toys, to worry that they, too, can disappear. I rolled over and looked at the clock, which reminded me I had to be in the city soon. Another widow and I had organized a financial seminar for the families today. I needed to know what to do with all those checks.

"Brigid, wake up," I called, sitting up on the edge of the bed, staring at the leaves Dave had woven around the room to make it feel like a jungle.

"I don't want to go," Brigid moaned from down the hall. The bed creaked and I pictured her sitting up.

"I know . . . ," I answered. There was nothing I would have liked more than to stay in Aidan's small bed, pull the flag quilt someone sent over my head, and sleep the past seven months away. I was exhausted from starting a 9/11 families organization, doing media interviews, crying at endless funerals, sorting through piles of mail, attending meetings and press conferences with politicians, and holding rallies to keep my husband's firehouse open. Most of all, I was sore with grief.

Brigid came into Aidan's room. Her chestnut hair was poking up in places and her eyes were beet red. "I feel horrible," she mumbled. We had become fiercely close since our husbands died, holding hands and tissues as we attended services together, calling each other when we caught a whiff of our husband on one of the shirts still hanging in the closet.

I made extra-strong coffee, and we sank into the soft cushions of my new chenille couch. The firefighters had come the week before to take my twelve-year-old faded white sofa away. They arrived with tools and joked as they worked, sawing and chopping the couch into smaller pieces. As I watched, a thousand memories floated away with the tiny specks of foam and wood. They carried my couch outside in carefully taped bundles, leaving old toys, crumbs, pencils, and coins scattered among the dust where it used to be.

"You got something here," one of the firefighters told me,

pointing to a dusty piece of paper on the floor. He stared at it in disbelief. "It's a $10,000 check from the Red Cross." A familiar flash of guilt traveled through me. When Dave started on the job, that amount would have been half a year's pay.

Another one stepped over to look. "You're kiddin'," he said. "You should cash that soon."

"I DON'T WANT IT!" I almost screamed, but an awkward silence filled the room instead. I felt responsible for all of it: their shameful salaries, how they all had to work second jobs to survive. I wondered if they were happy for me, or jealous and angry about the outpouring of support the other widows and I were receiving. Perhaps they were simply noting, as Dave used to do, that they were worth more dead than alive.

Despite our miserable hangovers, Brigid and I pulled ourselves together and headed to the seminar. A light rain fell as she drove her new Lexus SUV over the Brooklyn-Queens Expressway toward Manhattan. I loved to look at the old brown water towers that sat on Brooklyn rooftops like giant spools. We drove in silence through the dimly lit Battery Tunnel. I had learned two weeks before that Dave had run through it on foot to get to the World Trade Center. Squad 1 was stuck in traffic, and so he and the other firefighters jumped off the rig, following the lieutenant past cars and trucks that couldn't move. The deputy commissioner had told me how she'd seen Dave running past, smiling his wide-cheeked grin at her. "Be safe," he'd said. I put my hand on Brigid's thigh when we passed Ground Zero; her high-pitched wail always triggered my own tears. Small leafless trees lined the esplanade of the West Side Highway, their branches like thin wet arms against the gray sky. I remembered how after 9/11, the esplanade was lined with people holding signs and flags for the firefighters and police. They applauded when the firefighters passed to go look for bodies.

"Where's a garage?" Brigid asked as we neared the hotel.

"It's Sunday. We should be able to find a space," I said, cracking my window to listen to the sound of wet tires hiss on the pavement.

"I don't feel like looking," she said.

"They're everywhere. There's one right there!" I pointed to a meter, but Brigid drove past.

"I always go to a garage," she said.

"That's a waste of money if there's a spot."

"It's a convenience," she said, shaking her head. We didn't always agree about how to spend money. Brigid was used to having it and I was not. All my life, I'd cut coupons and shopped at thrift stores. Recently, I'd quit my day job as a gymnastics teacher to be a freelance writer, and Dave had decided to forgo working a second job so he could spend extra time with our son. When he died, we were living on $450 a week. Brigid always tried to make me feel better about the money I'd received. At restaurants, she'd insist I order steak instead of the special, but I couldn't help feeling like I was spending pieces of Dave himself.

We arrived at the hotel where the seminar was being held and sat in the front row of the generic meeting room. Blue folders full of financial information covered each seat. I riffled through the pages, trying to seem interested, but to me they seemed about as exciting as dental work. Dave had always tried to get me interested in our financial future, but I'd never paid much attention. Luckily, he'd had huge portions of his checks deducted so we would be comfortable when he retired or if he was ever killed.

Suze Orman entered the room holding her new book, *The Road to Wealth*. Her black leather jacket swished as she paced back and forth, her short blond hair flopping into her face.

"How we have been raised has a huge effect on how we view and manage money," she began. People nodded in agreement, and I thought of my grandfather Joe, of the way he pined for money for most of his life as if it were an unattainable woman. Adopted by a young couple in Portland, Maine, my grandfather quickly realized he'd been attained for labor instead of love. He spent most of his childhood working at the family-owned candy store, making malteds for his peers who attended school nearby. He tried his best but never earned his adopted parents' affection. Still, they promised he would inherit their wealth someday.

By the time my grandfather was a teenager, he'd moved to New York, where he worked the assembly line in a Tropicana factory. He met my grandmother in the elevator of their Bronx apartment building, and they lived there for many years, marrying, having kids, and anticipating their future wealth. But when his adopted parents finally died, the inheritance they left him was barely enough to cover the funeral expenses. By the time I met my grandfather, he had become a sad and defeated man who rarely rose from his green vinyl recliner. I was too young to understand what had happened, but I seemed to absorb from him the unspoken power that money could have over people's lives.

"Are you glazing over?" Suze Orman asked me suddenly, and I felt my face flush. I didn't know how long I'd been daydreaming, but I'd mentally left the room somewhere between laddered bonds and T-bills. I sat up taller in my chair to answer.

"I was just thinking how I should have been born when they

traded beads, because I find this all so overwhelming." Everyone chuckled, including Suze.

"Yes!" she said emphatically, her eyes stretching impossibly wide. "What we have begins with what we think!"

I thought about my own personal history with money, how my parents were hippies who prided themselves on being resourceful, who snuck Pathmark cream soda and rice cakes into the movies to save a few bucks. While my grandfather was obsessed with money, my father seemed repulsed by it. When he paid for batteries at the hardware store, he flung the bills down as if they were something disgusting. We owned cars so rusted that the street was visible below my feet, but somehow I never felt like I didn't have enough, and I never thought much about money. Sometimes, though, in the long, hot summers, when my parents' business as marriage and family therapists would slow down, I would lie in bed, moths pinging off my window screen, and listen to their hushed conversations about how to make ends meet. Their worried voices echoed up the stairs, and I couldn't help but worry, too.

Suze was talking about emotional responses to money now. A weatherworn woman in an FDNY cap asked her about the Victim Compensation Fund, which had been created by an act of Congress after 9/11 to compensate the families and prevent them from suing the airlines. I had attended numerous meetings and press conferences about the fund, whose restrictions came under fire from a number of politicians, including Attorney General Eliot Spitzer and Senators Hillary Clinton and Chuck Schumer. What at first had seemed like a benevolent act of Congress to help the victims' families suddenly began to seem like an ill-conceived effort to change the legal system by putting limits on the damages that could be recovered for pain and suffering in future lawsuits. I remembered attending another meeting about money in a dimly lit lecture hall on Third Avenue a few months before. Special Master Kenneth Feinberg, the man appointed to distribute the 9/11 victims' fund, presided over a room filled with victims' family members. He was hard to like, with the affected accent of a wealthy Bostonian and the cold countenance of someone who had never lost anyone he loved. He seemed surprised by the families' confusion and anger and answered questions by narrowing his bespectacled eyes and shrugging. At one point, a blond woman in her mid-thirties raised her hand and said, "My husband was killed and I am dying of cancer. He took out huge life insurance policies to protect me and our kids. Now, with these restrictions, I will get nothing from the fund." Feinberg rubbed his chin and placed his foot dramatically onto a chair. I had read somewhere that he wanted to be an actor but chose law instead. "I'm not going to tell you that some people won't slip through the cracks," he said flatly. And she cried right then and there. In the dark, someone cursed him, another mumbled, but all I heard were the muffled tears of unfathomable loss.

I hated being at meetings about the victims' fund, death and money, the subjects I most abhorred. Yet now they seemed to be the focus of everything I did. A few weeks after the meeting with Feinberg, I was asked to be a guest on the Brian Lehrer radio show on WNYC. I had been on once before, and I liked how literate and thoughtful the host was. At the appointed time, I dutifully called him from my home. We talked for a while about the work I was doing (mostly advocacy for the victims' families; creativity had left me), how I felt about the fund (shitty), then he went to the phones for questions. I hadn't known this was planned and had never done it before. I paced around my living room and kitchen, carefully considering the callers' questions, bracing myself for a storm that I felt coming. When the interview was almost over, a young woman called in screaming into the phone with indignation. "IT SEEMS LIKE YOU PEOPLE WANT TO BE SET FOR LIFE!"

I stared dumbly at the cracked linoleum on my kitchen floor, trying to collect my thoughts. "I understand that it might seem that way," I said, "but to me it is not about the money, it is a moral issue." I kept my voice low and steady. "The government has taken away our rights to sue who might be responsible, added restrictions that most adversely affect the middle-class family, and changed the legal system for the whole country." When we went off the air, the host thanked me and apologized about the last caller. I hung up the phone and burst into tears, wondering how a stranger could evoke so much emotion from me. I hated being judged, envied for being given something I never requested. It reminded me of Patsy Muller in junior high school, how all my friends talked behind her back because her eyes were too blue, her skin too smooth, her hair just like Farrah Fawcett's. How was any of that her fault?

After that show, I decided I would no longer do interviews about the fund. I had founded my organization to talk about firefighters' salaries, to help the 9/11 families get information about the site, and to ensure a dignified recovery at Ground Zero. This was all I was interested in doing.

"Bead lady, am I losing you again?" Suze said, breaking into my thoughts. She was smiling at me, her teeth perfect and straight. I shook my head no, even though I'd been lost from the very beginning.

The truth is money will never be something I want to focus on. The Monday after the meeting I quietly deposited my stack of checks, the teller's eyes widening as she punched them into her adding machine. I looked around nervously, wishing she would go faster so that no one, not firefighters, not friends, not even me, had to see them.

It has been almost five years since Dave died. I bought a house and a hybrid car and enjoy treating my friends to dinner. I am not ungrateful for the money, but in a way it's been as much of a burden as a blessing. At some point, the tide of empathy about 9/11 shifted, and the media began portraying widows as out-of-control rich women spending money on fancy cars and breast implants. The sums we received were exaggerated and printed in local papers. I lent money to friends who asked, then felt confused when they quietly slipped out of my life as though embarrassed. I hired a man Dave knew to repair some things around my house and later heard he'd charged me double the market value. Most of the firefighters have stopped visiting altogether.

I've felt overwhelmed by managing the money I've been given. Scared I would make mistakes or be taken advantage of by the dozens of financial advisers who solicited me after 9/11. Dave had always handled the money, and managing it felt like another task to fulfill alone.

It's most difficult during the holidays. Not only do memories of Dave take my breath away, but now that everyone knows I have money, deciding what to buy them is daunting. Do I purchase a nice bowl for my sister, like I might have five years ago, or replace the TV that she has been complaining is on the fritz? Will I be considered cheap if I spend less than I did last year? How much should I give to charity? When I finally cashed my checks, it took three sessions with my therapist to decide on an appropriate amount to give my mother-in-law and members of my family and how to go about setting up college funds for my nieces.

Christmas has passed. I bought my sister the television, re- placed the rickety stools in my parents' kitchen, and resisted buy- ing everything Aidan wanted on his list. I gave to a dozen charities and bought my eleven in-laws tickets to a Broadway show, as I have done for the last three years. It gets us together, and I don't have to schlep heavy gifts when Aidan and I attend the family gathering at my mother-in-law's home. Since Dave died, his mother has trans- formed herself into a living shrine to him, his photo printed on a gold pendant around her neck, 9/11 buttons adorning her shirts, FDNY hats and sweatshirts. The license plate on her car reads, "LTDVESQ1" (Lieutenant Dave, Squad 1), and she has a bumper sticker that reads, "Many Gave Some, Some Gave All." A banner of firefighters erecting the flag at Ground Zero blows in front of her house.

Inside, the house is cluttered with books, catalogs, photos of Dave, and 9/11 memorabilia. At Christmas, while my nieces were opening their gifts, my mother-in-law pulled me into the kitchen. In her small, wrinkled hand was a xeroxed copy of an application for funds, "next of kin" circled in blue pen.

"The people in my group told me about this stamp fund, and I got excited because I thought I would finally get what's due me," she said. My mother-in-law is a member of a parents' group that lost their firefighter sons. In the almost five years since their forma- tion, half of the parents have alienated their daughters-in-law with jealousy and resentment over the funds the widows have received. This fire has been fueled by those parents in the group whose sons were unmarried and who are therefore qualified to get money themselves. They tell my mother-in-law about every flag, every fund, every 9/11 locket and bear, and she requests them from me often before I have even received them.

"It says next of kin, so I was hoping if you weren't using it, I could have it," she said. I looked at the application. The funds they'd be distributing came to about $10,000.

My niece entered then and kissed me on the cheek. "I love them," she said, shuffling through the kitchen in the new slippers I'd bought her for Christmas. I tried to smile, to hide the heat rising to my face. I glanced at my mother-in-law, then headed for the bathroom, trying hard not to cry, wondering when she would stop, when it would be enough.

The following week I received a letter from her. Enclosed was a mortgage payment for her Winnebago, which she insisted she would have to sell if I did not give her the money. I felt emotionally blackmailed, angry that the neediness that had once frustrated Dave was now focused on me in a blatant showdown of loss. I considered telling her everything I felt, but I knew it was as fruitless as throwing a chair off a sinking ship, so I wrote a check instead. The hole that Dave has left in both our hearts is as wide as the ocean, and nothing can bring him back to us, not even a dollar a tear.

Porn Bought My Football

Chris Offutt

My parents were born within a few months of each other during the "dirty thirties," as my mother called the Depression. She came of age in Lexington, Kentucky, drawing lines up the backs of her legs with charcoal to simulate the seams of stockings she couldn't afford. Her father sold shoes at a department store. Mom's only aunt was a nun, and her favorite uncle was an undertaker who distinguished himself by embalming the racehorse Man o' War. Both sides of her family made a living in the unruly world that surrounded the horse-race industry. Mom's relatives included professional gamblers, bartenders, poker dealers, bookies, and jockeys. These were people of great loyalty to one another, close-knit and fierce, part of a force that successfully defended itself against organized mobsters from Ohio who tried to muscle in on the gambling. Within the loose circles of organized crime, Lexington is still regarded as an open city.

My father grew up on a dairy farm near Louisville. To save

the land during the Depression, my grandfather rented out the main house and moved his family into the sharecropper's quarters—a hundred-year-old log cabin with defensive gun ports bored through the walls. The water lines froze every winter. Dad was a dreamy child, a mama's boy who read escapist fiction and playacted stories from his imagination. The tedium of farmwork instilled in him an aversion to physical labor and a strong work ethic—both of which followed him throughout life. At age ten, he wrote his first novel, a Western adventure.

Dad attended the University of Louisville on a full academic scholarship financed by the Ford Foundation that compelled bright kids to skip their senior year of high school and go straight to college. After a difficult initial transition to the urban social life, Dad became editor of the school newspaper and president of his fraternity. He also won a college science-fiction-writing contest sponsored by *If* magazine. Dad graduated with a degree in English and began selling Procter & Gamble products to small country stores. Young and single, he was transferred to Lexington.

Mom went to Transylvania University for a year until economics forced her to quit and take a job in a bank. She met my father at a Catholic youth dance. At age twenty-two, they considered themselves old to be unwed and were eager to start a family.

They soon married, and I was born the following year. My parents' lives reflected the enthusiasm of the 1950s—they lived in a freshly built ranch house, owned a hardtop convertible, enjoyed martinis, and played records on a new hi-fi. Dad didn't like jazz or rock and roll, and Mom despised Elvis Presley because he reminded her of the greasy corner boys she'd been warned against. They preferred the crooning of Frank Sinatra. For Halloween they dressed as beatniks.

With three young children and a pregnant wife, Dad envisioned a brighter future selling insurance seventy-five miles east in the hills. He bought a house that had been empty for more than a year. Haldeman was the smallest outlying community, farthest from town, and had a poor reputation due to its bootlegger, drag races, poker games, and frequent bouts of gunplay. The two-story brick house in Haldeman offered everything my father wanted, including two bathrooms, a basement, a large attic, and a private dirt road. Just as important, Mr. Haldeman had built it for himself. After growing up in a sharecropper's cabin, my father had finally made it to the main house.

During the 1960s, eastern Kentucky experienced its greatest period of out-migration as thousands of people left for industrial jobs. Mom and Dad did the opposite. They moved into Appalachia and never left. I was five years old. My new hometown was founded in 1905 along with the Kentucky Firebrick Company, the biggest employer in the hills. Local mines provided clay for the manufacture of large yellow bricks that were transported north to line the kilns of steel mills. In the old days, Haldeman had its own water system, railroad station, barbershop, saloon, tennis court, and small hospital. The town ran on scrip, paper money issued by the company to its workers, redeemable only at the high-priced company store. Mr. Haldeman established an athletic association funded by a compulsory tax of every worker. The amount was equivalent to $50 a month by today's economic standards. This mandatory fee built a baseball diamond and basketball court where employees were permitted free access to watch games played with the equipment they'd been forced to buy.

In 1934 the workers produced sixty thousand bricks a day. They attempted to form a union affiliated with the AFL. The Kentucky Firebrick Company notified the county judge, who called in the National Guard to stop a strike. Mr. Haldeman recognized his inability to control the town he'd founded or the men he employed. Within a year, he sold the town to U.S. Steel, the biggest client for firebrick. Haldeman's glory was reduced to empty mines, rusty sections of train track, and dirt roads that dwindled into the underbrush. The water tanks went dry. The buildings commenced a slow collapse. By the time my parents arrived, the town had been in decline for thirty years.

Haldeman was composed mainly of out-of-work workingmen whose wives occasionally held menial jobs in town. Many of our neighbors heated with coal or wood, and some replaced broken windows with panels of cardboard. Others lacked indoor plumbing. People canned garden vegetables for the winter, slaughtered hogs in the fall, hunted year-round, and fished when they could. The chief source of income was tobacco. Many families lived on various forms of federal assistance. A hierarchy formed based on monthly income—military pension, physical disability, Aid to Dependent Children, Social Security. At the top of the heap was "the crazy check," a large amount received for emotional disability. So many people received welfare that the local bootlegger accepted food stamps, which he sold to store managers, who exchanged them with the government. Eventually the bootlegger cut out the middleman and improved his profits by dealing directly with corrupt state officials.

Kingsford Charcoal bought the brick-making facility and used the kilns to burn railroad ties soaked in creosote. The resulting smoke killed infants and the elderly, turned the creeks black, and produced a high rate of emphysema and asthma. At night, the smoke blended with fog to form an opaque wall. My mother drove the slowest speed possible, following my father, who walked a few feet ahead carrying a flashlight. Town people knew where we lived by the smell of our clothes. My parents led a legal drive to force the charcoal plant to curb its pollution. Rather than face a court battle and bad publicity, Kingsford shut down operation. The air was suddenly clear. Everyone could breathe easier.

Some people appreciated my parents' efforts, but many resented our family—we had moved into a dying town and dealt it a fatal blow. Worse, we'd done it from Mr. Haldeman's house, the biggest in the community. The air was no longer lethal, but men were out of work again. I knew nothing of this at the time. When I was ten, the woods, free from smoke, were suddenly open to me, and the charcoal factory became a vast playground for daylong games of cops and robbers, army, and bicycle tag. I came home exhausted, covered in soot from the kilns, my body scraped and bruised. The next day I went back for more.

My father flourished as an insurance salesman. One of my earliest memories is of waiting for him to come home. If he'd closed a sale, he honked the horn in a distinctive way, and supper would have an element of cheer. A silent horn signaled the family to be careful. By 1967, he was running his own agency in Morehead, overseeing several employees at two branch offices in nearby towns. People in other parts of the country may have been protesting the war and indulging the Summer of Love, but Dad was working sixty hours a week. He wore tailored three-piece suits and drove the only Mercedes in the hills.

In the meantime, Mom was single-handedly raising four kids. She shopped for food, prepared every meal, washed all the dishes, cleaned the house, did the laundry, and took care of repairs. Overwhelmed by domestic duties, she carried out her tasks with a grim determination. Mom seldom smiled and never laughed. She was smart but uneducated, and her life lacked the structure and sense of purpose a job would provide.

Both my parents severed relations with their own families and had no friends in Haldeman. I don't recall any adults from the community ever visiting our house. Mom and Dad preferred the upper echelon of town society, which meant hobnobbing with the professors of Morehead State University, doctors who worked at the small local hospital, and a few lawyers. Mom hid her intimidation behind a patina of politesse and cheer. Essentially, my parents sought upward mobility in a world where there was plenty of traction but nowhere to go. Dad had accomplished his early goals of family, career, and status but found little satisfaction with success. Through public feud and private grudge he began withdrawing from the society in which he strove to belong.

At night, he wrote longhand in the dank basement. The walls leaked with every storm. Periodic plumbing problems caused the septic tank to back up and fill the floor with detritus. Snakes and vermin were not uncommon. Our well was contaminated so badly that we mixed Clorox with tap water to drink. On weekends Dad sat at the dining room table and used three fingers to type what he'd written through the week. He struck the keys of his manual typewriter with such force that his glass of water slowly moved across the table. Every so often he slammed the carriage return into the glass, drenching his manuscript and yelling at whoever was handy. More and more, I explored the world outdoors.

Haldeman was a hill-and-hollow community—a zip code with a creek. Several dead-end dirt roads branched off the blacktop. We had a church, post office, grade school, and general store. George Molton offered country staples on long shelves that sagged from the weight of flour, sugar, cigarettes, candy, Vienna sausages, bread, crackers, and canned goods. Two refrigerators stood side by side, one full of pop, the other containing milk and eggs. To save money, George kept the lights off most of the time, creating perpetual shadows in the room. If the store was closed, I crossed the creek to George's house and borrowed the key. I went to the store, found the merchandise, returned the key, and paid for the goods.

Haldeman had two actual employers. The school hired the teachers, a janitor, a bus driver, a secretary, and two women in the cafeteria. Mrs. Franklin was the only teacher who lived in the community, and the only one who didn't threaten her students with violence or beat them with a length of lumber. The Haldeman post office employed one person, Avanelle Eldridge, who heated the building with a woodstove. The flag was permanently attached to a pole, which she stored on the floor at night. Each morning she carried the flagpole outside and strapped it to a hickory fence post. Avanelle read letters to the illiterate and delivered mail personally to the sick.

The Haldeman bootlegger was a legendary figure widely admired for his ability to outwit the law. He sold beer, wine, and whiskey from a one-room shack located in a wide spot at the top of a hill, well placed to watch traffic and defend against a robbery. People parked next to the building and made transactions through a sliding panel of wood. The state police monitored illegal alcohol sales with several regional posts, each of which covered vast territory. The bootlegger operated at the farthest edge of their jurisdiction, less than a hundred yards from the county line. Because of this carefully chosen spot, the state troopers of the next-closest post couldn't bother him. When politics forced an official arrest, the bootlegger made arrangements for someone other than himself to serve jail time. The business closed briefly, then reopened to the joy of the community and the dismay of the preachers.

I wore an army shirt as a jacket due to its deep pockets and ability to withstand briars in the woods. The shirt was too big, which protected me from my rough-and-tumble habits—riding my bicycle along game paths through the woods, plunging down slopes, splashing through creeks, climbing trees, leaping from cliffs, playing at the charcoal factory. Several of us boys roamed the hills together, grateful to be free from our respective homes. When thirsty, we stopped at people's houses and asked for water. Our only mutual rule was to be home by dark. We had camaraderie and the woods, and a shared boyhood of remarkable freedom.

The heavy yellow bricks were everywhere—in the woods and creeks, propping foundations, stacked as steps, and holding doors open. During winter, people tucked hot bricks in bed to warm their feet. Haldeman's original buildings commenced their gradual collapse—windows first, then roofs and floors, until finally the exterior walls began to crumble. Each dislodged brick bore the name of the town, a perpetual reminder of Haldeman's former prosperity.

The War on Poverty had begun, and young people arrived with half-baked ideas of how to help us. One group of do-gooders saw us kids running free in the woods and decided we needed a youth center. They arranged for delivery of concrete blocks and lumber, which vanished overnight, used by families for house repairs. This was their greatest form of assistance, although certainly unintended. At the time, we considered our saviors supremely ignorant.

Dad's late nights paid off with the publication of a few short stories, and on their basis he was invited to attend the 1969 World Science Fiction Convention in St. Louis. My mother accompanied him. It was the farthest either had traveled from Kentucky, and the longest they'd been away—four days. The convention introduced them to the counterculture. Faced with the outrageous styles of hippies, Mom no longer worried that wives of professors and doctors might judge her clothes. Few people in Rowan County knew that Dad wrote, but science-fiction fans sought his autograph, a dream come true for him.

My parents went to St. Louis with the confidence of people who are naive about their own degree of naïveté and came home astonished. They had never questioned the lives they led or the motivations for their decisions, but merely followed the accepted patterns—they hated communists, loved JFK, and flew the flag on national holidays. A gigantic Douay-Rheims Bible was always open by the supper table. They had four kids because the Church opposed birth control. At age thirty-five, my parents felt trapped by the lives they'd assembled. The fissures were undoubtedly in place before, but now the cracks had deepened, and the surface of their life was beginning to peel.

My parents were not particularly brave people, but in 1970 they made a courageous decision, the only risk they ever took. Dad shut down his insurance agency to pursue his dream of writing. He hired a carpenter to build a home office, and Mom placed a desk in their bedroom, where she typed his manuscripts for submission. She treated this as a serious job and felt good about herself. Dad was happy as well. He quit the Church and wrote a letter of resignation to the pope. The Bible disappeared, replaced unceremoniously by a massive unabridged dictionary. Dad grew long hair and a beard, and Mom trimmed her hair in a pixie cut. They traded the Mercedes and Mom's car for a Volkswagen. Dad began writing ten hours a day.

After school I climbed a dirt road and walked a path through the woods, entering the house to the sound of two typewriters clattering simultaneously, a continual noise that represented home. Money was suddenly tighter. I wore shoes wrapped in electrical tape, and in August we received a set of mail-order school clothes to last the year. My parents' experience with economic deprivation during childhood resulted in household thrift. Dad insisted on saving tiny slivers of soap, which he then re-formed into new soap. Mom carefully kept dry eggshells year-round to make a Christmas wreath for the front door. My parents never discussed family finances in front of me. The general feeling was that we always had a little money but never really knew where the next chunk was coming from. Everything relied on Dad's continuing to write, and our family geared itself to protect his time, space, and emotional stability.

Dad went from being always gone to always home. I didn't feel as if I'd gained a father, but lost my mother, who shifted her attention to him. The house was suddenly less a family center and more a place of work—we had to be quiet lest we invoke Dad's wrath. Mom made it clear that she was not to be bothered unless someone was bleeding. I avoided the house as much as possible, preferring to be alone in the woods, at my neighbors' homes, or exploring the remnants of Haldeman. Dad's change in occupation made us more like other families—the father was home, the mother was subservient, the kids desired to be away.

Molton's Store was two miles away by car, but I could cut the trip in half by walking out the ridge and following a trail down the hill. It wasn't a path in the strictest sense of the term, but more of a muddy gully in spring, a leaf-filled ditch in fall, a snowy crevice in winter. During summer it vanished into the thick underbrush of weeds and briars, overhung by dense foliage. The creek at the bottom of the hill held household garbage, sewage, and empty bottles thrown from cars. I often walked the creek hunting pop bottles, which were worth two cents apiece. I learned to discern at a glance the valuable pop bottles from mason jars, beer bottles, and telephone insulators. With luck I could find enough for a candy bar and cold Dr Pepper. George never complained about the muddy bottles filled with a layer of hardened silt or the foul odors from within. He carefully counted the bottles, handed me the money, and then waited with utmost patience while I calculated how to maximize my earnings.

I enjoyed sitting in the store and talking with customers, particularly the older ones who recalled the past. The road leading up my hill bore the improbable name of Broadway and was originally paved with brick. Broadway ended at the top of the hill where four ridges intersected, each with its own dirt lane. I lived on Clubhouse Road. Our house was not Mr. Haldeman's primary dwelling but his site for entertaining politicians, captains of industry, and Lexington horse people. Dad hadn't made it to the main house after all.

To support a family of six, my parents began mass-producing pornography for the burgeoning market in 1970. Dad had sold ten such books the year before, which Mom dutifully typed and mailed to editors. This was a simple business decision. The sexual freedom of the 1960s coincided with widespread availability of birth control pills. Pornography was in sudden demand. The books were tailored to various tastes: gay, lesbian, group, bondage, swap, interracial, incest, sadomasochism, even historical and science fiction. The publishers paid poorly, but their standards were low. Different pseudonyms were used for each subgenre.

An obsessive and dark sexuality began to permeate our house, and I spent more and more time in the woods. Several weekends a year Mom and Dad left the state for conventions where they wore revealing clothes and participated in the various activities of the counterculture. The conventions provided them with rock star status on the periphery of the sexual revolution. Working as a team, my parents produced over a hundred hard-core porn novels published under thirteen pseudonyms. Neither of them had ever been inside a dirty bookstore and vehemently denied that what they were creating was smut or porn. They said they were performing a kind of social service by providing sexual guides in the form of hard-core pornography.

In eastern Kentucky, an area oppressed as much by religious belief as by economics, my parents put forth the image of a close family financed by Dad's work as a science-fiction writer. I was taught to keep the real source of our family's income secret. In their efforts to protect themselves, they arranged for outgoing manuscripts to be postmarked in Lexington instead of Haldeman and later used my out-of-state return address for envelopes.

Once a month Mom drove me to Mount Sterling for orthodontic care. Porn straightened my teeth. Porn supplied me with shoes, food, and clothing and the only football on the hill. Not all the boys had gloves, but porn kept my hands warm in winter. Porn paid the mortgage. Porn bought clothes and food and medicine. Porn provided Christmas and birthday presents. Porn would have financed my high school dates had not the widespread knowledge of Dad's occupation interfered with my ability to acquire dates. It was an open secret but rarely mentioned, expressed instead in the silent judgment of a small town. People knew who I was because of my father's occupation.

For twenty years the only successful businesspeople in Haldeman were my parents, the bootlegger, and George Molton. Like Mr. Haldeman himself, each operated as an entrepreneur during a time that marked the end of an era for each particular enterprise. George Molton closed his store and died a few months later, still holding IOUs for several thousand dollars. His cash register was sold as an antique. When Morehead legalized the sale of alcohol, the bootlegger went out of business and opened a liquor store in town. My former grade school closed. The government shut the post office, rescinded the zip code, and changed the mailing address to town. The onset of AIDS ended the era of sexual freedom. The widespread availability of VCRs introduced a market in adult movies, which effectively eliminated the demand for written pornography.

All of my father's books are currently out of print, although early porn has become increasingly valuable in the collector's market. Serious academic courses in pornography are offered at major universities, and a number of schools include vintage porn in their libraries. Indiana University at Bloomington has a temperature-controlled, highly secure archival library that houses the largest collection of pornography in the United States. Soft-core porn pervades media advertising, television, movies, music, and video games. Hard-core porn has entered many homes via the Internet. This overt commercialization has given rise to a romantic nostalgia for the more innocent era of the 1970s, when sexuality was free and open, its creators tucked in out-of-the-way places.

My parents still live in the house where I grew up, but Dad no longer writes. His last book came out in 1992, the same year my first book was published. Mom went back to school and now works for a lawyer in town, answering the phone, running errands, and typing.

Progress is an odd beast in Haldeman. The dirt roads are paved now, and the piped-in water is sanitary enough to drink. These changes allow trailer courts to proliferate in a curious form of rural suburbanization. The population has increased. But there is no school to educate children, no store to buy goods, no place to mail letters. Without a zip code to mark its place in the federal system, my hometown will eventually vanish from official maps. The lovely wooded hills endure, but the people who remember the past are dying off. Only the bricks remain.

Treasure Me

Walter Kirn

Back when I was young and broke, and back when the girls I liked were broke as well, I used to steal gas from the service station I worked for and try to convince my little princesses that driving around in circles in the dark, sharing hits from a papery, weak joint and glugs from a screw-top bottle of warm peach wine, constituted a lavish big night out. The cost of those dates was rarely over $5, but my favorite dates were even cheaper. I'd appear after school at one of the two Dairy Queens where my tawny foxes liked to work and pepper them with doltish jokes and stories while they pumped sludgy hot fudge onto huge sundaes or spritzed Fantastik into the linty cracks where the freezers met the floors. If I hung around long enough and wouldn't shut up enough, my girls would pitch me Peanut Buster Parfait, the most expensive item on the board, and banish me to my parked Chevy until quitting time.

"What should we go and do tonight?" they'd ask when at last they plunked down next to me, reaching around to untie their smeared red aprons. "I think there's a pretty cool movie at the six-plex."

"Did you get paid this week?"

"Nope. Not yet." The cheats. I knew the whole system at both local Dairy Queens, and I knew when my girls' purses contained checks, zippered into the hidden sub-compartments where they kept pilfered sedatives and other guys' love notes.

"Me neither. Let's just watch TV in your folks' basement."

Because most of the girls I saw back then were Mormons and Mormonism is a patriarchal faith which believes, among other theological doozies, that its followers go to heaven as husband and wife except when the husband doesn't love the wife and can leave her drifting in icy cosmic solitude by refusing to speak her secret name (which he learned in the Mormon temple at their wedding but which his darling has no clue about), these girls were not given to talking back to males. They usually did whatever I suggested, even when that meant watching *Gilligan's Island* with our hands plunged inside each other's undies and a big-eyed kid brother right there on the couch with us. On the rare occasions when I did feel flush, though, and sprung for sixplex tickets and licorice fish, the Mormon girls were so heartbreakingly grateful that they would have offered up their virginity—if only they could get it back from me. That $2 peach wine played havoc with their memories.

But then I grew older, went east to a fine college, snagged a low-paying job at a high-style magazine, and found myself meeting women who made demands—expensive demands that they didn't fear would land them in cold, dark orbits around collapsing stars. Since I couldn't afford to court these beauties, I had to hang back and play the confidant as they sniveled about the oil brokers with Porsches and the conceptual artists with SoHo lofts who had the juice not only to date them but to marry them and support their children. Too often these fellows treated the women like whores, though, because they suspected the women wanted their money— the money they'd used to woo them in the first place by tucking platinum cards into their panties and sending them off to Saks.

Comforting beautiful women who'd been screwed at a time when I lacked the financial wherewithal to give them screwings of my own caused me to spend big dollars in my dreams and fantasize about luscious carnal returns. After hearing so many weepy tales about being sent back from the Hamptons in a cab after being flown out there in a helicopter, about having to read to Gran-Gran in her sickroom while sonny boy raced sailboats off the Cape, and about trembling outside some dashing congressman's office only to get a note from his top aide instructing the girl to abort "our little no-comment" and never return to the District of Columbia, I resolved that if Walter Kirn were ever rich enough to keep his lady in lobster salad, I wouldn't make her feel greedy and contemptible. I'd tell her in bed—where she'd gladly spend whole days with me, listening to my career plans and book ideas while lying beneath me spread-eagled on French sheets that I'd declined to ask the price of—that she deserved much, much better than I could give her. Secretly, I'd know she'd never get it, though, because there wasn't a softy in the solar system who'd spoil this brat the way I had. So why had I? Pride in my surplus, I imagined. Pride in the vast horn of plenty between my legs.

Years of work and thrift and decent luck eventually made it possible for me to start asking out the sort of pearly-whirlies who, I learned after traveling with a few of them, are the real reason that four-star hotel rooms have telephones within arm's reach of their toilets. No, the phones aren't there for 911 calls from aging fatties who've given themselves heart attacks by straining on the pot (my first assumption); they're there for women who realize during showers that their price-is-no-object highlighted, scorched hair could use a second small bottle of free conditioner brought to the room by a bellman who you, the boyfriend, aren't aware she even called and are startled by when he comes knocking and irked by when he lingers for a tip—which you have to hand him because your girlfriend's naked and also, another knock will soon reveal, because she's on the toilet phone again ordering fruit to snack on before dinner because it will take her another ninety minutes to lube her hair so that she'll look presentable for dinner. Which, after gobbling kiwis and melon wedges, she's not going to want, you just know it. But don't dare say it. If you do, her ego will drag you to the restaurant and invent an excuse for not eating anything, such as "It just feels dirty in this place." The check will be as high as always, though, because when the girl gets all squirrelly she drinks.

Having the money to put up with all this guff struck me at first as a privilege and a thrill, just as I'd fantasized it would. Love and sex and companionship, I philosophized, are the basins where all the world's cash flows drain to anyway. Skyscrapers and supertankers are merely solid-looking clouds of value vapor fated to rupture someday and rain their essences into calfskin handbags and lipsticked mouths. And this was how it should be, I concluded. Despite the changes in gender roles that got rolling in the 1960s and frightened me witless as a kid because every career that they opened to my mother seemed preferable to laundering my poop-streaked cotton briefs, I accepted that males were rainmakers for females.

Even women whose work paid better than mine did and whose political philosophies stressed economic and spiritual equality didn't mind gulping whatever I poured out. Their formally stated willingness to cover the check now and then, or half of the check, was enough to calm their consciences when old-school Walter handled the whole thing without their glimpsing so much as a glint of the Platinum MasterCard he'd learned that any phony can get as long as he pays a bumped-up annual fee. And heaven forbid if I ever forgot my wallet.

This happened once at a movie box office with a woman whose co-op apartment was worth a sum that would take me another decade to amass. She called me absentminded. A dope. A birdbrain. Moving higher, into metaphysics, she accused me of "not being present to life." That slit my gut. I was a writer, and surface absentmindedness indicates, in writers, core intensity. Those who never misplace their wallets may make terrific Air Force colonels, microbiologists, and scuba instructors, but they don't know the possibilities of the modern American short story. Instead of buying my ticket, or her own, my girlfriend taught me about responsibility by loaning me $40 for our admission, two Diet Cokes, a common vat of popcorn, and a private carton of Swedish Fish that she stashed like a wino's bottle under her coat and ate from as though she were doing something else, and only when she thought I wasn't watching. A feminist liberal Democrat but a goody-clutcher who asked me to repay her forty bucks when I found my cash card. She would have been glad to treat me, she avowed, but not under these particular circumstances, because it might reward my presentlessness.

The breakup scene that should have come that night and begun with my chewing up my girlfriend's twenties, swallowing them, and promising to return them as soon as I found a public bathroom was postponed for a mysterious seven months or so, during which my income suddenly jumped and I started buying stocks and mutual funds whose modest appreciation made me giddy. My revenge on my hurtful girlfriend, I decided, would be to ask her to marry me and then zip her up in a bag of total security that Houdini couldn't wiggle out of. Once I was providing everything, I reasoned, I could leave my wallet on the hall table and order her to walk back a mile and fetch it while I drank iced coffee and timed her on my Rolex.

But the woman rebuffed my proposal. She savaged it. She asked to know my annual income and the total value of my portfolio, and then told me the pumped-up sum I finally quoted was barely 10 percent of the amount she'd worked out with her therapist as the minimum she expected in a husband. The therapist business shivered my kidneys. So that's what passed in Manhattan for inner healing—sitting face-to-face with adding machines, tabulating spousal acceptability to the decimal point.

The woman I married after I fled New York and moved to rural Montana, where doctors don't practice Freudian accountancy, was impressed by the fact I owned a rust-free truck and let her order pizzas with extra cheese. She wasn't a bumpkin, just very, very young and accustomed to living off child-support checks that filtered down from her wealthy divorced father through her thrice-divorced, spendthrift movie star mother. The girl had grown up in Malibu and on film sets with little knowledge of where money came from other than good looks and better lawyers. Still, she seemed grateful for whatever came.

Which made me stingy with her—to compensate for her unappreciative predecessors and to save toward my new financial goal: exactly one-half of the figure specified by the woman who'd spurned me. Now that she wasn't around to make me feel small, I felt free to build up a stockpile on my own schedule. Living way out west gave me an edge. A mansion in Montana in 1990 equaled a summer beach house rental back east, and a college-age wife in Montana penciled out to about one night a month with a non-English-speaking New York escort. Getting ahead here was as easy as staying put.

As our nest egg swelled, I noticed something odd, though; my wife was competing with it for my affection. My experiences with women and money had made me fonder of money, which doesn't spend itself by calling a bellman to deliver a one-ounce bottle of hair conditioner and doesn't assault your manhood when you fall short of heaping it high enough to touch some mark drawn on the wall by its psychiatrist. Money sits still, demure, polite, and quiet, and lets a man contentedly stroke its neck. As a love object, it's like an Asian courtesan.

My wife decided she wanted me to herself, though. She also saw that the process of getting me back could yield fringe benefits. When she ordered a $6,000 oven from France, she not only weakened her rival—my treasury—but gained a world-class appliance with a warming drawer. The same with the designer boots she ordered and the long-distance charges she racked up jazzing with her best friend in California, who'd found herself in a similar predicament when her ambitious artist-husband got far ahead enough to utilize online trading software.

I watched my wife fight my money from a distance, confident that the conflict wouldn't break me unless it raged considerably hotter and dragged in our two young children. When it did heat up (household renovations), I reminded my wife that being able to pay the mortgage, fund an IRA, vacation in Florida, and order whatever the waiter recommended on our Friday nights in town didn't constitute a piece of the rock. Instead, we were dwelling in a financial sand castle that needed continuous firming up and fortifying.

No emergency, though. Not for now. But maybe someday. All it would take to wash the structure flat, in fact, was for Walter the writer to suffer a tiny aneurysm in the verbal region of his brain or—and I'd not yet contemplated this picture, but suddenly it was all that I could think about—keel over dead from the oppressive stress of single-handedly supporting a family on a lonely sphere of spinning stone crawling all over with hunger, disease, and strife and not necessarily protected by God. Perhaps even actively disliked by God, who found humans' greedy complacency revolting and couldn't wait to whip out his awesome dong and thunderously flood our puny palaces under a rising, salty yellow sea.

My outlook dimmed then, by the hour, until one morning I announced that in the great brutal existential scheme of things, the Kirn family was a poor band of huddled gypsies and the showy, hulking French stove where we sought warmth was an abomination before the Lord.

In the divorce proceedings that started soon afterward for all the classic unfathomable causes, among which money is always one but not one whose role can be defined or quantified, my wife called my bluff about our alleged poverty by taking half of what I'd come to fear was practically nothing but which seemed like a fortune when I forked over 50 percent of it. The half that she scored still felt like a fortune—to my mind, almost the size of the lost whole—while the half that I got seemed like two dimes tumbling loose inside a clothes dryer.

All the shining rivers of gold running and rushing toward love's deep blue sea. The streams can be dammed temporarily, of course, and their funds collected in pools of capital sufficient to finance football stadiums, navies, rock operas, oil wells, vaccination drives, pistachio plantations, and bullet trains, but over the long haul emotion will change them all back into diamond rings and dowries, candlelit dinners and alimony payments, eau de cologne and motel hot tubs, chocolates and sex toys, negligees and nurseries. It's the way of all flesh, and it cuts a deep, deep channel down.

On the second anniversary of my divorce, sitting home alone and feeling broke, I thought about all the wealth I'd tossed away on passion and affection over the years. The oddball small expenditures came back first. The tow truck bill for a crush's Honda Civic that I blew out two tires on driving through a construction site in search of a hidden blow-job spot. The three champagne cocktails I'd bought for a cute stranger who, in a flat, dislocated voice that might have belonged to a pull-string talking doll, accused me, when I tried to rub her knee, of having raped her ten years earlier in a town I'd never heard of. The antibiotic prescription for a girlfriend who claimed I'd given her a burning itch that I'm still sure she caught from someone else and had to purchase two more rounds of pills for when it crept out of her pipes into mine and then, when I thought the beastie was dead in both of us, slithered back into her.

Chiseled away at. Nibbled. Nickeled-and-dimed. Add in the jewels, the clothes, the meals, the travel, the phone bills, and the houses, and I realized that I may as well have gathered all my earnings and everything they entitled me to borrow and stuffed them inside an enormous heart-shaped box tied with a bow and crisscrossed with pink ribbons. Banks and brokerages were jokes. The principal, the interest, and the dividends all belong in a big red velvet box with a pretty card taped to the lid and no return address on the envelope.

"To whom it may concern," my card might read (I've revised it a thousand times while lying in bed), "this is all of it. All I have to give and all you'll ever get from me. I tried to hold back a small stake for myself, but that's impossible, I've found, because I keep dividing and dividing it and spending the bit that's left over on new companions, with whom I end up dividing it again. If it's not quite the sum you expected, kindly shove it. Love expects nothing except love in return, which means every penny here is a pure bonus that you'd be wise to donate to charity but which, my pampered darlings, I know you won't—and I didn't, either, when I had the chance. I bought you boots and movie candy instead."

At the bottom of the card, I'd draw a dollar sign whose traditional slashes through the S would take the form of feathered cupid's arrows, one pointing up, one pointing down. Then I'd slip a $5 bill inside the card the way my grandma did on birthdays until I turned thirty and she deemed me self-reliant, or tried to prod me into self-reliance by cutting off the annual stipend. I'd put the card inside the envelope, close the flap, and seal it with a kiss. Then I'd take the final step. I'd pick it up and lay it on the fire.

The American Dream

Isabel Rose

Here's a little peek through the blinds of my childhood: posh private school and ritzy summer camp, Broadway shows and the Metropolitan Museum of Art, a Sunday night series at the New York City Ballet and Mostly Mozart at the Philharmonic. By five, I was making toasts at the Shabbat dinner table. By eight, I could draw out the shy son of a Wall Street magnate. By twelve, I knew to eat *coquilles Saint-Jacques* with an oyster fork and to use the utensils above the plate only for dessert.

Although many of my school friends didn't live like I did, in a full-floor apartment on Fifth Avenue, enough people around me did for it not to seem embarrassing or strange. There were always the Bernsteins, my parents' best friends. Their daughter, Claudia, was my age, so we played together constantly. The Bernsteins' apartment—only a few blocks south on Fifth Avenue—was much nicer than ours, and their weekend home in East Hampton was twice as big as my family's place in Westchester.

Claudia and I spent countless hours of our childhood playing dress up in her mother's amazing collection of couture gowns and hiding in the numerous pantries and closets of my apartment. We never said, "Isn't it fun, wearing Armani and Valentino at five!?" We accepted the situation, as all children do. It just seemed normal.

Formality tinged with fear mixed with a soupçon of awe was the marinade of my childhood. It tasted as normal as roasted chicken and matzo ball soup. It was normal to be slightly afraid of the big, fancy living room in our apartment with the long taffeta curtains and the silk-covered sofa; normal to be slightly afraid of the cold white marble entrance hall at the Bernsteins' apartment with the twin orange Ming vases on pedestals as you entered; normal to be slightly afraid of the dark, lonely formal dining room in our apartment with its breakfront full of china dishes painted with fish; normal to be slightly afraid of Mr. and Mrs. Bernstein's bedroom, with its imposing art deco partners desk in front of the fireplace and a bed made with military precision covered in numerous tiered pillows you dreaded to displace.

I suppose one of the reasons our families spent so much time together was that neither party needed to feel self-conscious about its lifestyle. But for both Claudia and me, there was always the knowledge, stated or implied, that we were privileged—privileged in the sense that it was our great privilege to have so many opportunities at our fingertips—we knew that we needed to be sensitive around our less-fortunate friends and, if they were in either of our homes, we should work to set them at ease. And always there was the warning that some people would be jealous and act toward us with hostility. We were also told to beware of sycophants. I remember that was the word my parents used because Claudia and I looked it up in the *Webster's Dictionary* that I gave her for her twelfth birthday.

By that time, regardless of discussions with our parents, Claudia and I both knew we came from a pretty rarefied economic sphere. We went to the same school and played at other children's homes. We compared our observations and noted that some of our friends actually *shared* rooms with their siblings. And some of our friends' apartments didn't have a large, formal living room and a large, formal dining room, but instead had only a kitchen, a family room, and a bedroom or two.

We realized we were different because not every kid in our class was going on safari in Africa, or on a cruise, or to Japan, or on a yacht in the Caribbean over Christmas break, like we were; they were staying home in New York and ice-skating at Rockefeller Center. We realized we were different because we never babysat after school like many of our friends; we went to ballet class or took piano lessons or worked with our private tutors when any subject in school proved challenging. And in the summer it was always camp time, not summer-job time.

And if there was any doubt left in our minds as to our financial good fortune, *Forbes* magazine took care of that for us when we were fourteen, which was the year both our families made it onto their list of the four hundred wealthiest families in America. My father told me that the amount the magazine said our family was worth was based on misinformation. Nevertheless, it solidified in my mind the concept that I was really lucky, enough so that I mourned when our family stopped being listed after the real estate crash happened.

Luckily my parents were extremely grounded people who

truly emphasized core values. It was always clear that family was more important than fortune, that education surpassed any eccentric indulgences. My parents worked hard to handle things tastefully, like my Bat Mitzvah, which was celebrated with a luncheon in our temple's modest basement pavilion.

Claudia's family handled things differently. Her Bat Mitzvah was celebrated with two parties: the grown-ups and kids party, which took place at the Harmonie Club, a members-only, posh Jewish institution on Sixtieth Street not far from the Plaza. It featured six food stations for hors d'oeuvres, followed by a sit-down luncheon during which several prominent New Yorkers made toasts to Claudia, including a senator and a major magazine editor. After lunch a DJ helped the guests through a limbo contest, and then several men dressed as the Village People taught us how to do the "Y.M.C.A." song with proper hand motions. That night there was a kids-only party at Régines, a popular nightclub. I don't remember any alcohol being served, but I do remember Hannah Segal telling everyone she went to third base with Robby Ginsberg in the bathroom and a rumor that Brynn Westerfield was handing out cigarettes in the hallway out of view of the two or three parental chaperones. I did nothing more deplorable than win the hustle contest. Even so, it was the night I made the connection between money and bad behavior.

Thank goodness for religion. Religion kept me clean while around me through the 1980s classmates stayed up late studying for tests by snorting cocaine and drank themselves into near comas while they partied on the weekends. I spent every Friday night of my life until I was sixteen at home celebrating Shabbat. It may have been catered, but it was 100 percent wholesome.

Judaism gave me other deeply important life lessons. It was at

Hebrew school—to which I was driven in my parents' Mercedes station wagon by a chauffeur who wore jeans so as not to embarrass me—that I first learned about *tzedakah. Tzedakah* means "charity," and we were sent home from class with little cardboard boxes with slots in them to collect coins. Where these coins ended up I can't imagine, but we knew they were for those less fortunate than us.

My parents reinforced the importance of *tzedakah* at home, and we were encouraged from a young age to consider philanthropy as a part of our civic and personal duty. The importance of *tzedakah* was even further highlighted by my mother's seemingly endless toil on behalf of the many boards she served on and by the nights my father stayed out late because he was "at a board meeting," which seemed very important the way my mother said it.

Like all daughters, I was curious about my mother and observed her closely, eager to learn the tools I'd need to become a successful woman. I studied her life, and the lives of my enormously capable and intelligent aunts, and the lives of many of my mother's friends, including Claudia's mother.

These women were CEOs of the domestic and social spheres of their families' lives: running their homes (which were always beautiful, with fresh flowers on coffee tables and not a speck of dust anywhere), throwing parties (which flowed perfectly and were often catered), organizing gala dinners for their various excellent causes, booking extraordinary trips, keeping themselves in beautiful physical shape, signing their children up for the top camps and programs and schools.

The unspoken implication of my upbringing—and Claudia's—was that after we finished college, we would do something—exactly *what* was never discussed—and then, hopefully before we turned thirty (the age at which I had heard my mother say a woman has "missed the boat"), we would marry men of substance, like our fathers, and, in turn, become superb wives and mothers in our own right.

I'm quite certain that this assumption stemmed from a generational expectation on our parents' part and was not meant to be mean-spirited or explicitly undermining. Nor was it meant to belittle our achievements or talents. We were being prepared to marry the best: a diplomat, a bank president, a famous lawyer, a movie producer, even, perhaps, a big-time politician.

I went to Yale and Claudia went to Penn, where we both dated one lovely future man of substance after another. But then we graduated, and although we both returned to New York City, there our paths diverged: Claudia moved to the Upper East Side and began an internship at Christie's, while I moved to the Village and began my life as an actress.

After a year of acting classes and auditions, I got cast in a nine-month national tour of a Broadway show. Claudia and her boyfriend at the time, a first-year associate at Lazard Frères, threw me a huge going-away party at her apartment that was catered by Glorious Foods. For dessert, we all ate a giant cake designed to look like the program for the show I was doing. My boyfriend, a law student at Columbia, gave me a beautiful going-away present, too: a pair of sapphire earrings that he hoped I'd wear and think of him. We made an agreement to talk on the phone every night *no matter what,* and off I flew to L.A., the first stop on the odyssey that would change my life.

My boyfriend and I tried to keep our promise, but life on the road was lonely. It wasn't long before I broke up with him one teary weekend when he came to visit me in San Francisco. Of course I didn't mention that I was already paired off with a fellow cast member.

My Cast Member was different from the guys I had met at Yale. He hadn't had enough money to finish his own college experience and had been working as a bartender before landing the tour, which he was thrilled about because it meant nine months of a steady paycheck. I had viewed the job simply as something that might look good on my résumé and also as something that had caused me to cancel a long-awaited trip to Paris with my mother. It never occurred to me that it was a coveted condition in the acting world to earn a paycheck for nine consecutive months.

Claudia predicted my relationship with the Cast Member would end as soon as the tour reached its conclusion. It didn't, though. Not right away. I was too busy learning lessons. One major eye-opener was the debunking of my notion that someone who doesn't finish college must come from a home that doesn't value culture or intellectual pursuits. Visiting the apartment my Cast Member grew up in certainly challenged that. Every inch of wall space in the living/dining room in the Yonkers apartment was home to a book. There were stacks of them in the bathrooms and stacks on night tables and stacks under the beds and precarious stacks on windowsills that would clatter to the floor in frightening bookslides when one of the cats jumped on them.

The Cast Member was brilliant and could quote whole pages of Shakespeare, even from plays like *Troilus and Cressida.*

"Brilliance isn't enough," Claudia said when we were having a girls' night. "You aren't social equals. It won't last."

I hoped to prove Claudia wrong, but things did in fact erode after we abandoned the democracy of life on the road. For my twenty-fifth birthday, my parents bought a table of ten seats for me at a black-tie benefit at Lincoln Center. I was prepared to be without the Cast Member because he had told me ahead of time that he was scheduled to work a party that night. I wasn't prepared, however, to have him be the guy serving us drinks. And yet there he was: my Cast Member offering my parents and friends a choice of champagne or sparkling water while I stood by not knowing exactly how to behave.

To make matters worse, Claudia made a joke out of it, asking him to get us all sorts of complex drinks. I stopped looking him in the eye somewhere between her comment that he made a great Orgasm and her request for a Sex on the Beach. At the end of the night I asked him if he wanted to join us at a bar where we planned to have a nightcap.

"I gotta clean up after you pigs," he said. "See you tomorrow, toots. And happy birthday. You just enjoy yourself with your friends." He said the word "friends" as if it were covered in feces.

I made a point of seeing him the next night. We met at his favorite diner, where he scowled into his fries while I tried to ameliorate the embarrassment of the previous night.

"What can we do?" he said. "I'm not embarrassed about the way I make a living. But I gotta tell ya', I think your friend Claudia is a real piece of work."

I agreed wholeheartedly and denounced Claudia as my friend.

When the Cast Member and I were finished with our dinner at the diner, we went back to his place. It was a boiling night and he had no air conditioner, but I knew it was the wrong night to complain. He lived in a desolate part of town and slept on a futon that lay directly on the cement floor of his studio apartment. It was hell for me. I'd seen numerous roaches and slept lightly, convinced that every brush against my skin was some sort of creepy crawler trying to join us in the sheets. Luckily, I saw none that night, but as I lay awake I did make a note to replace the dead plant on the floor by the heater. Then I changed my mind. What could possibly survive in that sweatbox of an apartment? A cactus, I decided, making a note to pick one up for him in the morning.

The summer got hotter. The Cast Member refused to join me for refreshing days at my parents' summer place, where a pool eased the debilitating effect of the heat. Instead, he spent much of his time sulking about his lack of auditions, stalking around his steam room of an apartment in a pair of jeans, the turquoise cross necklace that banged against his chest and a beer in his hand his only adornments. He called me Stella because I told him he was posing as Marlon Brando and suggested that maybe he should just install an air conditioner and throw on a shirt instead of bathing in his own sweat from June through September.

He told me he couldn't afford one, and I told him that P. C. Richard was having a sale and that, if he worked a party every night for a week, he'd be able to afford one. He worked a party every night for a week, but there was still no AC. I told him I'd be happy to buy one for him as a gift, but he told me he wasn't comfortable with "my charity" and shot me a look that told me to drop the idea.

Claudia called the Cast Member "damaged goods" because she noticed he wore gym socks with his dress shoes when we met for drinks one night at the bar of a fancy restaurant. I also confided in her that the Cast Member had no AC, and *that* was grounds enough for her. That was the summer Claudia was being wooed by the heir to one of the world's biggest real estate empires. She spent most of her weekends being whisked over the LIE in a helicopter to his mansion at the beach.

I spent most of my weekends whisking myself to the window of the Cast Member's apartment in search of a breeze—*anything* to subdue the vicious heat in that apartment. As the mercury rose, I tried to convince the Cast Member to spend nights at my place. But he had two cats and felt that, on principle, we should spend equal amounts of time at our respective pads. I agreed, on principle. But one night I couldn't take it anymore. I felt as if the heat were searing my lungs. I thought he was still asleep as I tiptoed to his front door, but just as I got there he called out, "Nothing wrong with a little natural heat, princess. I hope your spoiled *tuchas* learns that lesson one day."

Okay, I said to myself as the taxi took me back to my air-conditioned apartment. So he's right. I *am* too spoiled to deal with the deprivation of no AC in the summer. But there was more to it. I also needed to eat in something other than a diner, which was the only kind of restaurant he could afford since he didn't like me to treat him. I needed to be with someone who didn't call my Ivy League friends a "hoity-toity" bunch. I needed to be with someone who didn't chew tobacco and spit the juice just past my big toe. I needed to be with someone who didn't find excuses every time I wanted to visit my parents on the Upper East Side because he didn't like to be in their "dressy" apartment in that "snooty" part of town.

It was time to throw in the towel and acknowledge who I was: a princess raised on the very Upper East Side he despised; a princess with the ability to buy someone a new apartment with central air if that's what it came down to.

All right, I said to myself as I got out of the cab and raced into the air-conditioned lobby of the building my family actually built. So it's time to move on.

I decided to infiltrate the "straight" world, meaning people who weren't actors and therefore had actual employment. By this time Claudia's boyfriend, an investment banker named Rob who wore pressed jeans and a blazer even on the weekends, had proposed, and I hoped their engagement party would prove fertile ground for "socially appropriate" boyfriends (to quote Claudia's favorite expression).

I tried. I really did. I discussed the Nasdaq (though I had no idea what it was) and my favorite golf courses (though I'd never played). I laughed with a group of guys about the Knicks (who I thought played football), and I told a story about once getting stuck for an hour on a ski lift in Vail to a guy who told me he had a ski "share" for the winter in Vermont.

Still, I ended up giving my phone number to the bartender, an adorable actor and writer, and went home without a single prospect from the professional pool. As I lay in bed that night, I pondered my plight. Most of my friends were in the arts and had no money. I knew many stable couples, but most were gay men who didn't know any single heterosexual men for me to date.

I contemplated Claudia's choice. Rob was from an upper-middle-class American Jewish family. He didn't have as much inherited wealth as Claudia, but he was earning over $2 million a year, so it seemed likely that one day he might be worth more than she was, especially given his mega-bonuses and Claudia's disinclination to work once married.

It wasn't just the money. Rob was sociable and considerate. He had a career that continued on a weekly basis. He had health coverage. He was able to spend the weekends with Claudia out of town. He accompanied Claudia when she had to go to a benefit or wanted to see theater or attend a concert; often, in fact, he was the one inviting *her* to join *him*. He certainly didn't mind going to a black-tie event; he owned two tuxedos, he told me one night, one single-breasted and one double. The only time *my* boyfriends wore a tux was when they donned their rental for a catering or bartending job.

I decided a life change was in order and applied to graduate school. I would be able to control my own schedule instead of running this way and that for auditions. I'd be able to stay put in New York instead of living out of a suitcase while doing regional theater. I'd be able to go away on the weekends and have dinner at normal hours instead of being locked into a show schedule working Tuesdays through Sundays with matinees on weekends. I'd be able to do a summer share in the Hamptons instead of summer stock in the Berkshires. In short, I could try to live the life Claudia had chosen and see if the right guy for me would follow suit.

In no time at all I met someone at a bar who worked on Wall Street. When he asked me what I did for a living, I told him the truth: I was about to start graduate school for fiction. Mr. Wall Street was a generous guy. For weeks he refused to let me touch the check, convinced I was a poor graduate student who could barely afford to eat. By the time I cleared up the confusion, we were an item.

The first time Claudia met Mr. Wall Street, he was walking toward us carrying a briefcase and wearing a suit. She said, "Oh my God, he has a job. Book a hall!" Rob was equally impressed. Mr. Wall Street was an Eagle Scout, an Ivy League grad, a financial wunderkind, and an expert on all things historical, political, and economic. He ran marathons in his free time and went vertical rock climbing to relax.

"The one thing every five-star general in the United States Army has in common," Rob said, "is that each one of them was an Eagle Scout."

My dates with Mr. Wall Street ranged from evenings in chic restaurants to canoeing down the Delaware River. There was nothing we felt we couldn't do together, and we celebrated "the range of our game."

Mr. Wall Street proposed to me just shy of my thirtieth birthday. I got an engagement ring. He got a prenup.

"How can we ever merge as a couple if your money is yours and my money is mine?" he asked, deeply upset. "We'll always be separated by it."

I suggested that we create a joint bank account and an investment account into which we could put equal amounts. He wasn't satisfied. It was the principle of it that bothered him. He tried to come up with clever loopholes. When my financial advisers and lawyer said no-go, he complained they were treating him like an idiot or, worse, like someone who had designs on my money.

"I need a prenup to protect myself from *you*," he announced one day in the midst of our prenup trauma. "One day I'll be worth more than you, and then we'll see who needs a legal document."

I agreed it was in *both* our best interests. We signed the prenup and tried to put the financial issues behind us, but tensions over money began to build.

I planned the honeymoon, choosing the same luxurious resorts in Bali that Claudia had gone to on her honeymoon. My Wall Streeter told me the trip would cost more than he wanted to spend and suggested we do something else, but I had no time to plan something else, and neither did he. I told him he should pay whatever he felt comfortable spending and I would pay the rest. He said he felt pressure to live beyond his comfort level, even though he earned a very substantial amount of money, and I told him that I didn't want to be held back from living the way I could, so he should find a way to get comfortable with the idea that sometimes I would pay more for things than he did. I told him that it would all be *our* money anyway as soon as we were married.

"It won't be," he said bitterly. "It never will be."

And it never was. Our divorce four years later was easy enough; what's his was his, what's mine was mine. Still, there was some question over how much he should pay for child support. I told him, in a moment of frustration, that I was prepared to raise our child without his financial participation, that his money meant nothing to me. In the silence that followed, I realized that was the single worst thing I ever said to him.

About a year after we split up, he called to share an insight. He said he realized now, dating a woman who came from a simple background, who struggled week to week to pay her rent, that she made him feel needed in ways I never could.

"Just the way she thanks me for dinner when I take her some-where nice—or even just to a coffee shop—it makes me feel so *use-ful.* As if all the hard work I do every day really *means* something. I never felt like I could impress *you.*"

I told him I was always grateful when he took me out to dinner and was thrilled by every gift he ever gave me no matter what the cost. He told me that my gratitude somehow wasn't convincing.

I applauded him on both his self-knowledge and his new-found happiness, but when I hung up the phone, I cried. How can I erase who I am and what I come from? I've traveled the world and eaten in restaurants with three stars in the Michelin guide. So what? Should I pretend not to know the difference between *tagine* and *tarte tatin* because my date might be intimidated by my knowl-edge? Do I have to find someone with the same background and so-phistication level in order to be happy?

Claudia said, "Indeed," when I ran the conundrum by her. "If the guy doesn't have three to five million in the bank, you should run."

"Why?" I cried, frightened I'd never find the right person if I first needed to know his net worth. "It's just not my style," I told her. "And I don't run in those circles anyway."

"Then run in them," she suggested.

Fear that I would be forced to compromise on my basic joys in life—hanging out with my creative friends and choosing partners based on their personality and our chemistry—was setting in fast, but then I met the Sculptor. He came from a big family fortune and had no problem with my financial profile. Finally I felt as if I'd found my male counterpart, until I discovered that he hadn't sculpted anything in years and that when he went to his "studio" he was actually at the gym or else checking his e-mail. I confronted him, and he said, "Darling, people like us don't have the same fire as people who come from more humble circumstances."

I said, "People like *who*?" and on with my search I went.

Thank goodness for the Film Editor. Not only did he share and value my work ethic; he took it to new heights. His professional dedication, in fact, was so outstanding I never saw him. The Film Editor—who was from Venezuela and had the most dreamy accent you've ever heard—worked late into the night and often worked on weekends. But I was willing to make the sacrifice, knowing that his crazy hours probably wouldn't last forever. He was building his career. My Wall Streeter had worked those same hours when we first met.

"Do you really want to repeat the situation?" Claudia asked. "You already played the role before. Besides, he'll hold you back. He's a fine fellow, but he isn't an asset."

I wondered what I'd be held back from and how it was that he couldn't be considered an asset when, in fact, he knew all kinds of people in the film business who might be of help to me in my career.

"Come on," Claudia said. "What is he going to do with himself at some big posh dinner party? He'll either never go with you because he'll be too busy, or he'll go and sulk the whole time because he doesn't know anyone and thinks we're all capitalist pigs."

It was true. The Film Editor went very few places with me. He said it wasn't his thing, and I didn't care. I went with friends and tried to enjoy whatever time we did spend together. Oh, how I loved the Film Editor! When his business needed a quick cash infusion, I decided to become an investor. I signed papers and had my lawyer and financial advisers look at them. When I made the error of telling Claudia what I had done, she nearly fainted.

"You're going to give away your entire inheritance because some guy with a sexy accent knows how to manipulate you?!" she cried.

I explained that I had become an investor, that I believed in the future success of his company. I asked what the difference was between her giving "grants" from her personal charitable foundation to struggling artists and my investing in the Film Editor's business except for the fact that I stood to potentially make my money back (and then some) whereas she was basically giving out money on the dole.

I decided to give her a bigger shock just for fun by telling her that my Film Editor and I had been discussing marriage.

"Has it occurred to you that he may want to marry you so he can get citizenship?" Claudia said.

I asked her why on earth that would matter, and she said, "You can't get a loan from a bank without being a citizen. If he marries you, he can get a loan for his business. Or else he can just get it from you."

"I don't think he's out to use me," I said. "He's a very proud man. Besides, I think I'm able to determine who's a sycophant and who isn't at this point in my life."

The Film Editor and I didn't make it in the long run. He didn't feel accepted by my friends, he told me. I suggested we hang out with *his* friends instead, but in the year and a half we were together, I never met one. He told me he worked too hard to have friendships, that at the end of his long days he went to the gym and then spent time with me. I asked him if he really had to work those long hours. I asked if he could get an assistant with the money I'd invested.

"It's about my eyes and ears and how I, personally, want to tell a story," he said.

I understood, but I knew I couldn't spend my life with someone I never saw. I also can't spend my life with someone who shuts me down socially. I love my friends and need to be with someone who feels comfortable socializing with any group no matter which part of town they're from and no matter how much money they do or don't have.

When I think about the Film Editor now, what I remember most is his telling me that he came to America with $200 in his pocket and slept in Central Park for a few nights until he hooked up with a friend from Venezuela who helped him get his first job.

"I'm living the American Dream," he would often say.

"So am I," I would yearn to add, but I kept the thought to myself because, although I am pursuing a career in the arts without the aid of any connections, I'm technically able to do so by living off the fruits of my ancestors' previous glory, and it somehow makes my modest successes lack the validity of the Film Editor's own first-generation achievements.

I was at a dinner not long ago honoring some philanthropists for their work improving the lives of inner-city African-American children. One of the speakers was an extremely distinguished black educator, and he said to the audience that inner-city kids have no role models in their own community and so needed to look beyond it for role models. And they need to believe in themselves a hundred times over because often no one else in their community will.

After the dinner I ran over to the speaker and said, "I know this is going to sound strange, but I, who grew up with so many advantages, had to do the same thing. Granted, I was always lucky enough to have food and shelter and many other privileges, but there were no women in my social world, or at least the social world of my parents, who worked. My own father once said to me, 'I think it's a kick that you've worked because it never occurred to me when I was raising you that you ever would.' "

Where in that is the message to strive? To dream? To aspire? I distinctly remember taking note of women like Dina Merrill, women who came from wealthy backgrounds and yet still chose to pursue their career dreams. I also remember taking note of either successful or wealthy women who married men who were either less successful or less wealthy than themselves: Patty Hearst, Meryl Streep, Elizabeth Taylor, and Madonna, to name a few.

Where is he? I wondered. Where is my man? I joined JDate and tried to select someone with a good job who was from a suburb

I knew to be affluent. Judging by this criteria, I did meet a very nice architect. We went out for a few weeks, but I didn't feel the sparks I know I need, so I ended it.

I met Claudia for coffee the other day, and she asked what happened to him.

"There was just no chemistry," I explained.

"Well, he wasn't impoverished," she said. Then she dug into her Louis Vuitton purse and pulled out a card. "You should call her," she said, handing it to me. "Dr. Marcelle Adams," it read, "therapist, relationship dysfunction a specialty."

"I don't have relationship dysfunction," I said, handing the card back. "I just have a healthy bank account."

There's no question: it would be great if I could meet a guy from a similar background with similar drive and interests. But I haven't met him. Instead, I've met whom I've met; I've learned what I've learned. And what I've learned is that you have to accept who you are and then find someone who also accepts who you are. You can't look away and say apologetically, "The Upper East Side," when someone asks you where you're from. You have to own it, which not a lot of people feel comfortable doing. When I told Claudia I was going to write this essay, she said, "I assume you're going to write under a pseudonym."

I shook my head.

Claudia looked shocked, then said, "You're not going to say that you're—you're—"

"What?" I asked. "Moderately wealthy? Am I going to say that I'm moderately wealthy?"

Claudia looked at me as if I'd said I was going to admit that I do animal sacrifices in my living room.

"Yes," I said. "I'm going to say that I'm moderately wealthy."

"Do you really want people to know that about you?" she asked, the worry and distaste clear on her face.

"I guess so," I said. "I guess I'm going to come out of my walk-in closet."

So there you go: I'm moderately wealthy. This means that I'm not as rich as Ivanka Trump or Paris Hilton, but also that I don't worry about paying my rent each month. I have a very keen understanding that if I don't invest wisely, I will end up back where my family started three generations ago. Still, for the time being, I'm what some people would call rich.

Does it mean I will end up with a man who's rich, too? That remains to be seen. I'm not convinced. I married a wealthy man the first time around, and money turned out to be one of our greatest sources of tension. I do know this: somewhere out there is a man who doesn't care; who's both grounded and honest enough to talk with me about the specific stresses finances always cause; who will work with me to find solutions that don't break us apart. And if I end up with a man who has less money—or no money—I don't want to argue every time I go to a restaurant over who's going to pay the bill. And I don't want to be held back in my life from enjoying those things I can afford to enjoy.

As for Claudia and her host of worries, well, I understand them. No one wants to see someone they care for get used. And no one wants to see someone they love choose a life of downward mobility. My hope is that no matter what man I choose, Claudia can come to accept him. Because if I stand under the chuppah one day again and the rabbi says, "For richer or poorer," I want those people who surround us to cheer us on and really mean it.

For Richer

Fred Leebron

I don't remember what my first argument with my wife about money was actually about, or when the last one occurred. Perhaps to Kathryn it is one long, continuous argument, but here's one thing I can say in my defense: I believe I have expressed less envy about money as I've become determined to make more of it and successful at doing so. So what I want to know is, isn't that a good development?

What I remember is this. I courted Kathryn with money I didn't have, running up bills on my one credit card, borrowing against national prize money a professor told me I was sure to win, and sputtering fumes of relief when the check did come in. In between our dates, we dined on Swanson Chicken Pot Pies and Kraft Macaroni & Cheese, and never went to movies, and drank Wiedemann beer and box wine. We were happy with the occasional dinner out. We were happy with what we had.

After we got married, we took one last fling at the penniless existence, using an award I won and our small savings from a year working in San Francisco—and selling our lousy furniture and our aging Subaru—to travel to Thailand, France, Mexico, and Guatemala. In Thailand we were rich, on our $350-per-month housing budget, eating out every night at the Chiang Mai bazaar, drinking bottle after bottle of Mekong whiskey, making up silly songs ("We're boats on the river, we're boats on the river, we're boats on the river Mekong"), attending free movies at the CIA-run American library. We loved our life there. It seemed, in Thailand, that our money went further than ever before, further than we even needed. I guess we were just your typical expats taking advantage of the strength of the American dollar in a more tentative economy. We were so naive about money that we didn't even realize this; we just thought Thailand was a "cheap" place to stay. Then we moved on to France, enticed by an invitation from our friends Ann and Jon, who were already living there during their year as travelers. The problem was we'd forgotten they were rich.

They'd chosen Vence, a town in the foothills above the Riviera, where our $350 housing budget got us laughed out of every realtor's office, where Ann turned to us after a fruitless first four days of apartment hunting to say, "What, would you rather we had told you not to come at all?" Frankly, yes, but who were we to admit that? We settled on an apartment with no heat and an outdoor bathroom, built on the top floor of a studio designed by Dubuffet. Every morning Kathryn had to blow-dry her legs to thaw them into movement. Ann never did use our bathroom, despite the many days she deigned to visit us from their two-bedroom flat with the washer and dryer. Once we were invited over to dinner, and we brought our usual cheapskate wine. We could hear her muttering in the kitchen,

"What did they bring us this time? Oh, that. Don't bother with that."

We left France early, skipping out on our lease agreement, skipping out on Ann and Jon, and wound up in Mexico, where we were nearly rich again, and then in Guatemala, where we were definitely rich. We returned to our "home" in San Francisco, out of money, to discover we were really poor. We had a friend lie about our income so we could qualify for a rental, found a charming fourth-floor walk-up overlooking Golden Gate Park, and got to work. Kathryn wanted to get pregnant. I'd forgotten about all that. We couldn't afford it, I told her. I told her we had absolutely nothing in savings, and any baby would want food, clothing, furniture, and a college savings account. I pointed out articles that said that the average American kid cost over one hundred grand from cradle to high school diploma. I told Kathryn she was nuts to want a baby in our financial state. "If we wait until we can afford it," she said, "it will never happen."

We got pregnant instantly, as if I had no say in the matter, as if as soon as I grudgingly consented to just give it a try it was a done deal. I felt doomed. I had just turned thirty and I had $109 in the bank. "I thought you said we were just going to give it a try," I said. "Well, this is what happens when you try," she replied, laughing. I wanted to be excited. I wanted to be the hunter. I wanted to be the protector. I wanted a lot of cash, and we were so under the gun that I made us have a rule that we couldn't even have coffee out. I made us keep track of every cent we spent. I can still see the columns of carefully inscribed numbers stretching across the tightly lined page marking off every single expense we incurred over every single goddamn day. Whatever we bought—soap, shampoo, toilet paper, toothpaste, coffee, printer paper—it was the cheapest brand. We took, between us, a total of twelve part-time jobs teaching, editing, ghostwriting, grant writing, and ad writing, and we began to sock away some money. I was frantic about money. I imagined the cost of each diaper disposed, each emptied little jar of food, and how we wouldn't be able to buy the next diaper or the next jar. When my nonprofit employer finally gave us benefits, we had to move from the great university hospital we had paid for ourselves to a suspect HMO, and Kathryn was upset. I was worried, sure, but I thought, at least it would all be covered, when it hadn't all been covered before. I felt we could breathe a little bit. Still, we gathered hand-me-downs and discarded furniture; we ate more mac and cheese and downgraded our chicken pot pie selection.

By the time the baby was due, we'd saved nearly $15,000, and we could have the occasional take-out meal. We bought a brand-new white sofa. A white sofa with a baby on the way. What were we thinking? I tried to tell myself we were doing fine.

Then Kathryn went into labor. What I remember first is that we called the taxi company and told them all the clichéd details, and they promised to arrive, and after thirty minutes they hadn't, and after another thirty they still hadn't, and we huddled on the first-floor landing of our fourth-floor walk-up, practically pleading for the goddamn taxi, and when it did arrive and the baby was still where it was supposed to be, I thought we were truly saved.

At the hospital, I wanted to thank this miraculous taxi guy, and I carefully counted out an exorbitant tip, very, very carefully, and only in the delivery room did it dawn on me that I'd miscalculated, that it was actually an incredibly awful tip, and I finally understood the awkward and incredulous look the taxi driver had given me and how I had forever and completely poisoned our karma.

Then our daughter arrived and was mishandled by a doctor who wasn't even licensed, who wasn't more than three weeks out of medical school, and our little girl was gasping and darkening and inhaling poison as she lay without help and the stunned "doctor" and the nurse muttered questions to each other as simple as "What do I do now?" and I watched the stooges and watched myself watching them, and I knew it was all my fault, all the fault of a little money, a lot of money, whatever money was the difference between a terrible tip and a wonderful tip, whatever money was the difference between that gorgeously luminous university hospital on the hill and this dimly lit HMO hospital in the valley. For days after, late at night and into the morning, the times when we were not allowed to be with our baby as she tried to survive, as we held each other in our cold, dark apartment and hoped the phone wouldn't ring, I promised Kathryn that if it didn't work out, we would go away again and be poor, happy expats once more; we would begin again by starting all the way over.

When we discovered that the taciturn, gloomy neonatologist who was managing our daughter's case was probably the best goddamn neonatologist in the city, I thought at least there's that. And when he saved her from her fate one long and endless and "cyclical" night, as the NICU nurse tersely termed it, when the respirator failed to have an effect on our daughter and they had to take her off it and "handbag" her to see if her lungs could again be made to have a meaningful relationship with oxygen, when she started off poorly and grew deathly ill and came out poorly again, when the neonatologist somehow managed to do that, and then she indeed came all the way back, I thought that maybe there was something to be said about the nonprofit lifestyle after all. She was alive and we were lower-middle-class and we were going to pull ourselves up as much as was necessary to restore order and safety. Everything was going to be all right.

But once a week I would load all the laundry into this cart thing we'd found on the street and roll it the five blocks to the Laundromat. People would stare at me from their BMWs and Cadillacs and Toyota Camrys, the weight of their assessment making me hunch my shoulders, and I felt enraged. I just wanted our own washer and dryer. I just wanted our own car. I didn't want to feel so inspected, so obviously deprived, so disdained, so pitied. So dirty. I was over thirty and regarded by strangers as on welfare.

"This is driving me nuts," I reported to Kathryn.

"Just get me the vacuum cleaner," she snapped. She used the vacuum cleaner to calm the baby's colic.

If only we had a car, our parenting book said, we could drive our screaming baby into serenity.

We kept working our jobs. One of us would take the baby, and the other would get on the word processor or race out to the bus. I'd refused to let us drop any of the twelve gigs. Soon we would have $17,000 in the bank, $18,000. One morning I called the Honda dealership downtown and dreamily asked about the cost of a tiny hatchback. Technically, once we factored in insurance and tax, it was still beyond us. Every week I kept rolling that cart out to do our laundry. Every week I stared back at the staring people passing me in their fancy cars.

"We've got to get out of here," I said.

From the ceiling strange orange goo dripped from a leak in the roof. The heat went on only when the landlord told it to. To get the baby to her checkups, we had to take three buses or wait a half hour for a $10 cab ride. All the exotic elements of being penniless—the unpredictable and eventful bus rides and the suspect and sometimes indeterminate food and the cold and drafty rooms and having to walk sometimes to get anywhere—suddenly took on a dangerous quality. Perhaps the lower-middle-class existence was an existence destined to be haunted by the possibility of the descent of evil. And if you didn't have the means to protect yourself, to rescue yourself, it was unlikely that anyone would intervene on your behalf. Every family needed to erect its own fortress, and in San Francisco the best we could do was pitch a pup tent. If we stayed here, somehow we were doomed.

"All right," Kathryn said. "We can go."

Over the years, we made our way to better jobs and more affordable towns, we lived in safer and cleaner neighborhoods, we stocked our refrigerator with fresher and healthier foods. We made what we thought was our last change when we moved to Charlotte, North Carolina, where we had a little more money, and we chose a safe, sanitized upscale apartment complex to have our second kid in. (And how I fought having that kid as well. When Kathryn called to tell me she was pregnant, I was at work, with a colleague breathing down my neck, and my wife and I hadn't yet completed the debate about whether to keep "trying" when we had just this minute only "tried" the once. "Fuck" was all I said when she gave me the news.) We wanted the children to be safe and comfortable. The hell with fun and adventure; we were all about comfort and safety. We wanted—and got—wall-to-wall carpeting, a washer-dryer, a microwave, a swimming pool, a neighborhood with take-out Thai food.

I was still contemplating how lucky we were when I first noticed the parade of Range Rovers and Lexuses outside my window. Charlotte, we learned, was the country's newest boomtown, and practically everyone around us was booming. There were six-thousand-square-foot homes and $15,000-per-year private schools and plush country clubs and a massive mall that was growing more massive by the minute, and the crux of every conversation wasn't "How much are you making?" so much as it was "Why aren't you making more?" Practically everyone in our neck of the woods had perfect teeth and perfect hair and perfectly attired children, and the subdivisions and neighborhoods had names like Foxcroft and Dilworth and Myers Park and the Arboretum, and the sound of each was like the sound of money, an endless chime of precious metals, the substantive chromes of their enormous imported cars ringing against the substantial facades of their magical homes. As I drove the swollen streets and saw the blur of behemoths, I would point to each one and say, "Congratulations," or, "Way to go," or, "Good for you," or sometimes, when I could not help myself, "Fuck you." Friends of ours called from around the country, up the coast, down the block, to announce their arrival in the land of six-figure incomes. We were so well below that tier that we went out and bought six little dolls and put them on the mantel of our fake fireplace. That's our six figures, we told ourselves.

Finally we moved to the middle of nowhere, to a place that the boom hadn't yet reached, and took steady jobs and stayed on when our better-located families and fancier friends thought we were sure to leave, and my envy had a nice long rest. After nine years we can now go out to dinner, buy gifts, and subscribe to all the parenting magazines, and my wife even sometimes makes the trip through the cash register without checking the stunning cost of randomly overpriced items such as our boy's ski goggles or our girl's shampoo. We appear to have landed in the contentment of the hinterland, ignorant of just how well the better-off are doing and grateful for our relatively uneventful and guarded lives. Our third child arrived with the least difficulty, our teeth get regularly cleaned, there is no private school within forty-five miles, and the only Range Rovers belong to the local college students. Still, I kept track of our money, although not to the extreme degree. Something gnawed at me; there was always something gnawing at me. I felt I would always keep track; I would always want more money, that even as we filled the kids' college accounts, there was a trapdoor underneath us, below which lurked something certain but indescribable, something I knew firsthand yet could not name. One day, when Kathryn pointed out an article in the newspaper that reported that money really mattered most when people got older, that money really determined in what kind of comfort you were going to die, that sealed it for me. We need more so that we won't die in a double-wide in a trailer park outside of Pittsburgh, we need more so that we won't die without the full complement of pain medication, we need more so that we won't die being hauled onto and off of bedpans by some stranger who smells of bourbon and couldn't care less whether our asses were still coated in what had brought us to that bedpan in the first place.

Some rich people, you think, will never die and will never experience discomfort or pain. Like George Hamilton or Jack Nicholson or Uma Thurman. They all look like they've been embalmed as a protective measure, that nothing will get to them, that they have literally been sealed off from the mortal world and can bear any expense therewith, that their toilet seats will be made of velvet and their bed rails will gleam with gold. I once had dinner with Uma Thurman, and she demanded to know whether everything was fresh, and she demanded to know the actual country of origin of the food, and I thought, That Uma Thurman, she can afford to live forever, and she has the resources to make it happen.

And so—after promising to start over thirteen years ago if tragedy befell us—I have started over indeed. I work two different jobs, teach all over the place, consult wherever I'm asked, and do anything else I can to secure my family's fortunes.

My wife thinks all I care about is money. In a way that hasn't changed much from the days when I barred us from having so much as even a cup of coffee outside our own kitchen. What I really care about is the comfort and safety and sanity of our burgeoning little family, and since money is what fuels that particular plane, we'd better make a bunch of it, or someday our plane is going to crash. I still fret about food wasted, about clothes newly bought that don't fit but are not returned, but it is all more about guarding against the threat of an attack on our fortress than it is about trying to build it brick by brick in the first place. I want to save every cent, not for the sake of enhancing our current life, but for the sake of securing it until death do us part and maybe beyond that.

Now, if I could only tie this all together for Kathryn, then maybe the next time she takes something to the cash register she'll read the damn tag beforehand, or maybe the next time she signs up for one of those magazines she barely reads she'll pause and say, "Is this really worth the twenty-five ninety-five that they're charging me?" That twenty-five ninety-five might be the last bit of morphine she'll need to get her to the land of bliss in her moment of absolute pain. That twenty-five ninety-five might help out one of our sons when that rock band he's trying to lead disintegrates and he's stuck in some nasty, money-hungry town. That twenty-five

ninety-five might be the cab fare our daughter is searching for
frantically in her apartment after her water breaks, when she
knows she needs much more than just what the meter will say,
when she'll want to leave a significant amount for the lasting karma
of a great tip.

For Poorer

Kathryn Rhett

My husband's grandfather, who retired as president of the Industrial Valley Bank, was the first Jewish banker in Philadelphia. He lived with his wife at the top of a hill, and when their two children grew up, he built them twin stone houses at the bottom, a family tree made architectural. He also built trust funds for the education of all his grandchildren, but my husband, being the fifth and last kid in his family to get his hands on the trust, knew it might run out before he finished college. Because of this, he found it urgent to finish in three years so as to accrue fewer loans, and to live in the infirmary one year, and work as an RA another, to pay for room and board.

Though Fred grew up on the Main Line and went to Princeton, his parents didn't make much, and he knew firsthand the humiliations of standing in the unemployment line with his dad and having only powdered milk at home. He was, to put it lightly, ambivalent about being in the rarefied environment of the Ivy League.

For three years, he stopped brushing his teeth as a form of social protest against the glossy superficiality of the Princeton elite. When we met, in graduate school, he slept on a mattress on the floor. To pay the bills, he worked for two Baltimore nonprofits, a bunch of nuns operating a literacy center out of a decrepit storefront and an institute for handicapped children. He was serious about his beliefs and yelled at me and my friends when we acted unintellectual (trading recipes was the crime). We both lived in apartments fizzing with cockroaches. Meeting for dinner at one or another apartment, we ate Swanson Chicken Pot Pies. We were not, seemingly, part of the American plan for upward mobility.

In those days, we entertained ourselves with reruns of *Taxi* on his roommate's small television set, a bottle of rye he kept in his bedroom (in memory of his grandmother, whose favorite drink it was), and dancing to the jukebox at the grad club. We ate macaroni and cheese, with frozen peas mixed in, and used my roommate's rowing machine for exercise. Sitting on my row house front porch swing on a fall afternoon, or lying in bed with the snow swirling outside, reading a Jane Austen novel, I felt content. Fred and I and our friends all lived communally, renting an apartment or house with two or three other people, sharing a kitchen and bathroom.

We didn't care about making money then. Rich people didn't intimidate us, because we didn't aspire to be them. Fred had once interviewed for a banking job, and the guy had said to him, "You have to care most about making money—do you?"

No, he didn't, and he didn't take the job. We made enough to live on. Every two weeks I stood in line at the credit union to deposit my paycheck. I balanced my checkbook, paid the rent and utilities. Fred had a car, I didn't. My furniture came from Goodwill, my parents' garage, and yard sales. I had a students' health insurance plan through the university. One year I had some arguments with my father and went to see a counselor; after the allowable eight visits, I called myself cured. I liked riding the bus, drinking happy hour specials, and making creative outfits from old clothes. In one thrift shop I came upon the cast-off vintage wardrobe of a woman who had been exactly my size, and felt that I had communed with the dead somehow by wearing her plaid day dress, her black cocktail dress. Who needed money to have an interesting life?

After our marriage, Fred and I cobbled together a lot of part-time jobs to get by. We were living in San Francisco because he had a fellowship that gave us a reason to move there, but it didn't cover the rent. We updated a law enforcement guide to driver's licenses of the fifty states. We wrote promotional copy for a baseball pitching machine manufacturer. I edited dissertations for grad students in anthropology and proofread for a university press and for banking, law, environmental, and graphic design firms. Even now, certain theorists' names (Jürgen Habermas) and kinds of books (Russian military history) and categories of documents (environmental impact reports) make me shiver. But this life of constantly trying to make ends meet was not what we had imagined for ourselves. We wanted to travel, to live lightly. We targeted July as our departure month and started saving money so we could quit our jobs and go away for a year.

We sold our books, furniture, and car. We advertised our sofa and chairs in the newspaper and set out the smaller things on the sidewalk to sell. I loved getting rid of stuff, owning only what I would use. My friend Jane helped me trundle garbage bags full of clothes down to the thrift store. Another friend bought our old gold Subaru and our table with the pretty spiral-lathed legs. Easy come, easy go, I thought. I felt adventurous and free. After working dozens of jobs, we would have our reward. We were headed to Thailand, then to France, and then we would figure out the rest. We bought backpacks and Birkenstock sandals and got vaccinations and visas. We put the remainder of our stuff in a rented storage facility and took a shuttle van to the airport.

We had a budget that, after we'd figured costs for plane tickets, would allow us to travel for a whole year. When we arrived in our first motel room, in Bangkok, after midnight, I eyed the cheap, mildewed shower curtain, the larger-than-usual cockroach, and the dripping air conditioner with a definite anxiety. How would I sleep in a place like this? Not very well, it turned out, but in the morning as we walked along a dirt alley lined with banana trees, I felt exuberant that we had made it, farther away from home than I had ever been.

We rented a new, clean kitchen-less row house on a dirt street in the northern city of Chiang Mai, where we wrote at home and in the air-conditioned U.S. Information Agency library, ate at street market stalls, and rode red pickup trucks around town, the group taxis that everyone took. At night we played cards and drank local whiskey mixed with water. A friend of a friend in Chiang Mai showed us around the local temples and let us hang out at his house, an open-air place full of animals like his pet loris, who would sit on our shoulders and hold our hair with its babylike fingers. We were broke, but we didn't feel deprived. Backpackers streamed through town, Australians on their round-the-world trips, American white kids wearing dreadlocks and baggy pants bought in Goa. Our fellow travelers, like our fellow grad students, looked no better-off than we were.

Then we made the mistake of moving to France. We settled in the town of Vence, living near a pair of married friends who were spending the year abroad. Their version of roughing it looked a lot better than our version. Whereas in graduate school all four of us had lived in similarly fixed-up, crummy apartments, now they lived in a well-heated flat and had bought a used car, while we lived in a cold artist's studio with an outdoor bathroom and walked everywhere. We cooked spaghetti most nights and drank cheap wine ("Let's open ours," we overheard our friend say from the kitchen as her husband presented her with the bottle we had brought). As the snows advanced down the Maritime Alps toward the edge of town, we sneaked into our landlord's woodshed to make off with a few logs for a fire. Suddenly I felt poor.

So a few months later, after we flew to the States for a family wedding, we decided to head south rather than back to France. We flew to Texas on frequent-flier miles, then traveled by train to Mexico City and on to the inland town of Oaxaca. We rented a one-bedroom apartment there, in a motel-style building arranged around an interior courtyard. I loved doing laundry on the roof in a large sink, hanging it up to dry on clotheslines with a view of the valley and surrounding hills. We met neighbors who were permanent expats, making their retirement checks from the States go further across the border. They showed us the American library and the best places to buy a laundry tub, limes, and red beans. Though the first chicken I bought appeared to have been murdered, I got used to shopping at market stalls rather than stores.

We budgeted a certain amount of money for every day, and if we had extra, we bought pottery or went to see an American movie. Money was very tangible then, paper bills in my hand, coins in a purse, doled out for mangoes or a bus ride. Our money has become so intangible now, our paychecks deposited and health insurance withheld automatically. Back then I knew exactly how much I carried in my wallet and how long it had to last.

When we felt comfortable and a little bored in Oaxaca, we headed to Guatemala, on a twelve-hour bus to San Cristóbal de las Casas, and then on another twelve-hour trip that involved seven different vehicles, including school buses and a van. We kept retrieving our bags from the roof of one vehicle and then running to the next, and along with us, grabbing bags and running, were people from Switzerland, Germany, and France, all headed for Panajachel on Lake Atitlán.

The nickname for Panajachel was Gringotenango, the refuge for American and European hippies. They walked into the bank with tangled hair to cash their AmEx traveler's checks, dressing in more native clothes than the natives did, in embroidered vests, striped pants, long skirts that trailed in the dust. Gringo wholesalers trolled the main street past a hundred textile stalls, buying cloth caps, wallets, belts, and woven bags. The friendship bracelets were displayed in tied bundles for their convenience. Fred and I watched them fill their VW vans with worry dolls and quilts to sell in the States, and felt superior. "How would you like your every relationship with a Guatemalan person to be based on a financial transaction?" we asked.

Panajachel was a trading crossroads, where money and textiles changed hands all day long, soldiers with machine guns stood guard in the crowded bank lobby, and vans stuffed full of quilts and Hacky Sacks turned and climbed up a hill for the long drive north. The town represented a crossroads for us, too. What would we do next? Fred imagined us in a little white house on a tree-lined street in a small city. Reading Mary McCarthy's novel *Birds of America*, I ached for a future, wanting to be her character Rosamund, the perfect mother who cooked every recipe from *The Fannie Farmer Cookbook* as a game and made cranberry sauce in heart-shaped molds. In Oaxaca, I had watched pregnant women walk the town square in pastel Peter Pan–collared maternity dresses and wanted a baby. Not just as an idea anymore, but a baby to hold. Baby fever, Fred called my state of mind, as if it were an illness that would pass. But it didn't. One day we walked by an orphanage, and I thought, Who would let us adopt a baby? We have no jobs, no safety net.

And then I felt small-minded for worrying about security and practicality. I wished to be free and wild and romantic, taking to heart lines of Rimbaud like "Finally I came to regard as sacred the disorder of my mind." Order attracted me too much, and I kept lists of what I read, and bought. Copying out friends' recipes, I criticized myself for being such a housewife and office girl. Being this way while traveling seemed acceptable, part of the survivalist, can-do, pioneer spirit that drives low-budget expatriates. Being this way while at home, though, would leave me with a middle-class imagi-nation, limited and literal, making a cozy nest with everything in its place. On the day we boarded an old school bus and wound up the hill away from Panajachel and toward the many crossroads where we could catch buses heading north (I linger over their names, Cuatro Caminos, the four ways where two highways met, or Los Encuentros, the encounters), we left the free-minded pursuit of what we might do and chose instead the typical American Dream.

When we returned to our old city, San Francisco, we acted as if we were still traveling and kept to a budget, writing every expenditure on small white lined pages in a notebook. I remember coming into the apartment and sitting down to enter my purchases: $0.35 for a newspaper, $28.00 for a monthly subway pass, $4.70 for produce. This helped us feel in control of our money, however little of it there was. We liked a certain coffee shop in our neighborhood, but months passed before we could afford to go there: $9.50 for two cappuccinos and a piece of carrot cake. We worked for a nonprofit ad agency, writing copy about sacred Native American lands in New Mexico, a rain forest in Japan, and institutional racism in Albuquerque and El Paso. Fred worked for a think tank in Berkeley. I picked up my editing and proofreading clients again.

We bought health insurance that would cover pregnancy and delivery, and so finally we could start trying. Our friend from France was already pregnant, and of course they had a car. She only took jobs she wanted to take, whereas, pregnant with our first child, I temped for seven months at the Southern Pacific Railroad's environmental group, filing by spill site. (Coalinga, Lemon Cove, Salida, all the lovely California names where poison got dumped out of train cars.) When Fred got cheaper health insurance through his job as a fund developer for nonprofit low-income housing, we switched health care providers instantly, though I had liked the midwives and obstetricians where I was. Instead of being seen at a respected university teaching hospital, I now visited the dreary Kaiser Permanente hospital on a heavily trafficked boulevard near a Toys "R" Us. The Kaiser industrial companies' clinics for their construction, shipyard, and steel-mill workers in the 1930s and 1940s had opened to public enrollment in 1945. In 1990, a year before we joined, Kaiser Permanente was the biggest HMO in the United States, with 6.5 million members.

If it was good enough for millions of people, it was good enough for us, I reasoned, and after collecting recommendations for an obstetrician, I found a woman I really liked who was unassailably competent and kind. However, Kaiser being the sort of factory hospital that it is, there was never a guarantee that my doctor would be on duty when I had the baby.

In fact, too few obstetricians were on duty the night our daughter was delivered. After I received epidural anesthesia, my blood pressure dropped, I had to be given oxygen, and the monitors showed fetal distress. Despite these warning signs, a brand-new resident delivered the baby without supervision, and she forgot a basic procedure: to suction out the baby's mouth with a rubber suction bulb before cutting the umbilical cord. Our daughter had excreted meconium during her oxygen-deprivation distress, a common occurrence, and once the umbilical cord was cut and she then took her first mouth breath, she inhaled the toxic stuff. It was the nurse who saw the baby turning dusky red and ran with her out of the room. My husband ran, too. Together they fumbled with light switches, and resuscitation equipment in another room. But the baby's lungs shut down, reverting protectively to their fetal breathing state, which works with an umbilical cord. A ventilator was used to force oxygen through her lungs the right way. The neonatologist told us she might die and that if she survived, she had a good chance of being impaired.

We quickly learned that what had happened was completely unnecessary, that she had been a healthy baby until the resident forgot to suction her mouth. Unbelievable, we muttered. Suddenly we didn't trust anyone. My family called around to determine if the neonatologist was regarded as competent (he was). When I saw the resident leave the nursery one day, I wanted to scream at her, "Stay away from my baby!" Her eyes met mine with a cool flicker and she said nothing, and I hated her for her gracelessness as well as her mistake. Now our baby might have to be transported by ambulance to another, more expensive hospital, the same one where we used to be insured. They had a higher-level intensive care nursery there and a lung-bypass machine. But they warned us that she might die during transport so we made the difficult decision to keep her at Kaiser. We sat over her warming bed, and on the eighth day we were told she might have stabilized, and on the eleventh day we brought her home. She was fragile, we were warned, susceptible to infection for the first year. She couldn't travel, shouldn't be in crowded stores or restaurants. Every few weeks, an infant development specialist came to our apartment to check her progress. The good reports made us ecstatic, and the bad ones made us brood. "My poor baby," I would say as I rocked her, knowing I had failed her. If we had stayed with the midwives, maybe I would have made it through labor without the epidural that made my blood pressure drop, that started the whole terrible sequence of events.

In the months after the baby came home, I felt bitter about money. First we'd had to wait to try getting pregnant until we could afford health insurance. Then we had to switch to an inferior hospital because it would cost us less. I looked at the expensive hospital, lit green cubes on a hillside, as I walked to one of my jobs. We didn't own a car. If our daughter had cerebral palsy or developmental delay, we could sue the hospital. But without visible harm, our attorney advised us, we wouldn't win a settlement. Our daughter could never get health insurance on her own, Blue Cross of California informed us, because of her condition at birth. She would always have to be insured through us, the sort of insurance where preexisting conditions don't disqualify you.

As she grew older, Fred and I argued about whether to have a second child.

He asked, "Do you want another child just so you can have a better birth experience?"

I asked, "Do you not want another child because you're afraid?"

"No," he said tiredly. "It's just that it will take away from our time together, we won't be able to travel as much, and we'll be poorer."

"I'm close to my sister," I said. "What if I didn't have her? I think being an only child would be sad." Some old friends who were staying with us agreed with me, arguing with Fred that giving our daughter a sibling would be the best thing we could do for her. Fred felt cornered, outnumbered. We came to an easy decision and stopped using birth control, but it was the kind of argument that is unwinnable. By the next month, I was pregnant, and he felt, in some way, that our friends were responsible. He even developed a theory: one night, when he had gone to sleep early, the husband of this couple had slept with me and impregnated me. "I am the most goddamn faithful wife on the planet," I countered coldly. "The baby is yours."

We were both afraid. Fred felt trapped by the pregnancy and worried about the outcome. I wrote down bargains: please let the child be healthy, or—let's qualify that and not ask for too much— it would be okay if the baby had a genetic disorder or deformity, or was a bit premature, or had jaundice, but a serious problem such as a heart dysfunction requiring surgery might be pushing the limits of what I could stand. My father had just had open-heart surgery because of a congenital mitral valve defect. My knees weak, I watched his ventilator and checked the numbers on his oxygen monitor. Being with him in the ICU reminded me of being with our daughter, and made me understand that trauma only sensitized us to further trauma, rather than preparing us. The repetition was not numbing but worse. We did everything we could to make sure that this second birth would not be a repeat of the first, carefully choosing a private obstetrical practice, making sure every doctor there knew our history.

We were deep into the pursuit of stable careers, teaching at a university, and had excellent health insurance, when our second child was born, at the state-of-the-art Carolinas Medical Center in Charlotte, North Carolina. Instead of a resident and a nurse, a whole team, including an anesthesiologist and a pediatrician, stood by as our son was born, healthy. But twelve hours later he turned blue for a minute, a "blue spell" they called it, and he was admitted to the intensive care nursery for observation. We did some research.

"I think it's his heart," Fred said. We were very quiet. We couldn't believe this was happening again, the baby in intensive care, the research, the phone calls to relatives. We requested an ultrasound on the baby's heart. "Too expensive," we were told. "We'll have to wait and see."

We felt sarcastic, tight-lipped. I tried to be civil to the nurses, who kept wanting to give the baby formula instead of calling me to come down and feed him, just as the Kaiser nurses had. "You would think," I said to Fred, "that in these past four years the nurses might have become less ignorant about breast-feeding." "You would think," Fred said, "they would save themselves some money by ordering the damn test on the first day. How much do you think it costs to keep a baby in the NICU?" Three days later, the medical team ordered an ultrasound on the baby's heart and found a hole. The expensive health insurance did not fail us, though. Visits to the pediatric cardiologist were fully covered.

When we were first married, we had lived a purely bohemian life of cheap food and thrift-shop clothes and freedom, but it didn't square with having children. It was one thing for the two of us to live in Guatemala, where the medical care consisted of a team of American doctors arriving at a town across the lake once a week. (They climbed out of a motorboat in green scrubs every Saturday morning, and their patients formed a line that wound around the church.) But we couldn't gamble like that on good luck and health now. What if one of the children had an emergency?

We now required of ourselves that we carry full family coverage health insurance. We lived in a generic (wall-to-wall white carpeting) town house in Charlotte, a place with central air that was insect-free. But while I depended on our new washer and dryer, and wouldn't want to do without a car again, I hadn't quite dispensed with the romance of the rebel artiste. Now it seemed a question, though, of not whether to compromise but which compromises to make.

A few years ago we moved out of the city and settled in a town where our paychecks go a lot further than they used to. The difference between France and Thailand, say. And yet still we fight about money, about expenses large and small.

Recently, for example, I reminded my husband that we should send a gift certificate for our nephew's birthday. "Don't be such a perfectionist!" he said.

"Perfectionist? His birthday was a month ago."

"We've got a lot of other things staring us in the eye— taxes . . ."

"This isn't a chore, it's a gift."

"Why are you such a pain?"

I buy all the gifts. He grouses about them. But he's pleased to announce them. "We sent Stephen a graduation card," he tells his sister, though I've bought the card, written it, argued with him about the amount of the check, addressed and stamped the thing.

He doesn't give to charity, either. Years ago he would say, "I'll donate my time, or write something for them. I'd rather do that than give money." But then he wouldn't. I volunteer at the kids' elementary school, serving breakfast, which he thinks a waste of time. And when I buy a few boxes of cereal for the school, he thinks it a waste of money, too. I write checks to Planned Parenthood, to UNICEF, to the Special Olympics. When the boy up the block sells pizza for the high school band, or our friend Clara sells Girl Scout Cookies, I buy them. Not an excessive amount. My husband rolls his eyes. "How much money are you giving those people?" he hisses, as if I were handing out cash to some meth users who showed up on the porch.

Meanwhile, he buys bottle upon bottle of Chardonnay (I drink half), doesn't blink too hard at an extravagant dinner out, and just bought a cashmere zip cardigan in Saint-Tropez that cost more than all my yearly checks to my high school, college, and assorted charities combined.

But these moments of reckless extravagance don't keep him from bickering with me about our minor expenses. Grocery bills, for example.

"You didn't buy applesauce," I say, unloading the half-filled bag he's returned with.

My husband shrugs. "We had another jar already."

"We used that."

In a way, both of us act as if we grew up during a war, or during the Depression. I want the cabinets fully stocked, with backups. It might be because of the 1989 San Francisco earthquake, after which we prepared, as suggested by public authorities, an "earthquake station" with first aid supplies, water, food, flashlights, radio, and a wrench to turn off the gas. It might be Y2K, when we stocked the basement with three days' worth of water and food, as well as a battery-powered radio, for when the country's digital systems would all crash at the century's turn. It might be September 11, with all its resultant advice to lay in quantities of duct tape and canned food. My husband will eat the scraps off of everybody's plates. He hates wasted food. I throw away moldy leftovers before he sees them. When he's the one doing the shopping, I don't add the long-term supply needs to the list, things we might not be cooking in the next three days but we should have in stock: black beans, chicken broth, brownie mix. He shops from day to day. I shop as if a blizzard were predicted.

It was a startling moment when I first realized I had ended up not with a rebel artiste but with a man who was obsessed with making money and socking it away. Had Fred always been this way? Yes, he had. His grandfather was a banker, I reminded myself. But in the early years, before we had kids, we could both pretend that how much we had in the bank didn't matter.

Even now, usually around Christmas, I sometimes wish for a husband like Pa Ingalls, the sort who wore plaid flannel shirts and carved children's toys out of wood while sitting by the fire, who played fiddle while the children clapped, who made much out of little. The happy family in its cozy home while winter roared outside would survive anything. But Fred is different. He would rather make more money than less, and to his way of thinking, money will keep a person safer than happiness or love. From the moment I was pregnant with our first child to this moment when our third child is two years old, he has spent most of his waking hours working.

The other day I yelled at him that he was a success-obsessed mercenary whereas I could quit my job, work at Wal-Mart, and happily live in a trailer. But that isn't exactly true. Maybe I chose him because I knew, at the age of twenty-three, that he would protect our economic status fiercely, that he might act bohemian at the start, but that a boy raised in Main Line, Philadelphia, with sisters who wore large diamond rings, a guy with "Phi Beta Kappa" and "Fulbright fellow" on his résumé, would not let me end up poor. And he hasn't.

Wining

Daniel Handler

Do you want to know what a $1,200 bottle of wine tastes like? Of course you do. That's the first thing my literary agent wanted to know when I told her I was going to participate in an anthology about money by spending the fee on a bottle of wine and writing about it. "I'll fly out," she said. A few years back, she almost died in a car accident, and she told me that as the car spun her around and around she thought to herself, "I'm glad I had all those delicious meals." "I'll fly out and drink it with you. What do you think it tastes like?"

The next day she called me again. "I don't think you should write this essay," she said. "Twelve hundred dollars on a bottle of wine? It's immoral. People are going to attack you. People are going to call you an immoral person."

"That's what I'm interested in," I said. "I keep telling people about this bottle of wine. First everybody wants some, and then everybody thinks it's immoral. This is the thing with money. If more people knew how money worked, they wouldn't be so stupid about it. They wouldn't give tax breaks to rich people like us."

"It's true," she said. "Hey, did I tell you how much money I saved on those tax breaks?"

I sighed. I'd just learned how much I saved, and let me tell you, it's much more than any bottle of wine costs. At least I hope it is. "Yes," I said into the phone. My literary agent is a wonderful person, and offhand I'd wish her all the money in the world. But if she had all the money in the world, then I wouldn't have any money for myself. This is the thing with money, and it makes me want to have a drink, although not necessarily one that costs $1,200.

Still, though, my drinks cost more than they used to. I can't say I've been poor—I grew up in comfortable circumstances, and my parents would have taken me back in rather than see me starve—but for sure I've been broke. After graduating from an expensive university, I spent my days trying to make a living writing fiction, and I spent my nights doing the cheapest possible thing, which was going with my friends to a taqueria down the street and drinking very cheap margaritas. We'd spend our loose change on the jukebox, and when the mariachi band stopped by and started playing, the manager would unplug the jukebox, and all the songs we'd chosen would be gone forever. I considered this a substantial financial loss.

A few years later, I moved to New York City. I spent my days trying to make a living writing fiction and my nights doing the cheapest possible thing, which had to be a lot cheaper than going to the taqueria down the street because I had less money and because New York City seemed to require not only more money than I had—which went without saying—but more money than I had any hope of having, then or anytime in the future, no matter how elaborate my dreams of success, and my dreams of success were getting more and more difficult to conjure up. My first novel hadn't sold, and every day I tried to concentrate on writing my second novel, but instead I kept reminding myself that even if this novel sold for a record-breaking amount, which it was not going to, I couldn't afford to be living in the city where I was living, trying to write the novel that in no way would ever sell for a record-breaking amount. After spending my days like this, I would get thirsty at night, and the cheapest possible thing turned out to be having people over to our apartment to play cards and drink bourbon. We had two kinds of bourbon: the cheap stuff that we drank all the time and the bottle of fancy bourbon someone had given us that we drank on special occasions, like on the night my book finally sold. As it turns out, I was wrong: the novel did sell for a record-breaking amount. It sold for the least amount of money my literary agent had ever negotiated for a work of fiction.

There were times when I felt like jumping out the window of my apartment, but I could only afford to live on the second floor, and I would just have landed on one of the loud, laughing people lined up outside, cocktails in their hands, for an unaffordable steak house. The steak house had its menu posted outside, and whenever I walked past it, I would see how much they were charging for a piece of meat. It was immoral. The people standing outside the restaurant were immoral, and so were the cocktails they were holding. It was immoral to do anything but the cheapest possible thing in New York City, because the cheapest possible thing was already expensive, and it was immoral to stand outside laughing, because if someone lived on the second floor of a nearby apartment building he could hear you as he poured the cheap bourbon and dealt the cards. The cards, too, were arguably immoral, as they came from

my father's bridge club, a group of men in such comfortable circumstances that they opened a fresh deck of cards at the start of
each bridge night; but my father mailed the opened decks to me, as
a gift to a guy who was broke, so it wasn't quite as immoral as the
cocktails the people were drinking outside the steak house, as the
people outside the steak house never offered me so much as one
measly sip, even when I was walking back to my apartment from
my only steady means of earning money, which was a gig reading
and summarizing manuscripts sent to my literary agent, a gig
clearly given to me out of pity and which paid so little that occasionally the day's money would already be spent on the way back to
the apartment, mostly because my homeward path took me past
the Strand Bookstore, which sold brand-new, dubiously acquired
hardback books for half price, which my literary agent told me was
immoral, but in my opinion not as immoral as a broke writer not
being able to afford new books at full price.

This fine-tuned moral philosophy has never left me. The ways
of people with more money than I had at that time in my life continue to be immoral, and even as my life has progressed, I have not
wavered. Even now, when I can afford it, I do not go to that steak
house in New York and fork over an immoral sum for a piece of
meat. Instead, I go to another steak house, farther uptown. It's
more expensive.

In fact, nearly everything now is more expensive. After years
of trying to make a living writing fiction, I began to make a living
writing fiction, and then a nice living, and then a nicer living than
one ought to make writing fiction, as opposed to, say, healing the
sick or teaching people to read. Children's books I had written more
or less on a lark did something that honestly had not occurred to
me, even in my desperate fantasies of ways in which I would no

longer be broke. They began to sell, immoral amounts of copies to total strangers, and then one day my movie agent—a kind and hilarious man, good of heart and startling of brain, who can talk authoritatively and brilliantly about more books than anyone else I know, and who spends an immoral amount of money on furniture—called me and said, "I hear the money train pulling in to the station."

This was such an immoral statement that I spent the rest of the day sitting on the couch staring into space until my wife came home and I told her the news. "My movie agent hears the money train pulling in to the station," I said.

"Great," she said. "Maybe I can quit my stupid job and start to do the work I want to do. Maybe we could buy a house. First let's have a drink."

We did all those things—quitting the stupid job, which was immoral not only for what it entailed but for the measly pay it granted my wife, and starting the work she wanted to do, which is not only moral but noble, like writing fiction, although thank goodness not that. And we bought a house, for an unspeakably immoral sum of money. But first we had a drink. We still had two kinds of bourbon in our home: the stuff we drank all the time, which used to be the fancy bourbon we drank on special occasions, and the stuff we drank on special occasions, which was immorally expensive. We learned of this immorally expensive bourbon from the menu of the restaurant of equally immoral expense, where a glass of it cost more than we spent on a bottle of bourbon before the money train pulled in to the station. We ordered it anyway, telling ourselves that it wasn't technically immoral because my publisher was paying for dinner. It was delicious. The next day we bought a bottle of the stuff, which we paid for ourselves. This is the bourbon we drank the night the money train pulled in to the station, and it's the bourbon we served as a nightcap to the last few stragglers at a party we threw after we bought the house and filled it with furniture and art. It's the bourbon a few friends sipped, all of whom suddenly had less money than me, before they left our house and got into the cars the valets had waiting. My wife and I had debated the valet parking for quite some time: it seemed like a noble thing to do for our guests, but it also felt not like the kind of nobility associated with good deeds but like the kind of nobility associated with fancy parties in expensive homes. Which was what we were throwing. So we paid for the valets. The next morning my fears were realized when a friend e-mailed me saying he was offended by the valets and that it was a sign I was an immoral sellout. I wrote back groveling, explaining my justifications, which I now saw as absolutely immoral. My friend wrote back to say he was kidding and that he appreciated the valet parking. I wrote back saying he ought to stay late next time, because the stragglers got to sample some very delicious bourbon.

This is the thing with money, right here, the simultaneous thrill of what it can buy and shame of knowing it ought not to buy such things, and knowing that no matter how much you give away—and in an earlier draft I had a paragraph here about how much money I give away, only to cut it out as it had no bearing on the subject at hand—it cannot mitigate money's immoral circumstances, and drinking the expensive stuff anyway, because it tastes better. Everyone knows money cannot buy happiness, but it is very easy to be unhappy in a crummy apartment overlooking the laughing immoral rich people drinking and waiting for steak. I found it so easy I did it several times a day. It is more difficult to be unhappy in a resort where someone unloads your car while you're checking in, and someone else parks it in the lot down the road—our dusty

and battered sedan looking pretty shabby among the shiny immoral luxury automobiles owned by the other guests—and then
takes you to your bungalow in a shiny SUV. In the daytime you hike
the trails of the grounds, where the staff has placed enormous vats
filled with ice and bottles of mineral water at convenient intervals,
or you swim in the pools, emerging to find that your towel has been
invisibly refolded while you were underwater. At night you sit in
the restaurant and stare out at the darkening, restless sea, and con-
sume delicious, vaguely healthy food, before retiring to your bungalow, where someone has set up logs and kindling in the fireplace.
I found it very difficult to be unhappy there, the one time I went
with my wife. The only way I could become unhappy was by reminding myself that it was immoral to spend the money it cost to
stay there, even if my wife was very pregnant and wanted to go to
an incredibly relaxing place, even if we were only going there one
time. It was immoral, I told myself, soaking in the infinity pool and
gazing at the view.

Twice. We went there twice. My life has been like this for a
few years now—not as long as I was broke, but long enough that I
know I won't be thrown out of my place if the check for the freelance writing project doesn't arrive on time, because my place is an
expensive house and the money for the writing project is going to
be spent on a bottle of wine. To acquire it, I e-mailed a friend who
works as a freelance wine writer. I expected a reply that went something like this: "It is immoral to spend $1,200 on a bottle of wine,
particularly if you don't really know anything about wine and
you're just doing it for a lark and to give you something to write
about. If you're hard up for ways to spend $1,200, why don't you
give it to me, you fuck." Instead, my friend told me to call a certain
shop and "ask for Dade or Elizabeth, and tell them you're looking

for a bottle of DRC or Jayer (jai-lay) or Leroy (le-wah) from a good vintage and ask if they can help you," and he kept on writing like I knew what he was talking about. "Naturally, this is for retail sales. It's harder to find expensive bottles like this retail. You could also easily go in and order something that pricey at that restaurant I told you about. If that's what you want to do, make sure you talk to Raj." I was scared to talk to Dade or Elizabeth, let alone Raj, so I left the procurement of the wine to my assistant, who I used to think ought only to do tasks that an assistant might do if I had an office job—otherwise it would be immoral—and who now picks up my dry cleaning and who once hired a man to come over to our house—I wish I were kidding—to change a lightbulb. It was hard to reach. The wine, disappointingly, looked like any bottle of wine, with French words all over it and a surprisingly recent year stenciled at the top. I kept it in a paper bag, afraid I would forget it was the $1,200 bottle, and stored it in the basement next to three bottles of what used to be the good bourbon and now is the everyday bourbon, left over from another party we held. Then I called my friends Nat and Jodi, who are probably the brokest people I know, to come over and drink it with us. They have two children. It has occurred to me, more than once, that I should buy them a house. Why shouldn't I? Why haven't I? I suppose that it would end the friendship, but they have other friends; they may never be able to afford a house.

"Really?" Nat said. "Great! What can be bring? Should we bring cobbler? Maybe cobbler is too acidic for the wine."

I thought maybe he hadn't heard me. "It's *twelve hundred dollars*," I said. "Don't you think that's immoral?"

"Was the money going to go to charity?" he asked. "Where did you get a $1,200 bottle of wine, anyway?"

"I bought it," I said. "I bought it with money they're paying me to write an essay about money."

"So the money was going to you," Nat said.

"It was already mine," I said. "I mean, I guess I could have given the money away, but I didn't think that would be much of an essay."

"See you at seven," he said. At seven they arrived, having brought the cobbler over on bicycles. I made Nat open the wine because I was too nervous to open it myself, and because he had once been, no kidding, a butler. We had a crystal decanter someone had given us for our wedding, but after some discussion we decided it wasn't for wine, so Nat just poured the wine into glasses and we all stared at it, letting it breathe. I broiled some steaks and we sat down.

"So, you really have no moral qualms about this bottle of wine?" I asked.

"None whatsoever," Nat said. "Why should I? People should spend money. They spend money to buy things. If you don't have a problem if it's art they buy, why should it be a problem if it's wine?"

"But it's *wine*," my wife said. "We'll drink it, and then it'll be gone."

"Ephemeral is preferable," Nat said. "As opposed to, say, a car that could run someone over and kill them and eventually end up clogging up a junkyard."

"So you would buy a $1,200 bottle of wine?" I asked. "If you could afford it?"

"Never," Nat said.

"What if it's the best wine ever?" Jodi said. "Or, what if you were supporting a noble industry? What if this were the last vineyard that made wine the old-fashioned way, without any ma-chines, or—"

"There's nothing that would change my mind," Nat said. "I'd never spend $1,200 on a bottle of wine."

"But you just said," I said, "you don't have any moral qualms about it."

"I don't have any moral qualms about spending *your* money on a bottle of wine," Nat said, with an enormous grin. "Let's drink it."

We drank it. I had the end of this essay all planned out, be-fore I drank the wine, in which I'd say it tasted delicious but left a bad taste in my mouth—get it?—but it turns out it just tasted like wine. (The next day Nat sent me an article in which various free-lance wine writers agreed.) It tasted red and smooth—I'm not good with the wine adjectives—and if I had to choose a fruit it tasted most like, I'd say grapes. It didn't even taste very old, but then again it wasn't very old. It was made in a year I was still broke. It was not worth $1,200, even though it apparently was. None of us knew what to say about it, so we talked about other things until the wine bottle was empty and the meal was over.

"Aren't you relieved?" Nat asked me. "What if you fell in love with how it tasted, and for the rest of your life you'd be sad and nos-talgic for the one time that you—"

"Or," I said, "I'd buy it from time to time."

He'd forgotten for a moment that I could do this. "Would you really?" he asked. "Would you really spend $1,200 on a bottle of wine?"

"Never," I said. We'd finished the meal, and I was walking across our house to fetch some of the good bourbon, as a nightcap.

We keep the good bourbon in the cupboard of an antique wooden table from Denmark we bought on a recent trip to New York City and had shipped back to our place. It stands in the living room, which is stuffed with hardcover books bought at full price, and watching over it is a large piece of artwork by Alexander Calder, which I never in a million years thought I would own. It didn't cost that much. What am I saying? Of course it did. But I could give it up. My wife and I have lived in crummy apartments, and we could do it again if we had to. But we don't have to. We don't have to, and we are happier, no doubt about it, for not having to. There is something wrong with this, I know there is, but I can't quite delineate the thing that is wrong with it, and this is the thing with money.

"This is *delicious*!" Nat said when he tasted the bourbon. "Now, *this*, my friend, is *good*. This is *delicious*. This is *good*."

"I know," I said. "It's delicious. Everybody wants some."

"Of course everybody wants some," he said. "Everybody should have some. How much does a thing like this cost?"

Dirty Work

Lydia Millet

In college I never had to pinch pennies. My mother paid for my education with income from her family's peach farm in Georgia; she wanted me to give all my time to learning and none to working at minimum wage. So I was lucky, and when I graduated I had no experience needing money. My mother made it clear that when it came to subsidies, the buck pretty much stopped here: I was now on my own. I'd done well in school, and I thought, being smart and all, that I'd be welcomed into the world of toil with open arms. Employers would pay top dollar, I figured, for a primo brain like mine.

As it happened, my brain did not call out to them. This was January 1991 in Los Angeles, and the economy wasn't looking its best. To make ends meet, I was sharing an apartment with a graduate student at UCLA and a tiny, furtive woman from England who had come to California to learn how to scream. She was taking a course in primal scream therapy and had to practice regularly; but luckily, in the apartment with the student and me, she wasn't yet grappling with the full-fledged scream. She was working up to it, and now and then she would beetle through the living room all hunched up, close her door meekly, and let out a plaintive ululation.

I spent my days faxing off numerous résumés, then settling in to watch bad television, wait for calls that never came, and listen to the muffled wailing of the English. This lasted for weeks, and then months—not surprisingly, I now realize, since there was nothing on my résumé but a bachelor's degree and, under a heading that ran something like "Special Skills," the twin virtues of opera singing and fluent German. (It turned out I didn't have the résumé thing quite down pat.) I tried to get myself hired out as a temp, a typist, even a live-in servant, but got no takers.

Finally someone took pity. I was hired as an assistant to a producer of after-school specials in Studio City who'd had her heyday in the 1970s and continued, despite a deafening lack of interest from both network and cable TV, to scribble out egregious treatments, in her large, loopy script, for shows about teens coming to grips with puberty. She fired me just a few weeks in, after making me put a car cover on her pearly white Jaguar every time she parked it and then losing her temper one day when a bird shat on the vinyl; that afternoon she heaved a five-gallon bottle of Sparkletts water at my head.

It missed.

My next job was as a receptionist and general dogsbody for a lawyer who was trying to get into the movie-agent business, drove a slick little Mercedes, wore Armani suits from Hong Kong, and had almost no clients. He fired me, too, when he ran out of money, but not before pressing me into service as a perpetrator of fraud: I had to pass myself off, by mail, as an expert in feature-film screenplay doctoring, and the lawyer set up a false identity for me. When naive and hopeful scribes in the middle of the country sent us their scripts, it was I who was in charge of writing up expensive reports on how the work could be improved to make it sell. Although I figured I could criticize as well as the next guy, I was, of course, completely unqualified. I didn't make a living wage being fraudulent—it was about $200 a week before taxes—so on weekends, to make ends meet, I freelanced for a down-market catering company that did corporate picnics, helping set up carnival games for kids and scoop potato salad onto paper plates.

After the screenplay job dried up, I was unemployed and desperate again, late with my contribution to the rent and living off ramen. I asked my mother for money a couple of times, and she sent it, but I felt humiliated and sullied. For the first time I saw how desperation can erode a personality, how the elements of a whole I'd always thought was solid and fixed—my moods, my mannerisms, my whimsies and choices, in short the parts that constituted me—were nothing but a luxury of ease.

Then I heard from my roommate's friend that there was a copy editor position going begging at a magazine company in Beverly Hills. She was leaving the job herself to travel in Europe with her boyfriend and could put in a good word for me; all I had to do was take a proofreading test, and all the proofreading marks I needed to know to pass that test with flying colors were right there in the dictionary under "Proofreaders' Marks." I imagined myself at a polished wooden desk with a wide office window behind me showing a panorama of the city. There, glasses perched on my nose and with an air of professionalism, I perused articles in *Scientific American* and possibly *The New Republic* to make sure their erudition was perfect.

The company turned out to be LFP, Inc., otherwise known as Larry Flynt Publications, home of the *Hustler* family. I had never seen modern porn, much less read it; the closest I'd come was the Marquis de Sade, whom I precociously tried to write a paper about when I was in high school.

Beyond *Hustler*, LFP was the home of scores of other periodicals, including *S.W.A.T.: Special Weapons & Tactics for the Prepared American*, a gun magazine edited by a former cop, and *Fighting Knives*, edited by a former mercenary. These were the ones—unpopular beats, and therefore always available to the newest rookie in the copy pool—to which I was first assigned. It turned out the magazines were easy assignments for a copy editor, since neither the ex-cop nor the ex-mercenary cared too much about correct grammar or spelling. Basically, these broadsheets were a no-brainer where dangling participles and *i* before *e* were concerned; it was the content that could stop you in your tracks, if you had any moral quibbles with the Second Amendment or, for that matter, blood sports.

I didn't feel pure helping to churn out rags whose classified ads hawked lock-picking sets, shock collars for attack dogs, DIY chemical weapons, and mysterious manuals on how to create a completely new identity in three easy steps. Plus, I actually liked grammar and spelling and was starting to miss them.

But then there was the question of need. My LFP salary wasn't big bucks, but it was a lot better than nothing. It was also better than the clown costume I'd had to don at those company picnics when the real clown didn't show. In L.A. clowns are always moonlighting actors, so they can be called away at the last minute by the all-powerful lure of *the audition*. And when these magical auditions drop from the sky, people like me are summoned, people with no clowning skills and indeed no love of clowning, people whose balloon-animal repertoire is limited to snakes and worms. Shoehorned fifteen minutes before the picnics began into the spare costume, which was caked with the rancid sweat of many second-string clowns before me, I was given a ratty blond wig that looked like something from Twisted Sister. I had to do my own clown makeup with the aid of nothing but a side-view mirror. When they saw me headed for them, gaily smiling and prancing, children blubbered with fear.

I would not go back there.

So it was a relief when the copy chief switched me over to two new titles, *Hustler* and *Busty Beauties*. Both featured naked women with plastic parts; *Hustler* even contained the odd rape joke. And though I was unreservedly pleased to leave the world of weaponeering, I paged through these and recalled with queasiness a Take Back the Night march I'd walked in just a few months before. I'd held a sign that said, NO ONE DESERVES TO BE A PUNCHING BAG, at the urging of an eager friend, and felt sheepish but well-meaning.

But the world of *Hustler* was complex.

First there was the magazine itself, which had some idiosyncrasies. In a section of profoundly lame photo gags called Bits & Pieces, women might be pictured naked and on all fours eating out of dog bowls or smeared with filth; this in itself was apparently the punch line. In the cartoons, visible minorities, gays, and the handicapped were often the butt of profoundly stupid jokes, and in the Hot Letters section, which recounted sexual fantasies and misadventures, I recall a standout piece that spun a merry tale of the abuse of a girl born with a tail. And although I didn't object to the idea of porn as a tool for masturbation, I didn't see why it had to be so vicious.

But the rent was due, and I had no other prospects. Surely, I reasoned, correcting a few typos did not make me an accessory to a crime, did it?

For better or worse, the cynical attitude of the magazine was tongue-in-cheek; in day-to-day life, all but a few of the editorial staffers appeared to get along fine with both women and minorities. Formulaic hatespeak was their best attempt at edginess; they were trying to give the magazine's readership, which included legions of convicts, what they thought it wanted.

And that was unfortunate. Back when it first came out, *Hustler* had been a rebel magazine—tawdry, crude, and in-your-face, with a quasi-libertarian political bent. One cover bore an image of the Easter Bunny crucified. But by the time I worked there, Larry himself had been shot and sidelined; the magazine had been gutted of all political relevance, retaining the crudeness and the tawdriness but none of the fighting spirit. It had become glossy and more or less corporate, inasmuch as a brand name identified with spread legs and shining "pink" can be called corporate. The last remnant of its once-political character was a single page called Asshole of the Month, where right- and left-wing public figures alike were taken to task for their hypocrisy.

Then there was the staff—not only of *Hustler* but of its sister publications, which ranged from quiet and refined to borderline criminal (I was present at the ugly birth of *Hustler's Barely Legal,* a magazine that purports to feature girls almost, but not quite, too young to be porn models: despite its fakery, this among all the magazines nauseated me the most). The mainstream magazines, about photography and independent filmmaking and speedboats, were published out of a building across the street; all the smut monthlies and other fragments of counterculture—tattooing, heavy metal— were ghettoized in our building. Thus we staffers were also divided, with the purveyors of decency separated from bottom-feeders like me by the well-trafficked breadth of Wilshire Boulevard. We tended to stay on our own side of the street; we rarely socialized with those outside our caste.

And those who worked on the clean magazines turned up their noses at us, their smutty counterparts. They had paid their dues by starting where we were now, but having risen through the ranks to the lofty heights of *Hot Boat* and *Big Beautiful Woman*— not a porn magazine, despite its title—they liked to hold themselves apart.

The culture of the "porn side," as we called it, was a roiling melting pot of fetishists, outcasts, and freaks; we had editors who dealt guns on the side and who invited dominatrices into their offices to discipline them and had furniture broken over their heads; we had jolly married cross-dressers, art directors who wore linen by day and poured themselves into baby-powdered latex by night. We had identical twins with rhyming names, meth heads, wannabe rappers, mournful Goths, aspiring romance novelists who came to work in head-to-toe purple spandex; we had willowy Southern belles and aging, closeted queens in bad toupees; we had men who loved large breasts with such a passion that they made it their mission to proselytize them and slept in their offices the better to do God's work.

But this hodgepodge society was ruled by a conservative government, severe and autocratic battle-axes in Personnel, preppy executives who had MBAs from Princeton, and mustache-wearing, paunchy suits in Distribution who drank their coffee out of mugs that said, "Number One Dad." (I always wondered who the Number Two and Number Three Dads were, and whether they lived with the rest of the family.) Personnel liked to issue memos so punitive, and yet so poorly spelled, that they appeared to be a joke: "Those employees caught wearing shorts that ended more than three inches above the knee would be sent home to change immediately and have their pay docked; open-toed sandals were not permitted. ABSOLUTELY NO ECXEPTIONS!!!"

This in an office where the walls were papered with posters of naked women in absurdly contorted positions, exposed in such fleshly depth you could practically discuss the weather with their Fallopian tubes.

And then, within the culture of the porn side, there was the subculture of the copy pool—a group made up largely of overeducated grammarians in their early twenties, all holding degrees in the humanities, all mildly relieved to have landed paying jobs but building reserves of self-loathing as they slogged through their daily tasks. I shared an office with a punk-rock-girl-cum-music critic who hid her sharp intelligence inside a quiet demeanor and a Chaucer scholar who was saving up to go back to school and finish his Ph.D. My other best friends were an alarmingly well-read and gregarious copy editor from the "straight side" of the street, who liked to come slumming and visit us, and a slyly humorous MFA from CalArts, one of the porn editors, who spent his downtime hacking into other staffers' computers. Rob knew everyone's secrets, including mine; his own secret was being gay. *Hustler*'s editorial core was strictly and defensively homophobic.

Unlike the editors of *S.W.A.T.* and *Fighting Knives,* the editor of *Hustler* knew how to spell, and he was committed, believe it or not, to stylistic correctness. He was also a towering pillar of rage, waiting for the smallest excuse to burst into flames. He was an advocate of the stick, not the carrot; his management technique hinged on verbal abuse at high volumes, which almost always devolved into a vituperative personal attack. More than once he roared at me so fiercely and relentlessly—over a comma splice or a split infinitive, I don't remember now—that I burst into tears standing right in front of him, trembling and crying silently while trying to hide it. Dan was on a hair trigger, and I, a sheltered girl fresh out of college and hailing from a hometown where everyone was liberal and nice, was coming to understand that the working world had absolutely no decent use for my primo brain.

I had almost never been yelled at in my life—and certainly not by a foulmouthed middle-aged man who insulted my clothes and hair and had the power to get me fired.

Dan was plain mean; a number of other male coworkers were halfhearted, half-joking sexual harassers. I remember one who used to come into my office, during the brief period when I lived nearby and rode my bike to work, and stroke my bicycle seat. I kept the bike leaned up against the desk in front of me, since there was nowhere else to store it, and he would press his flabby belly against the bike frame, stroke the still-warm seat, and then raise his fingers to his face, inhaling. It was sickening, but he was such a moron it never occurred to me to complain. In the curious, off-kilter confines of our office all encounters had a slight surreality, distinct from the world outside. So it never occurred to me to complain about anyone, if the truth be told, with the possible exception of my editor, whose abuse of all his employees was famous throughout the company. Even with him, I never took it as far as I might have. The fact was

I thought most of the ruckus was absurd; and when it wasn't absurd, it had a quality of pathos that rendered most personal contact fundamentally unthreatening.

Both the staffers and the readers of our magazine seemed to me stricken with unfulfilled longing—and not just for the obvious. We got reams of letters from men in prison, and though they typically began by expressing their appreciation for the models, in no uncertain terms, and sometimes asking for dates or telephone numbers, they often ended by spiraling off into philosophical territory: meditations on God, the universe, mysticism, and morality. They liked to confess they had done wrong and were paying their dues. Some of them had theories about metaphysics that tended to exonerate them; others seemed to be asking for absolution. They were lonely souls reaching out for none other than us, their friends at the Beverly Hills headquarters of *Hustler,* and part of me was fascinated. For the first time in my pleasant life I was getting to know people I had not chosen to know; I was seeing into a world I had never before seen, a world normally closed to me.

Not that I actually responded to the letters; some of the other girls on staff had jailhouse pen pals, and one or two even kept up correspondences with serial killers. (The magazine attracted those guys; when we ran a feature on Richard Ramirez—the so-called Night Stalker, rapist, and killer convicted of thirteen murders—he called personally to tell us about a typo.) I couldn't have been less interested in forgiving the killers and rapists their trespasses. What I was interested in was observing: I watched the ways in which underpaid copy slaves and convicts alike sought desperately to distinguish themselves, the loneliness of that desperation paired with the longing for a community—any community. I came to see how these twin galaxies were home to all of us.

And then there was the fact that the bunker mentality in the copy pool made for the forging of solid friendships. At the time, we felt we were in the trenches together, though we knew we would have made lousy soldiers. Ours were tawdry but (fairly) comfortable trenches; our lives were not in danger, only our immortal souls. The more we gazed unseeing at the naked women on all fours, the caricatures of race and religion, the more subtly we were diminished. And in the afternoons, when there was no copy coming through, we often crawled onto the carpeting beneath our large desks and fell asleep. If you pulled your chair toward the desk, it was private and dark down there, and no one ever noticed.

And finally there came a time when I wasn't so sanguine about making my living off the flesh of others. For one thing, the novelty wore off and the job became, as many jobs will, thankless. You can only do the same thing for so many hundreds of days in a row without its losing its magic. I began to feel jaded, and the feeling didn't jibe with my sense of myself as an idealist, as one who had a debt to a world that had always been kind to her and wished to repay it.

Also, there was the shame. My parents had admitted to their friends and neighbors that I was working as an editor for a porn king; when I first started at LFP, it had been a humorous anecdote, though even when they first told it, their smiles looked slightly pained. But after several years, the neighbors were starting to suspect "editor" was a euphemism and my parents had raised a lowlife slut. My father joked weakly about the job, but his heart didn't seem to be in it.

Then came the final straw: the blow-up sheep episode.

The editorial staff was constantly receiving sex-toy freebies in the mail, in the hopes these items would get used as props in photo spreads and garner free publicity for the manufacturers. (We also had a found-object category: readers sent us potatoes and carrots shaped like penises, fossils they believed looked like vulvae, and of course many, many nude pictures of their own attributes. There was a paraplegic rodeo clown who sent us his whole life story in naked Polaroids.) A couple of the editors kept a pile of this merchandise in their office, which we called the playroom, and on coffee breaks we would amble in there and pick through the pile, ogling the newest products. We would toss around hairy pink beach balls, snack on penis-shaped chocolate bars and cherry-flavored edible panties, and tap out our cigarettes into ashtrays built right into the hands of startled-looking love dolls with open mouths.

It was a love doll that proved to be my undoing.

One day I sauntered into the playroom and picked up the latest in a long line of blow-up toys, this one not in humanoid but in ungulate form. It was a sheep named Lulu, with long eyelashes on lids that opened and closed slowly. She was made of black plastic and still had her new-car smell.

The two editors in the playroom typed on their computers, paying no attention.

"Look at this," I said, "a black sheep!"

"A sheep of love," drawled my friend Rob.

"It doesn't have one of those mouth holes," I mused. "So how are you supposed to—"

"Under the tail, I believe," said Rob, and turned away to open a desk drawer and pull out a stapler.

His young, wholesome-looking office mate, Steve, rumored to be quite a perv, smiled jauntily. "Yep, right there, under the tail," he said happily. "Thar she blows. Go, Lulu."

"This? This little hole right here?" I said, turning the sheep upside down. "Wow. It's so tiny."

And quick as a wink, because I had nothing better to do and I was twenty-two, I wriggled my right forefinger into the depression.

It was a terrible mistake.

Even as I was beginning to stick the finger in—I see it now in slow motion—Rob looked up from his drawer and saw what I was doing. In slow-mo, he raises his hands. His mouth opens. He shakes his head. His mouth forms the consonant *n*, then the vowel *o*. As his hands rise, the stapler falls from one of them, hitting the carpet and bouncing. But he is too late. My finger is poking into the sheep. On my face, a stricken look. A look of sheer horror.

"Oops," said Steve, still grinning. "You probably shouldn't have done that. I tested it."

Then I remember dropping poor Lulu on the floor, where she lay, puffy legs in the air, like one deceased. I ran down the corridor in a wild panic, the corporate wall art a blur of pastel sailboats. I remember the sink, and the soap squirting from the dispenser. More, and more, and more. I remember washing my hands in agitation repeatedly, like an OCD hygiene freak. I remember feeling I was going to throw up.

This was not where, as a young girl imagining a glowing future, I had pictured myself.

As I walked back from the restroom toward my office, pale and sickly, I passed someone else in the hallway. He was purple-faced with fury, running fast toward the men's restroom. But there was more than fury in his face. There was also alarm.

He was holding his right hand away from his body as though it could contaminate him.

It was Dan. As I learned later, he had entered the playroom right after me, found the boys laughing merrily, and in a good mood had himself picked up Lulu.

That was the day I opened the *Los Angeles Times* to the help-wanted ads again; that was the day the small, hunched-over woman from England let out her first full and unfettered scream.

I left the job a few weeks later, not too much richer but at least well fed, clutching my last paycheck in one dirty paw.

On Selling Drugs, Badly

Brett Martin

There ought to be a long, convoluted German word for the particular feeling of being at a wedding filled with college acquaintances in, let's call it 1996—when the world (and the friends) were suddenly awash in weird Internet money. It's not envy, exactly. Or bitterness. Nor Marxist disdain or some brand of reverse bohemian snobbery or any of the other emotions one might expect upon discovering that the people with whom you'd scrounged keg money only a few years before were suddenly rich beyond anyone's wildest dreams—at least, as turned out to be crucial, on paper.

It was more a sense of confusion, dislocation, the distinct feeling that one had gone to the bathroom halfway through the movie and missed a crucial plot point. I can remember standing with two erstwhile radical theater folks—he a composer of rock operas who had since taken a job, and stock options, at a successful Internet media company and she an actress who had married an engineer at a lucrative software firm—and listening as they discussed the "problem of money." The "problem of money," it seemed, was how to square one's liberal convictions with the fact that one suddenly had gobs of it. At twenty-three years old, with triple digits in my checking account, I had about as much to add to this conversation as I would if they were discussing how to kill a hobbit. And since my own problem of money was best addressed by the nearby free bar, I wandered away, consumed with that nameless emotion. Call it *whatthefückenfreude*.

Of course, Internet stocks have since given way to any number of other speculations—from real estate to Beanie Babies. It's no secret that Americans understand, on something approaching a genetic level, the innate goodness of buying low and selling high. I'm no different, but in each case the question of my participating has been moot. There are those who play the game and those who don't, and I am decidedly in the latter camp. It never occurred to me to join in on the lucrative markets of the past decade, any more than it would have occurred to me to climb down onto the field at Shea Stadium and try to pitch.

Again, this conviction doesn't come from either idealism or self-pity. I like money very much. And I admire people who know how to get it. My reluctance to participate is based on the most practical of reasons: if I were ever to invest, I would fail. In fact, I would likely bring all my friends, family, and perhaps the whole country down with me. I know this because I have been a failure at the easiest, most lucrative market of them all. I may be the only person in history to have lost money selling drugs.

For a short period in college, I was the worst marijuana dealer there has ever been—a disgrace to slick professionals standing on street corners all over the world. Everything that could go wrong to a small start-up operation did go wrong, and it was enough to turn me against entrepreneurship forever.

As so often happens in business, the problem began with my choice of partners. Or, more precisely, with my partners' choice of me. Growing up in Brooklyn, I was a precocious substance abuser; by the time I reached college, the age most of my peers were experimenting with mind-altering chemicals for the first time, I had already mostly left drugs behind. After spending ages fifteen through seventeen in a state of more or less constant stonedness, I had fortunately reached the point where I realized that I just didn't like it anymore. (When I say "fortunately," I mean the realization, not the fact; I would give quite a lot to be able to enjoy smoking pot the way I once did—minus the paranoia, the mouth full of wet wool, and the overwhelming urge to crawl into the nearest closet and go to sleep.)

In my mind at least, not being a pot smoker gave me a certain been-there-done-that cachet compared with my giddy classmates. And it certainly gave me an edge when it came to functioning at early-morning classes. Still, it was one thing to leave drugs behind and quite another to leave drug *culture* behind—particularly at a small, progressive liberal arts college in western Massachusetts desperately, but not very effectively, trying to shed its image as a "hippie school." I may no longer have been using drugs to get high, but when it came to using them to define my identity—in the most adolescent terms of hip versus square, cool versus lame—I had a monkey on my back the size of Mighty Joe Young.

So I was susceptible whenever my friends M. and H. came knocking. I would be lying on my bed and they would come slinking into the room, barely suppressing giggles. "Oh no," I'd say, well aware of what was coming. "Absolutely not. Get out."

Ignoring me, M. would whip out a calculator. "Now, let's see," H. would say as M. dutifully punched in the numbers. "As you know, dude, there's a serious dry spell on campus. M. knows a guy who knows a guy and we can buy a pound. People will buy an eighth for $50 . . ."

"Please stop," I'd moan. But by that time M. would be finished with his calculations. "If we each put in $150, we stand to make $1,200," he would report gravely, holding the calculator up to my face. There the digits were, in black and white. He would lean in close to my face and enunciate, "Twelve *hundred* dollars."

"It would literally be impossible to fail," H. would say, and I'd be hooked, as much out of camaraderie as profit motive. Lord knows what we would have done with $1,200 anyway; I imagine Domino's Pizza would have been very happy.

So we'd trundle out to one of those western Massachusetts towns beyond the warm embrace of the colleges, the areas where real people lived—"Massatucky," as one friend dubbed it—to score our magical pound of weed, the one that would make us rich. The first time, I remember pulling up at some dark and sagging house where the dealer got M. and H. stoned before handing off a bag of dope the size and shape of an airline pillow and sending us on our way.

In the car, we turned the bag over and over, passing it back and forth between us, not quite believing that there could be something so big. With its sharp corners and Ziploc top, the bag had the same proportions as a street nickel bag, only magnified 1,000 percent, like one of those massive bottles of champagne you see for decoration in old-school French restaurants. Hands shaking, we wrapped it loosely in a blanket on the backseat and drove home at six miles per hour.

From there, of course, everything would go wrong. I should have known that the prognosis was bad when we were dividing the stash up and M. and H. began negotiating how much they would be allowed to keep for themselves. In the dining hall, I would watch them attack the cereal and sundae bars and imagine those calculator digits whirring backward.

It goes without saying that the "dry spell" would quickly end the moment we got our hands on our supply and that the campus would instantly be flooded with superior, cheaper product. Or that M. would be carrying half the stash when he got stopped for speeding on the Massachusetts Turnpike and that he'd be forced to throw it into the woods by the side of the road.

It occurs to me, as I write this, that it may look like the boys were actually engaged in an elaborate scam to get me to pay for a third of their drugs; I can only wish that they had had such business sense. We were not a model of bookkeeping efficiency. We had serious issues in the accounts receivable department. Our market, remember, was mostly our friends, and they didn't always have cash on hand. As with all dealers, the first taste was free. So, sadly, was the second, third, and fourth. Within a few days of our big score, my thinking would shift from how much profit we were going to make to how to minimize the blossoming deficit.

I wish I could say that such monetary incompetence was the result of some inherited fatal flaw; that I was doomed by genetics to fail. Sadly, it is not so. My father is a certified public accountant and financial adviser. He is also a college professor of accounting, so surely he possesses the skills to pass on some basic microeconomic theory. So how did I wind up with financial skills limited to painstakingly parsing the final sequence of *Trading Places*?

The answer is that my family is the rare one that is familiar with money and knows how to handle money, but is adamant about not overly caring about money. Early in my parents' marriage, when my mother was a public school teacher and I had yet to come along, it was an annual routine for my father to quit his job every June, when school let out. My parents would grab their backpacks and go to Europe, often arriving back at JFK with just enough cash to take a taxi home, if that. Then my father would take a new job.

Over time, these included cabdriver, stockbroker, garbage man, optician, and writer for a television show starring a chimpanzee named Kokomo Jr.—all part of a restless search to balance financial need with happiness. One of the cornerstone pieces of my family's folklore took place when my father was working in the New York City comptroller's office, a job he detested. One day, he quit and was taking the elevator down the long tower of the New York Municipal Building when his boss jumped in to convince him to stay. As the elevator's floor counter ticked downward, the boss's offer of a raise went up. And when the doors opened in the lobby, my father walked away forever.

To a family of first-generation immigrants who had lived through the Depression, this behavior must have appeared to border on the insane. My grandfather and his brothers had all found blue-collar and municipal jobs—solid jobs that paid a decent wage but were never expected to offer more than that, certainly not a sense of personal satisfaction. To the similar family my father married into, his peripatetic employment was downright alarming.

My mother's uncle Phil, a bald and burly man who owned bars and vending machines and flirted with the fringes of the Brooklyn Jewish underworld (he claimed to be able to count any number of quarters simply by hearing them jangle in your pocket), once told me, "Your father was smart. Anyone could see that. But he was *weird.*"

Luckily, the weirdo and his equally brave wife found their way. My family's standard of living steadily increased along with my age. Another favorite family story suggests that I was sufficiently spoiled by age nine, when my mother informed me that we couldn't buy my favored brand of orange juice—the not-from-concentrate kind, with no pulp—because it was too expensive. "Wait a minute," I said, in a mixture of genuine outrage and confusion. "Are we *poor?*"

We weren't of course. In fact, what I saw as a sign of crushing destitution—next up would be the distended bellies and fly-covered faces so popular in the fund-raising poverty porn of the same period—was probably the precise definition of middle class: comfortable but forced to make choices. What my parents taught me wasn't that money isn't important (my father is not a hippie; he is an accountant); it was the rare notion that there is such a thing as *enough* money. So we owned crappy cars but traveled across the country and overseas. We lived in a small house but ate at new restaurants. And to their infinite credit (or at least my infinite relief), my parents' priorities had included saving for their children's college education, which meant that by the time I got to college, I had to make far fewer choices of my own—and had a far greater margin for error. In this way, I like to think of my selling drugs as nothing less than the fulfillment of the American Dream.

When I look back at that time, I feel a certain amount of shame, but it has nothing to do with breaking the law. It's how little the money mattered to me. I hardly even thought about it. I worked summers, and had since high school, but I also received a monthly check from my parents. Between the allowance and my savings, there was more than enough to cover my living expenses while leaving extra for ill-advised schemes. I was far from the wealthiest kid in my circle of friends (M., for instance, was the son of a highly successful importer of Asian products), but I took little notice of the fact that some were forever buying wildly expensive, state-of-the-art stereos and spending January break in Saint Moritz—or, it has to be said, that others were working in the cafeteria and passing up ordering pizza to save money for textbooks.

It wasn't until embarrassingly late in the day that my bubble of naïveté showed signs of bursting. It was senior year, when my attention was increasingly consumed with worries about how I might fashion a life outside of school. That cold, cruel winter, when no fewer than thirteen official blizzards swept across Massachusetts, as though conjured by my own anxiety, I had a premonition of dot-com weddings to come. I was standing alone in the parking lot near the dorms. I had been struggling to start my car, a shit-brown 1979 Oldsmobile Delta 88 that I had inherited from my parents and that died an average of once every two weeks. As if for the first time, my eyes traveled over rows of my friends' shiny SUVs. All of them had high-tech roof racks—for skis and kayaks and fancy mountain bikes. Wait a minute, I thought, in almost the exact tone in which I must have bemoaned the inferior orange juice. Are they *rich*?

I had taken from my parents a somewhat indifferent approach to money. What was shameful was that, unlike them, I hadn't paid for it with much discomfort. Where they had been forced to fashion their way of life and their priorities out of whole cloth, mine had been handed to me—the very essence, it seems to me, of privilege. And while this might cost me plenty of investment opportunities in the future, for the time being I intuitively understood that it made me invincible.

One day, word spread across campus that the administration had gotten wind that drugs were being dealt in the dorms—no doubt they were shocked, *shocked*—and would be cracking down. Sure enough, after class one afternoon I came into our floor's student lounge to find H. on the couch, warily regarding two men sitting across from him. They were middle-aged and wore close haircuts, shiny white sneakers, and tie-dyed T-shirts. One, oddly, was grasping a Super Soaker water pistol. They seemed to be doing their best to slouch.

"Um, what's up?" I asked, putting down my bag.

"These are apparently the new transfer students," H. said, taking a sip from a can of soda.

"S'up?" said the one with the water gun.

We all sat there for a minute or two.

Then the other man seemed to be struck by a great idea. "Hey," he said. "Do you guys know where we can get some drugs?"

"Drugs?" I said. "I'm not sure I understand."

"C'mon," the other guy said. "We really want to get high."

As good stoners and apprentice pushers, we knew what we were supposed to do here. It was a widely accepted fact that undercover police officers were not allowed to lie if you asked them directly whether or not they were cops. In truth, I had always assumed this was an urban legend, something like owning a dragon if you spoke his name or having to invite a vampire into your home. Still, it seemed worth a shot.

"Hey, you guys wouldn't happen to be narcs, would you?" H. asked.

"I'll ask the questions around here," the one with the water gun barked, playfully brandishing the weapon at us.

"Seriously, are you cops?"

"Do we look like cops?"

Holy shit, I thought, it actually works.

"Well, nice to meet you," I said, picking up my bag.

"Yeah, good luck." H. smiled as we headed out of the room. "See you guys around."

But we never did again.

That was invincibility at work. In part, its source was strictly socioeconomic—even in the feverish early days of the War on Drugs, white middle-class students at liberal northeastern colleges weren't exactly at the top of the DEA's target list, especially not those without enough sense to even turn a profit. But having come through unscathed, I like to believe there was also some magic at work. Because it never crossed our minds that we might face serious consequences for what we were doing, it became literally impossible. What's written off as youthful stupidity can also be, I have to believe, a source of real protective power. But it's a fragile and irretrievable one. Which is why I'm sure that if a pound of marijuana ever made its way into my home today, I could count the seconds before the door was being broken down by federal agents ready to haul me off to prison. Once that sense of invulnerability is gone, it's gone. But I'd give up a hundred times that $1,200 for the slightest chance of ever getting it back.

Of course, as we know, I wound up with neither. After three or four go-rounds, I started locking my door whenever H. and M. came knocking. I never really considered chasing my losses—in the end, maybe $700—by getting into more serious drugs. I had known a coke dealer in high school who had gotten so paranoid that he'd call me up in the middle of the night and speak only in code.

"I've been doing some great skiing," he'd say, confidingly.

"Sorry?"

"The *skiing*. It's really good."

"Do you mean you have quality cocaine?" I'd say, and he'd shriek and hang up.

I was pretty dumb, but I was sufficiently smart not to test the limits of my bubble of privilege too strenuously and to try to stay inside as long as possible.

What I had learned about money from my failed business was this: There's easy money and there's hard money. But there's no medium-hard money. Either cash flies in through the window, or you're going to have to work like a dog to get it. M., H., and I just didn't want or need the money badly enough, and so we suffered the effects of what I've come to think of as the Bad Karma of Casual Enterprise.

And so, you investors, speculators, great men of risk and reward—go forth without fear. I won't bring the whole party crashing down by dipping so much as a toe in the market. I'll just be over by the open bar. "Enough" is a fine philosophy, and I'm thankful for it. But it's no way to do business. And I know enough to just say no.

What This Cost Me

Susan Choi

If we're just talking about money—hahaha! "just" . . .
"money"—I guess I'm happy to be able to predict it will not cost
me much. You won't, from a purely monetary point of view, find it
hard to pay me back. Of course I won't know, until I'm finished,
how long this is going to take, but even if it takes a week—and this
is possible, because things are going very poorly, but more on that
later—I still think you'll find that it won't be expensive. Find other
readers to share the expense; it'll cost even less. Let's do the numbers, as Kai Ryssdal on *Marketplace* says. The babysitter costs $12
an hour, or $60 a writing day (10:00 a.m. until 3:00), or $300 a writing week. The "office," which is really just my upstairs neighbor's
apartment while he's in Toronto, for an indefinite period of time,
during which he's not subletting, which means he doesn't lose
money letting me work here, is $200 a month—and this, here, is a
funny part of the equation, because this cost is almost entirely un-

tethered from value, by which I mean I insist on giving my neighbor this money to make me feel better, not because it represents the worth of the privilege to me, or the worth of the bother to him. He and his boyfriend don't live here, but they don't want to sell; they're not allowed to sublet according to the bylaws of our building, so they're not, technically, supposed to be profiting from our arrangement. At the same time, they've left the electricity on—but this is so that they can use the apartment as a pied-à-terre on the weekends they come back to the city, not so that I can plug in my laptop computer. And they pay monthly maintenance ($450), but they have to do that anyway, too. In other words, I'm a phantom in their living arrangements; I occupy a space that doesn't really exist and that can't be reallocated for greater profit. Yet at the same time, the ability to escape my own apartment, where my fourteen-month-old son and his babysitter have the run of the rooms, in order to perform actions consistent with my role as a "writer," is invaluable to me; I could call it a $200-a-month value or a $2,000-a-month value. What is it worth? If I were renting a real office, I would pay a lot more, and I'd pass on that cost to the reader. Should I charge you for the number of days that I'm actually sitting here writing? Or the number of days from the day that I start on this essay (today) until the day that I'm done? I try to come up here the same five days a week the babysitter comes to my apartment, except for the days that I'm shopping or drinking with girlfriends or crying, sitting in my parked car, because I can't get work done, or the days that I'm taking the baby to the doctor (the sitter gets paid anyway) or to baby swim class ($110 for seven sessions) or to his grandparents for the long weekend (we drive, but gas isn't so cheap anymore, and we get all our meals, but the psychic toll that these people exact! How to put a price on it?), so that, when it really comes down to it, for every five days I'm paying the sitter, I'm only writing for three, and that's quite optimistic, and for most of those three days I'm really not writing at all. I hope you won't find it unfair when I tell you that, having considered the issue for the past fifteen minutes, I've decided I have to charge for the number of days this takes me, start to finish, including the days I'm not writing—after all, I'd pay my neighbor the $200 even if a month passed during which I didn't come here at all. Does it really seem all that expensive? If you divide the $200 by 20—an average of four weeks a month, five workdays every week—and then add in the cost of the sitter, it turns out that, amazingly, just $70 a day buys you all this good writing. Even if I'm only up here an average of three days, not five. *Someone* has to buy Cheerios, get new struts for the car, take the baby to doctor appointments. Arguably, I should pass on these costs to you, too—not all of them, of course, but the commensurate portion without which my life, during the time it takes me to write this, would completely collapse. That's a hard cost to calculate— and of course the burden of calculation falls on me, too. It's not as if you're going to wave the rounding-up wand and say, "Oh, well, let's just give you a thousand dollars a week so you can get this shit done. So you can get your life all taken care of and do this great writing." You might argue that the baby isn't really an artistic necessity. Why should you bear the costs of his baby swim classes, his shoes, his little T-shirts, his cheese sticks, and his crackers, not to mention his health care and his eventual education? Do I, the writer, really need all that stuff—under the rubric of well-cared-for baby—to provide you with writing? It would be simpler if you just paid me a wage—there wouldn't be all this guilty self-justification, all this snide inventory. But it's always like this. I write things, I get paid inconsistent amounts, there's never a clear connection, a precise valuation. Except now, that's what we're trying to do. Figure out what it cost me and how much you owe.

Not to spoil the mesmerizing rhythm of my prose, but I feel constrained to point out, as I generally wouldn't, that it's a new day now. Yesterday I wrote 984 words in just about an hour and a half, a good value for you, and I also had nothing nicer for lunch than two slices of pizza and a can of seltzer ($4.90). I really hate eating pizza for lunch. It's not good pizza, and with repeated exposure it's actually sick-making, but the plain economics of it dictates that having two slices of pizza is the most cost-effective way for me to get fed, because it's not just cheap but fast, the pizza place being right across the street, so that going there is faster than the mediocre sandwich place four blocks away, and, less obviously, faster than the enormous effort involved in keeping groceries in the house and packing myself a cold lunch. I just can't do it. Some weeks it happens, but the economy of scale never kicks in, the time involved in acquiring healthful foodstuffs (we live in a borderline neighborhood—no butcher, no fish, no decent produce, only a dubious grocery that serves well exclusively for paper products and beer) is always so extensive that the cost outweighs the benefits. Hugely. If I were to always, always pack my own lunch, my real writing-day/paid-for-writing-day ratio would descend even further, down to two and a half, perhaps two, for every five. If I have pizza for lunch, the number of paid writing minutes I spend unproductively is a mere fifteen, max—I'm not swanning out to Lupa on your dime. On a side note, this morning the sitter was fifteen minutes late. Fifteen minutes, whether of a sitter's lateness or a writer's lunch, is three bucks, but it's not like I'll deduct that from her pay; I'm not petty.

Many of us—okay, many of us who are women with children—routinely pay someone so we can be paid ourselves. It's such a fundamental universal arrangement it's almost beneath commentary. We all know that the idea is to pay that other person, almost always another woman with her own children, many times less than we ourselves are being paid; we don't ask where *her* children are spending the day, and we chalk it up, the wage earners among us, to the cost of doing business. Well, if that's you, that's great. Far be it from me to wax self-righteous; after all, I *emulate* this arrangement, like a kid playing grown-up! N.B.: I didn't say I do it. I *pretend.* I *pretend* I can afford to pay a sitter $300 a week, and a neighbor $200 a month, because this base expenditure, not including the pizza, the cell phone, the laptop, the blah blah blah, of $1,400 a month—until very recently the same figure as my rent, now better known as a figure equal to seven-eighths of my mortgage—is just the cost of doing business, a cost clearly outweighed by the income generated thereby. I spend the $1,400 a month because doing so enables me to *make* at least $1,400 a month—and preferably more!—from my writing.

It's embarrassing to have to admit that actually I'm $1,400 times X in the red, if X equals the number of months I've been working this way, with the sitter, and the office: coincidentally, also fourteen, the baby's adorable age (he's an adorable baby, and I need him—you can already see that my work requires him, in a way). But embarrassing for whom? For me? Or for the person or persons supposed to be paying me: you? It wasn't out of anger or frustration but just the basic desire to treat myself half decently that at the end of the previous sentence I did, in fact, walk the four blocks to the mediocre sandwich place instead of having pizza again, but as always, it just wasn't worth it. I left here at noon, and, believe it or not, it's twelve-thirty now and I haven't even eaten the sandwich yet. The sandwich place is incredibly slow, and also overpriced. The sandwich just cost me $8, without a beverage. Not to mention the $6 for the half hour wasted. Sometimes, in the middle of my workday, I become so anxious and upset trying to acquire a decent, inexpensive, time-efficient lunch I almost make myself sick, and then I'm no longer hungry. Which is, I suppose, one solution. When I told my husband last night at dinner* about this essay I'm writing, he was really delighted, and not just because, as you've probably guessed, it's my husband who subsidizes my "career." Yeah, fourteen hundred times X in the red: How exactly was that working out? Now you know. My husband, an actual wage earner, holder of 1.666 full-time jobs, reaper of benefits, funder of 401(k)s; it's my husband who bankrolls the sitter so that I can "work." It wasn't always thus. Time was, just a few years ago, I sold a book it had taken me five years to write and made a nice piece of money. I was able to pay back my husband for the loans he had floated me; he wasn't my husband back then, and we still maintained separate accounts. Then a couple of different things happened. First, we got married and mingled our funds. We spent what remained of my book advance on an apartment. Then the baby was born. Now, I'm not blaming the baby for anything, but something happened in connection with him that I hadn't predicted. My husband and I had al-

---

*Despite a recent resolution to watch our budget, we did, in fact, eat dinner out again (God help me: pizza!) because, as is almost always the case, I hadn't gone grocery shopping.

ways assumed that I would remain what I'd been, a reasonably successful, respected, self-respecting writer. A professional woman who
happened to have given birth. And it was *because* of these assumptions, it was *in line* with these assumptions, that we acquired the
sitter, the office, the monthly expenditure. Because I was a professional writer, *n'est-ce pas?* The way of doing business had changed,
the cost of doing business had changed (there must have been costs
previously, but they were by-the-by, intermingled with everyday
life, difficult to distinguish, only put into rigorous form for income
tax deductions), but the business itself was the same. The thing
was, it wasn't. Something had changed, for the worse. The mea-
sures we'd taken to dignify me seemed instead to have transformed
me into a hobbyist. I handed over my son to the sitter and took my
laptop bag up to my office, day in and day out, where I then sat and
felt like a fraud, an amateur "scribbler," a self-indulgent, wasteful,
neglectful mother and parasite wife.

I rarely wrote, and when I did, I wrote shit.

And why use the past tense?

So that when you say to me, "Just explain what it costs, just
assemble an invoice, just say what you need to get back in the black
and so out of this rut," even as you ask for a number, you're admitting the cost can't be figured that way! The arrangement has *cost*
me in ways that a mere check for $19,600 can't hope to address,
though it would be a start.

When I was first trying to be a "real" writer, first trying to
finish a novel, my efforts were untethered from value, just like my
strange presence in my neighbor's apartment. Money didn't touch
on the process. No one paid me to write, but at the same time I paid
no one so that I could write. I worked a forty-hour week at a day
job, and during evenings and weekends I secretly scratched my am-

bition. Believe me, I didn't even dream of being paid for that novel, and when I actually was, I felt like I'd won the lottery, not simply been compensated for several years of hard work. It's a good thing I felt that way, too—that the fruits of my writerly labors had no value at all—because if I hadn't, I might have started to notice that from the compensation point of view, I would have done a lot better mopping the floor at McDonald's. Young artists are told the satisfaction of making their art should be payment enough, but even if it were, and it isn't, all young artists get old, and some even have babies. Babies who need new little jackets as the fall weather comes. Who could probably use closed-toe shoes since it does sometimes *snow.*

You probably don't see the baby's warm feet as a business expense, and perhaps there's no reason you should. As my accountant tries to tell me each spring, right around April 10, in that narrowing window of time when I'm no longer being childishly hostile to him but I haven't yet burst into tears, the category of business expenses for writers is extremely elastic already. It's a little unseemly, my gentle accountant implies (not in so many words), to insist on expensing the bootees when I already get to write off so much else. Believe me, I don't fail to appreciate—neither should you!—that because I can write off my e-mail, the movies I see, books I read, magazines I recycle, pens I lose, reams of paper I waste, the happy result is I don't pass on those costs to the reader. And yet there are so many others: strange, vaporous costs that resist inventory. Tangential needs I require to be filled (those wee feet, snugly laced!) ere my mind can assemble a phrase . . . and on the opposite side of the ledger, those phantasmal losses I suffer, on-the-job injuries that no doctor can see. Reader, can I shock you a moment by rending the veil? Will you mind if I rupture this same warp and woof that I've woven? The baby is no longer fourteen months old. He is *seventeen and three-quarters* months old. The pizza and sandwich are no longer the sole foods I've eaten. These pages you're reading have lain for months, all but abandoned, though the dolorous thoughts they have spawned, the reckonings of accounts, have retardingly wended their ways into other arenas, like a river of goo. There were other things I was supposed to be doing, the past 114 or so days. Other things that might have earned me some income, and produced the effect of an unburdened mind, which in turn could produce yet more writing, more income, and so on until I was rich! . . . But instead there's been costly stagnation. Unremunerative meditation. You could almost think time had stood still, if it weren't for the baby. The baby, who has learned both to walk and to speak his first words ("dog"; "hi!"; "apple") in the time since I wrote my first sentence.

How do I bill for time spent, under such weird conditions? I know that you're bristling, checking the calendar, recalling those 984 words in an hour and a half, and then thinking, "What happened? She was such a good value!" Believe me, I know how you feel. An example: I'm not proud of this, but with regard to the sitter I really only want to have to pay for the hours I use. Right? If the sitter comes, fine. If, instead, my husband takes me and the baby to Rome, we clearly do not need the sitter while on our *vacanza*. Do I really have to pay for her time *and* our tickets *and* our beautiful Campo de' Fiori apartment? It's difficult to admit that we're responsible, in a broad, beyond-the-balance-sheet way, for the persons whose unique services we regularly enjoy. I don't call myself a saint for concluding that when in Rome, you pay the sitter anyway. It's not her fault you don't need her that week. I'm not claiming I dance for sheer joy when I pay for Thanksgiving, and Christmas, and the Fourth of July, and the days that she's sick . . .

when, by dint of these basic acknowledgments, I affirm it's her *job*. Just the same as it's my job to write this for you, even if you've been skimming, and diverting your eyes to the game on TV, and even if it has for some reason taken me almost four months.

I used to know a woman—perhaps this is off the subject, you tell me—who was also a writer, but a magazine writer, which meant she was actually paid a regular, and very generous, salary. Her magazine concerned fashion and lifestyle, and she wrote, generally, about purses and belts, just to give you the vaguest idea. I write about, according to my reviewers, race and identity and social belonging, not that I'm trying to do apples and oranges. Anyway, despite her generous (six figures!) salary, this woman had problems, and she got hooked on drugs. Her magazine gave her a leave, fully paid, but it also—recognizing that mere money wouldn't fix things—arranged for her to spend a month at a gorgeous rehab/spa facility somewhere in the Southwest, and it flew her boyfriend out there, and it bought her new clothes. At the time I was dumbstruck, although I suppose if my astonishment could have been given voice it might have said something like "Wow: it really matters to Condor's Nest Inc. [not its actual name] that X remain able to write about purses and belts." Clearly, X was valued. Her well-being mattered to those who employed her. She wasn't told that her baby—I'm sorry, her drug problem—made her too costly to still be an asset.

Of course, we can't all be such stellar employers. My own finances are at such a break-even state I can't possibly offer my sitter health care or a pension. And you—I know that regarding your duties to me, you've been doing the best you can. We all try to live by a small inward light and to feel we've done well by our fellows. Just because I know that it's right to pay my sitter on the days that she's sick doesn't mean you owe me the same sort of respect, as expressed in hard cash. I'm as surprised as you are that the writing of this "took" four months ($5,600), not to mention *took* four months, stole those months of my life during which I had thought I would finish my novel and sell it, for an unguessable but I would hope at least positive sum, instead of sitting through matinee movies ($10 a ticket) and then treating myself to an overpriced lunch ($27 on average) while prevaricating to the sitter ("a doctor's appointment"). Sometimes, just to make the day pass, I lie in bed thinking of how great it would be to get a check in the mail for $25,000, not that I'm saying these pages have cost me that much, what with the $19,600 before you came along and the $5,600 spent since and the cost of the lunches and the unknown amount of lost income—tens of thousands of dollars?—from losing the will to write anything else. But money alone can't erase our suspicions that our lives are a waste, that our efforts, far from channeling into great works, simply dribble away. In the end, it's a terrible measuring stick of our selves. Once, long ago, I remember deciding I'd charge you for all of the days this would take, from beginning to end. I hadn't realized I'd have to untether those days from their value. Who could have guessed that I'd wind up pretending those days were as worthless to me as to you? Today, the 117th day I've been working for you, I've brought the word count to 3,524 (through "word count"), and that feels like about three days' work, for a regular person. Let's just call it $60.00 times 3 for the sitter plus $30.00 (three days in the office) plus $4.90 plus $8.00 plus, oh, Christ, I don't know, $8.00 again for three lunches makes $230.90. And if you don't object, dinner tonight; to finally finish, I once again skipped grocery shopping. I'm sure our takeout will cost less than $40; if you agree that that's fair, I'll append the receipt to this essay.

My Vow of Poverty

At approximately the age of twenty-five, I took what I have called thereafter an informal vow of poverty. I wanted to emancipate my practical mind from the necessity of earning money. It was a way of unfettering myself, of lightening the load and achieving the social objectives that I was nurturing at that age. I was nonmaterialistic by instinct; the normal American way of life seemed over-acquisitive to me. My idea was to serve those in the criminal justice system whom I deemed victims, those who might not otherwise have the means to hire me. Living without much money, without property, without buying anything, would allow me the freedom to pursue social justice.

It was relatively easy to live like this then. It was the 1960s, and I was living partly in San Francisco and partly in Bolinas (about forty miles north of the city). There was a "free box" in Bolinas that everyone added to—embroidering the clothes and cleaning the items that were deposited there. Our rent at the time was about

$50 a month. I had five children, all born at home. My family lived on practically nothing, but I never felt that we were in need.

Even my law office had nominal expenses. I could really live on about $100 a week, and I certainly felt the force, the freedom of not having to earn money. Because I didn't worry about making a living, I was able to represent countless people of principle who had been arrested, mostly for so-called victimless crimes. Most could not afford to pay me. I became what is called a pro bono, a no-fee radical lawyer, and was soon taking on some of the most controversial cases of that era.

I represented many of the people who came out of movements born in the 1960s—Black Panthers, White Panthers, the New World Liberation Front, the Symbionese Liberation Army, later the Hells Angels, after that, various prison gangs. I became pro-marijuana, pro–Black Panther, pro–Hells Angels, pro–prison gangs. I became anti-police, anti–law and order, anti-informant, anti–undercover narcotic officer, anti–death penalty, even anti-lawyer. Any case that contained an element of racism, I rushed to help. Any case involving police brutality, illegal search and seizure, or governmental misconduct, I took free of charge. I put my own scant resources into most of them. I wasn't just a pro bono lawyer; I was a lawyer who paid to take the case. I put up my own money to pay the costs of litigation. I felt privileged to contribute to the cause of social justice and was respected by the "movement" population. Not making money became my trademark and my pride. "From each according to his ability, to each according to his need" became my creed.

In many ways, my upbringing had prepared me to live by this philosophy. I was born into the working-class strata in San Francisco in 1934. My father never went beyond the third grade and was a candy maker, a jelly bean specialist; my mother was a homemaker whose education had stopped at the fourth grade. But they both valued education, and my brothers and I all went on to earn advanced degrees. We were raised to respect law and order and to embrace the work ethic. But my parents were not materialistic. They didn't have much, but they didn't desire much, either. They passed these values down to me. When I graduated from Stanford with a philosophy degree, I had no intention of pursuing a profession that would reward me financially. I ultimately chose to get a law degree because it seemed a useful tool, one that would allow me to provide more liberties and a greater share of prosperity to underprivileged people.

As a result of my vow of poverty, I never bought anything new. I was the lawyer with an old car, with no insurance, the one who wore old suits and colorful ties, the one who brought cheese sandwiches in a brown paper bag to eat as lunch during court break. I disavowed credit cards. I disavowed bank accounts. I disavowed anything that wasn't absolutely necessary in order to practice law or raise a family. There were no embellishments, no hotels, no fancy restaurants. All my clothes were secondhand, nothing fit perfectly; my cars were constantly being towed for too many parking tickets. I grew my hair long and developed a counterculture mentality. I participated in various drug experimentations, became a dance freak at the rock-and-roll forums of the day, and yet never gave up my law practice. I lived a full life, sometimes barely sleeping, going to court all day, then dancing at the Straight Theater all night.

My essential beliefs and my philosophy about the practice of law were shaped by the time I spent in Haight-Ashbury. Thirty years later, I still live much as I did then. I still have no new clothes. I am still garbed in the leftovers of St. Vincent de Paul and the Salvation Army. I still identify with the antiestablishment and with those on the margins of society.

My belief system has crystallized. I don't believe in the private ownership of property. I don't believe in probate laws that allow you to pass property or other inheritance from one generation to the next. I don't believe in corporations that amass great wealth and perpetuate themselves over many lifetimes. I don't believe in acquiring anything that isn't necessary for the well-being of mind and body. I don't believe in excess. I don't believe in savings. I don't believe in investments. I don't believe in stocks and bonds. I don't believe in money in the bank.

My aesthetic and spiritual development is still ongoing; it is my most precious possession: the love of the outdoors, of nature, of the migratory fowl that abound in northern California. What I prize are long walks by the sea, dawns that are red and penetrating, trees that dance in the rain and the wind. These are the things that I have acquired—images, not possessions, experiences, not objects.

The truth is I feel lucky. I feel that I escaped. I am not a keeper or a servant of possessions. I am not caught in a neurotic compulsion to obtain things. I don't want a new wristwatch; I don't want any wristwatch. I don't want the newest mobile phone—I don't have any mobile phone! I don't want a computer. I don't want to learn how to do e-mail. I don't want to pay my bills electronically; I don't want bills. I don't want credit. And yet every day I participate in the routine life of a lawyer within society, within the bowels of the establishment. I have not dropped out. I am not a drug fiend. I enjoy relationships with the outlaws I represent. My children have all been college-educated, thanks to my wealthy artist-brother; ironically, the lawyer-brother just gets by, and the artist-brother has made millions.

I have specialized in pro bono cases for my entire career. My practice has been to put money from any paying cases into nonpaying ones. This has allowed me the freedom to be committed to what the Black Panthers used to call "selfless service to the people." It has allowed me to develop deep empathy and compassion for those who are victims of the system. It has allowed me to take risks that I would not have taken if I were fearful of being dispossessed of my material wealth. My contemporaries, most of whom have an objective of monetary success, seem to me like caged birds. We sing the same song and we see the same dawn, the laws of gravity are equally distributed, but they are ultimately imprisoned by the materialism that confines their spirit and imagination. I feel like a free bird.

And yet within thirty days I expect to go to federal prison for the second time, for a misdemeanor conviction of willful failure to pay federal income taxes. I am what many would regard as a tax protester, a tax resister, one who ultimately represents the dissident voice in respect to tax duties and responsibilities. I don't believe that that assessment is valid, but I have no trepidation about being incarcerated. It is my just due. People in prison are my allies, my associates; they are high-risk personalities; they are creative-minded; they have been defiant; they have been independent—all attributes that I respect and admire. Most people I meet are capitalistic, bourgeois, non-spiritual, non-aesthetic, pragmatic, and prudent, and I find I have very little rapport with them. Frankly, I would much rather sit down for a fertile hour of conversation in jail with a prisoner than sit in some comfortable restaurant or saloon talking to routine acquaintances. That fateful day in Haight-Ashbury, when I decided to take a vow of poverty, I did not know where it would lead me. I feel very fortunate.

Notes on Bling

Steven Rinehart

When I was eighteen, I wanted a nice car. Then, for a few decades afterward, I really, really *didn't* want a nice car. The thought of pedestrians watching me drive down the street nauseated me. I wanted a nice car when I was eighteen because the one I had was shitty. I'm not sure what I would even have done with a nice car, but with my shitty one and two friends I held up a gas station at knifepoint for $115 I didn't need. Later that night, in my jail cell, I wondered, since we had used my car, whether or not it would be taken away. If it weren't taken away, then at some point, when I got out of jail, I'd be seen driving it, by everyone I knew. It was the first dawning of shame in that whole experience. Shame came into that scenario slowly, through the imagery of being looked at, talked about, whispered about.

I was in that cell for three days, from a Saturday night through a Tuesday morning with a Veterans Day holiday in between, and for the first part of that I shared my jail cell with a skinny African-American kid named Kim Franklin. I know his name was Kim Franklin because the guards every once in a while would yell, "Kim Franklin!" and his head would turn slightly to look at them. He had to turn his head slightly because he had only one eye. His black eye patch included the initials K.F. haphazardly festooned in tiny rhinestones. It was odd, silly. Did he think that it somehow looked good? That eye patch must have really gotten to the guards, because they picked on him ceaselessly. Me they left alone.

When I robbed the gas station, I was wearing my class ring, my very first piece of jewelry. I was eighteen, and in a mindless way very proud of my high school graduating class. OTHS, O'Fallon Township High School, Illinois. It was my first semester of college, and I was supposed to be attending engineering classes at Washington University in St. Louis, just across the Mississippi River. I was supposed to be marching every Thursday in my Air Force ROTC uniform, but I couldn't quite bear wearing it, or marching, even though I was on a full scholarship. The class ring I did wear, though, along with my high school letter jacket with the numerals 78 and patches all over it for various football and track accomplishments I can't recall today.

They took my class ring and my letter jacket away from me when they booked me. I got them back when my parents were finally able to post my bond. I even got back the $115 in small bills we had stolen, but not right away, not for months. But in my cell I had no ring, no jacket, no wallet, and, as far as I knew, no car anymore. In return, the guards gave me cigarettes, which I didn't smoke, and a deck of cards. They didn't give Kim Franklin anything, but he had his glittering eye patch. It announced to everyone who Kim Franklin was, in shorthand, the way my class ring did, my letter jacket—at least until they were taken from me.

When I hear the word "bling," I think of glowering black rappers. I think of diamonds, gold jewelry, gold-and-diamond-bedecked teeth, rings of silver, rhinestone-studded fingernails. But Elvis was like this, too, wasn't he? Doesn't Tom Jones wear jewelry on his hairy chest? Elizabeth Taylor had that huge ring she got from the Welsh guy, the drunk—they made fun of it on Lucille Ball's show. White people gaudy themselves up, don't they, if they're not terribly sophisticated? For terribly sophisticated white folks, there are Rolex watches. I remember a story I heard that endeared George H. W. Bush to me, how when he was vice president they made fun of him behind his back for wearing a preppy fabric watchband. It got back to him, and by the time he was president he'd switched.

My father had a nice Seiko watch, and he always wore a very large garnet ring. His birthstone. My mother gave it to him at some point on their anniversary. I have it now, or my daughter does. She's holding it for me. I tried to wear it, but it's not my taste. My wedding ring is very narrow, as narrow a wedding band as I have ever seen on a man. It seems right for me: skinny, a bit dull, a somewhat shiny life preserver.

I once, a few years after the robbery, took to wearing a silver chain around my neck. It was a gift from my father; he'd heard they were fashionable. I was living in Waikiki, thinking about returning to school. I wore it for about a month until some drunks at a party jumped me and it was ripped from my neck as I tried to squeeze, whimpering, under a bed. One of the attackers came into the store where I worked about a week later, when he had sobered up, and sheepishly tried to pay for it. But I told him not to worry about it. It was nothing I would ever wear again. In fact, I couldn't remember any reason why I wore it in the first place. Had I wanted to show off, to attract attention? I had no girlfriend; it must have been simple vanity. I had looked at myself in the mirror with my silver choker and liked what I saw.

My car had cost me $200; it was a 1968 Ford Mustang with lots of rust and very, very bad brakes and a loud radio. It was probably filthy. It probably had marijuana residue in it, packed into the filth in the carpets. I think there might have been some dope hidden behind the radio or some such nonsense. It wasn't my dope, I never bought the stuff, but I'd smoke it if somebody else had it. They would buy it, and I would buy the gasoline and drive. The car was smoky gray or tan. It was wholly unremarkable.

I went on a date just after the robbery; the girl's father came out to inspect the car. He seemed mad when he went back inside his house. Did he know who I was? I bet he did. That was a smallish town, and everyone read the paper. But something about my ride seemed to make him angry. If what had made him angry was that this felon wanted to take his daughter out and pull off her pants, he would have gotten mad right when he met me and shook my hand. But he was only angry after he saw my car. My filthy getaway car with the rust and very, very bad brakes.

Kim Franklin and I were in the St. Clair County Jail, in Belleville, Illinois. Kim probably lived nearby in East St. Louis, a shithole my two friends and I only visited to buy liquor underage, or, every once in a while, cruise slowly past the houses they had lived in as kids before their fathers had moved them into nicely redlined O'Fallon, where the only black families allowed were from the military base out in the countryside. When we cruised East St. Louis, we were invariably quite drunk, and they would sob, curse. What had happened to their neighborhood? They would scream, *"Dirty Nigger Fucking Niggers,"* out the car window, lights would come on inside the houses, we'd race away, my crappy muffler *blat-blatting* into the air all the way back to O'Fallon. It was exciting and mysterious to me, this passion about a place, this hatred. I'd grown up on military bases in Europe, where we'd express ourselves by yelling, "Scheisskopf," at the dirty German kids on the other side of the chain-link fence during rock fights. They were poor. They had nothing back then, in the 1960s, at least in the little villages around Wiesbaden. Their stores had the best toys; we bought them and broke them instantly and left the pieces in the street. The dollar went a long way then.

The gas station we stuck up was exactly halfway between the two towns, halfway between East St. Louis and O'Fallon, on a meandering north-south highway spotted with dry cleaners, pawnshops, and muffler-replacement franchises. None of us needed the money; we had jobs, college was little more than a distraction— high school you could skip without penalty. The robbery was a mutual dare more than anything; we'd driven around for hours, cursing one another's cowardice, making fervent, shifting alliances against whoever was that moment's holdout, when the alcohol and cheap diet amphetamines had added their tiny push and we just did it. Maybe we knew we were blessedly lucky, that we were untouchable, although I don't remember feeling that way. I do remember sitting in the car on the dark side street before we leaped out to do the deed, and feeling that most of all I wanted to get out of there—that neighborhood, that car, all of it—and that this surely would be the quickest way.

So I knew what I had done to be in that particular jail, but I've wondered for twenty-five years what it was that Kim Franklin did. I don't believe I asked him, even though it was the standard opening line in that situation, the icebreaker, just like in the movies. "What are you in for?"

"Kim Franklin!" the guards yelled every half hour or so, and then cracked up.

What do you think a lawyer tells his jewelry-laden client to wear to court? Extra rings of gold? "More loops, Dog, layer it up! Juries go for that." No, he tells him to dress conservatively, leave the jewelry at home. Had I stood trial, he would have said, cut your hair, wear a suit. Maybe even wear my Air Force ROTC uniform. He would have told them I was a National Merit Scholar finalist, a five-letter athlete, a scholarship-wielding chemical engineering major. Look at my client, just look at him. Bathe in his normalness, his unvarnished Caucasian scared shitlessness. Notice nary a carat on him; even his hair is sporting the Dry Look.

At Kim Franklin's trial, or hearing, the judge or jury would have wondered, "I don't know if he did it, he probably did, but what the fuck is *up* with that eye patch? Lift it up, Kim, show me the goods." Would he even have a suit he could have worn? I have no idea. Today I'd like to believe I would have given him the $115 in small bills we stole from the Sunoco station to buy a good suit for his trial. But only if I could have gotten a guarantee that he wouldn't have bought jewelry with it. Christ, he might have bought over half of a shitty Mustang.

I myself saw lots of people come and go through that cell—it was Veterans Day weekend, I was white, I would post bond when the judge showed up on Tuesday. I could be spared the jump-suits, the trip to the back of the St. Clair County Jail. I could inhabit the much preferable holding cell for three days, no problem. Not so for Kim Franklin. He knew it and the guards knew it; they knew it every time they yelled his name. He wasn't long for the holding cell—he'd come in after me and he'd leave before me, there was no doubt at all, and not out to the street.

But for the few hours Kim and I shared the cell, we did have company: a hammer murderer, a rapist, two funny thieves, an old smelly man who said, "Amen," at the end of every sentence, then again, briefly, on some path to wherever insanity was taking him, that hammer murderer. During this same time my friends shared their cell with a guy who had tried to hijack a nuclear submarine—a guy whose life I later plagiarized and tried to sell, unsuccessfully, as a debut novel. All of them and Kim Franklin ended up in orange jumpsuits eventually. All of them and Kim Franklin ended up in the back eventually, but before they did we dined on hot dogs to-gether, we shat together, we talked about crime, we talked about the criminals who only just moments before had been put in orange jumpsuits and sent to the back, where every now and then, late at night, came the sound of men screaming in women's voices.

The two funny thieves had tried to steal a car in a mall parking lot. They had consulted privately in one corner of the hold-ing cell, and then later came to the public conclusion over a lunch of boiled hot dogs that at that particular mall there must have been security patrols on the roof. They figured that they'd raised the suspicions of the rooftop patrols by repeatedly seeming to forget which car was theirs. The funny thieves concocted, this time directly in front of us, a better plan for a different mall involving a shopping cart full of empty boxes.

The funny thieves had wanted a nice car, something of value. Probably they would have sold it for parts or perhaps filed off some identifying serial number and sold it in one piece. But I'm pretty sure they hadn't been looking to steal $200 Mustangs; that would have made very little sense—why risk jail for a stupid $200? The hammer murderer had killed his girlfriend—it might have been his wife—during an argument about money. The submarine hijacker had planned to ransom the thing for millions. Kim Franklin had his rhinestones. Regardless of what any of us thought was valuable, we had none of it in that holding cell, just our clothes, and whenever one of the hangdog, shuffling trustees came out from the back in his orange jumpsuit to sweep up or bring us our hot dogs, I wouldn't have traded my Levi's for a Porsche.

I did end up wearing an orange jumpsuit, after all, but only for about a half hour. I needed to be outfitted for the lineup in clothing that would more or less match the guys they'd pulled out of the back to stand next to me. I suppose they figured it was better to put me in a jumpsuit than give those guys their clothes back or drag half a dozen regularly dressed lowlifes off the street. I stood in the middle of a lineup, in my bright orange jumpsuit, easily a head taller than the tallest of them, the hue of my jumpsuit exponentially brighter than the faded saffron of the others. I stood in my eighteen-year-old fresh-facedness with a half-dozen mustachioed, girlfriend-beating, heroin-injecting thugs awaiting trial, on charges no doubt considerably less serious than mine.

After the lineup, I compared notes with my friends in the cell next to mine. We spoke in whispers, a concrete wall between us, one of those situations you see in prison movies that require the use of a hand mirror on a stick. It turned out that in theirs, too, they were a little extra conspicuous. In their lineup everyone but them was black. "They'll throw that out," I said. "I mean, Christ."

"Kim Franklin!" the guards yelled for the last time, and he was gone.

Somewhere near my final hours in jail, a white guy came into the cell, and all he did was jump up every time the guards walked by, which was all the time, and lie to them.

"Are you John Cooper?" the guards asked him more than once.

"No, that's my cousin," he said once. "No, that's another name," he said another time. But no matter what, fifteen minutes later, the guard would walk by again and say, "John Cooper," and the white guy would twist his neck so fast it might have been on an industrial swivel and deny it. But the guards never laughed; they'd shake their heads and walk away.

"They're messing with me," he told me later.

"What'd you do?" I asked.

"Speeding tickets," he said. "They picked me up on a bond." Later he said it was shoplifting. I think he might have been high, but I'm not sure. For someone who had as many Mexican seeds crushed into the carpet of his shitty Mustang as I did, I'd always been a poor judge of other people's mental states.

"What did you guys do?" he asked.

"Armed robbery," I said. I'd been thoroughly briefed by that time by my lawyer and the detectives on the pertinent Illinois statutes. Some years earlier the state of Illinois had decided on a few heinous crimes for which probation would never be offered—

armed robbery was probably fairly high up on that list. "It's a Class X felony," I said. "Fifteen years, no chance of probation." I was getting used to saying it, trying it out on my tongue. Fifteen years.

"Well, enjoy Menard," he said.

Menard is the name of the Illinois state prison at Menard. I've thought many times about writing a book with the title *Enjoy Menard.* Spending my twenties at Menard was a future held up in front of me for months like a severed head. I'd turn away and still it was there. Whose head? I think you know by now whose head.

The kid behind the cash register at the Sunoco station actually farted in fear when we burst in. "No alarms, sport," my friend said. I don't know where he heard that expression. *The Rockford Files?* I held the door, one of the others held a knife. The kid popped open the cash drawer and backed up against the window by the deicers and oilcans. He held up his hands, palms forward. There were only a few bills in the register, until I told the kid to lift up the change divider and hand over the twenties stashed underneath. My friend had reminded us to do that; he'd once worked in a gas station himself. After grabbing the money, we ran out, jumped into my shitty car parked a half a block away, and headed back to O'Fallon.

The knife was smallish. If it had been a gun, it would have been a snub-nosed. The snub-nosed knife was never found, even when I blubbered to the detective that I'd be happy to accompany him out to the field where, the night before, we'd thrown it, chortling wildly at our own cleverness in remembering to get rid of it. Had we ever gone to trial, the lack of the knife would have been helpful to us. We actually *were* clever to have gotten rid of it. It was physical evidence—the *only* physical evidence, if you don't count the $115 in small bills.

After we chucked the knife, we drove back to our town, our safely white drive-around-the-main-drag-all-night-in-your-shitty-Mustang town, and pulled in to the Burger Chef restaurant parking lot. I'd pulled in to the Burger Chef parking lot hundreds of times, but never with a police car roaring up behind me, expelling two officers, one of whom I'd been in Boy Scouts with before I dropped out due to a mild disgust with the sadism involved. I turned off the ignition and sat back, as though it were all a movie and I'd predicted the ending.

The two cops were very *Adam-12* about the whole thing, crouching first alongside their fenders before skittering up to each side of our car. I barely even paid attention to them. I just sat there. The only place I looked was next to me at the plate-glass window of the Burger Chef, lined with half of my graduating class. I'm sure I was still looking at them lined up there when the nearest cop got to about three feet from my window with his revolver pointed at my face. For some reason, I remember that behind the gun he wore a bright metal wristwatch, a big one. I think he was crying. I know somebody was. It was a fucking tearful moment for somebody.

The lead detective was an old black guy who typed up my confession so carefully I can still hear the sound of the keys. He typed it up while I waited, so I could sign it before he went home for his long weekend. I heard later that he put in a good word for us. Lots of people put in good words for us. The mother of a girl I'd secretly loved all through high school wrote a letter to the editors of the local paper excoriating them for the huge headline they'd printed about our arrest. It was wonderful, but we clearly didn't deserve it. We'd been full of ourselves, we'd tempted fate, treated girls too young to know any better worse than they would ever deserve, and mocked them afterward. We acted as though we were a generation of young lions, like we were entitled to have our way with everyone and everything, the way I imagined men acted in the months before they went to Vietnam. But we weren't going to Vietnam; we weren't going anywhere.

In the end the judge must have been impressed with us as well, or with our expensive attorneys. Six months after the crime, he threw out the case with the agreement of the state's attorney and over the vehement protests of the station owner. He didn't have the heart to send us to Menard for a decade, and since he had no ability to lower the sentence, he dismissed it. By then, the Air Force and Washington University had washed their hands of me. I'd discovered, very briefly, LSD, and dated a girl who had either wanted to save me or thought I was newly interesting. I showed up at the St. Clair County courthouse with my parents on a bright April day and twenty minutes later walked out into a brick courtyard like a reptile who'd successfully shed a dingy and ill-fitting skin. Six months after that, I fled to Hawaii, where I learned how to sell expensive clothes to rich people and celebrities who had packed poorly, and where, very briefly, I'd sport a silver chain around my neck and think that I looked good in it.

Kim Franklin's face was nice, smooth, with the kind of skin often referred to as mocha. He was thin, shy; his arms were long. He wore dark pants that were too big for him; twenty years before that would be considered stylish. He wore a long-sleeved knit shirt with a collar. His hair was neat and short, his teeth even and very white. He sat with his elbows on his knees when he wasn't on the toilet, his eyes leaking tears.

Before I could write about him, I took $115 out of my wallet— that's a lie, I took $115 out of my pocket. I don't keep money in my wallet. I keep health insurance cards, credit cards, and scraps of paper in my wallet, which has seen better days. To write this essay, I took $115 out of my front pocket and handed it to an old black man begging for coins on the sidewalk. He had a knit cap in the summer and a tweed jacket. His pants were clean, but his socks were dirty. I had to wait until nobody would see me and I could slip the tight roll into his cup and walk away very quickly before he could say anything. It wasn't modesty that made me flee the scene, or altruism, or even, at this point in my life, shame. It was, really, nothing but fear. The fear that nearly three decades later my continued arrogance and privilege are just the currency of a fool who will, finally, be stripped, fitted for a jumpsuit, and called to go to the back with the others. But not today, and probably not soon, and thank God for that.

Mad Money

Andy Behrman

It's the height of the 1980s in Manhattan. Hidden in my freezer, behind two huge bottles of Absolut vodka and a few pints of Häagen-Dazs ice cream, are stacks of $100 bills, the proceeds from my art-counterfeiting efforts in Europe and Japan. My "cold cash," as my friends and I refer to it, is organized in neat rubber-banded piles of $10,000. There's probably about $200,000 in all. I take five or six wads and stuff them into my coat pocket, then I grab a few $20 bills that are in a kitchen drawer and a fresh roll of quarters.

In the elevator, I organize the loot in my coat pocket—rubber-banded money, loose $20 bills, and the roll of quarters—no wallet necessary. I bought one in Milan about a month ago for credit cards, but I don't really use it. I like rubber-banding my credit cards, too. It makes me feel like a bit of a gangster. But I don't use credit cards when I go shopping, even though I have six or seven of them with no limit. I only use them for business expenses so I can be reimbursed by my employer, a successful downtown artist. He's the one I've been counterfeiting.

When I get down to the lobby, I remember a fistful of change that I found the night before and threw into a baggie. I run back upstairs to get it. It comes to about $8, and I slip it into the pocket of my coat. Oddly, my left pocket, the one with the change, is heavier than my right pocket. Eight dollars in the left, $50,060 in the right. Go figure.

I hail a cab and tell the driver to take me to Barneys. The fare is $6.00. I apologize as I hand him the baggy of change. "It's about $8.00," I tell him. (It's actually $7.80. I know because I counted it six times the night before.) Feeling guilty, I take four quarters out of my roll and throw those in, too. "Buy yourself a lottery ticket— I think this Saturday is your night," I say. His big cocoa-colored hand is full of coins from the baggy. "Thanks. Have a good day," he tells me. I don't know if he's perturbed with having to deal with all the coins or thinks he's struck it rich and gotten ten bucks for a quick crosstown trip. Anyhow, he smiles at me and continues on his way. His next passenger will probably give him ten bucks for a $9.60 trip, so I'm a "king tipper" after all, I think.

The doorman at Barneys opens the revolving door for me. "Good afternoon," he says as I walk into a wall of fragrance. I avoid being spritzed to death by focusing on a wall of cashmere sweaters about twenty-five yards away, ignoring the offers to "try" Helmut Lang or "enjoy" Moschino. I don't want to try or enjoy anything. I'm on a mission to shop. I want to lighten my coat pocket and spend real money.

Natalie, my regular saleswoman, acknowledges me with a nod

and finishes up quickly with her customer. "Good afternoon, Mr. Behrman," she says. "What can I help you with today? A gift for someone or something for yourself?"

"I just need a couple of sweaters I can wear with jeans," I tell her. She comes back with ten and I like them all. I try on a navy blue one. It fits perfectly. Natalie tells me that she also has it in black and heather. "Which one would you like?" she asks me. "I'll take all three," I respond. They're $550 each. She shows me a black turtleneck that I realize I need desperately. It comes in navy blue, too, and I take both of them, $275 each. I'm losing patience with sweaters, and we move on to casual shirts. I take seven of the eight she shows me. Another $1,200.

I thank her and head to the shoe department. On the way there, I take off my coat because I'm getting a bit anxious and feeling kind of hot. I tell the salesman, a fresh-faced wannabe model in his early twenties, that I'm looking for boots—nothing more descriptive. He brings me four pairs. I try them on. "I'll take these three," I tell him after a moment. He seems pleased. The total is $2,200. I undo some more cash from the rubber band and pay him. I get a few bucks in change and a receipt.

I feel like I can't spend my money fast enough, but I can't even think what I need. I take the escalator upstairs and start picking out jackets and jeans and shirts furiously, just making big piles of them. I don't bother asking a salesman for help, but I notice from the corner of my eye another wannabe model looking at me. "Buying gifts?" he asks me. "No, clothing the homeless," I tell him. "Well, you couldn't have come to a better place," he says. I put the pile on the counter. He rings it up and it comes to $7,000.

I feel like the ceiling is going to cave in on me and the walls are closing in. It's time to get the hell out of Barneys. On the way out, I'm forced to walk past the fragrance guys and girls again. "No thank you, I just use the strips in the magazines," I tell them. It's true. I would never spend $200 on a cologne when I can get it for free in *Vanity Fair*. Never.

I'm on Madison Avenue now. I'm carrying four huge bags and have spent more than $12,000. My throat is dry and I'm sweating. I have to find a cab and get home. One pulls up. "Eighty-ninth and Broadway, please," I tell the driver. I throw my head back as he drives me across town, and I look through the back window. There are a bunch of puffy white clouds, nimbus clouds, I think, moving incredibly fast across the bright blue sky of winter. They're moving as fast as the panic in my head. I feel like I've been in the cab for-ever, but we're not even across the park yet. I wish I had some Klonopin with me. As soon as I get home, I'll take one. Finally we pull up to my building. The meter says $7, and I give the driver a $20 bill. "Keep the change," I tell him.

As soon as I get inside my apartment, I drop the bags and col-lapse on my couch, trying to recover from my day. This time I blew my money at Barneys, but I've done the same at the Food Empo-rium, laying out $300 on cleaning supplies—cases of Lysol, Soft Scrub, Windex, Pledge, two dozen rolls of toilet paper, a half a dozen paper towels. These manic spending sprees always leave me in the same state. Confused, agitated, and utterly exhausted.

But I'm not done spending money yet. I know I'll get a second wind and go out to a club later. I take a shower to revive myself, us-ing a mini-shampoo and mini-conditioner from the large collection of things I've stolen from hotels lately. I steal toilet paper, too. Even though it's bulky, I can usually get two or three rolls into my suitcase. In my bathroom closet, I have more than fifty rolls, all in different hotel wrappings: gold labels from the Four Seasons and even fancier ones in beautiful paper from hotels in Tokyo and Paris.

I get out of the shower, dripping wet, and admire myself in the mirror. "Am I going to get laid tonight?" I ask myself. I throw on a pair of jeans, a white T-shirt, and one of my new sweaters from Barneys and take a cab to Scores. I like watching these hot, innocent girls from the Midwest strip and am even more intrigued by how they work the crowd of young horny businessmen for cash. Tonight, like many nights, there's a bachelor party—a group of guys in their midtwenties whom all of the girls are paying attention to because each guy has a fistful of $20 bills.

I'm reminded of my own days stripping, almost ten years ago, and the thrill of having men put wads of cash in my socks. All I had to do was shake my ass and get my dick hard for a bunch of horny old men, and I'd leave the theater with a few hundred dollars and a client for the night. I invite a beautiful girl named Amber to come back to my apartment for a private show. "And make sure you bring your boyfriend," I tell her. "Can't do that, but I've got a friend I usually do duos with who's working tonight," she tells me. She writes my address down on a card and says they'll be at my place by 3:00 a.m. I offer Amber a wad of crisp green bills—$500 as a deposit for the night. "Honey, I trust you. Pay me later," she says.

When I get home, I tell the doorman to let my friends up without buzzing. I make myself a vodka tonic, go upstairs to my bedroom, light some of my new Diptyque candles, and wait for them. I'm wearing a pair of jeans and a T-shirt I bought in Tokyo that says "Trust Fund." A little while later, there's a knock at my door. I invite the two of them in. Amber is wearing a full-length fur coat—I don't know if it's real—but she opens it up and is only wearing a pair of panties underneath. She giggles. Travis, a blond and tanned young man, shakes my hand. "Pleased to meet you, mate," he says. The two of them come in, and I take Amber's coat. "Nice titties, huh?" says Travis. "I used to bang her for two years at a club in Amsterdam and really make those fuckers bounce." He goes into the kitchen and looks around. Then he grabs a beer from the freezer and spots my cash. "We're here to show you the best you've ever seen and put a dent in that motherfucking pile," he tells me.

When we all wake up in the morning, I've blown more than $3,000, and Travis and Amber have put on the show of their lives. They get dressed and I walk them downstairs. On the way out, Travis pulls his pants down and shows off his ass. "This one, mate, is on me," he says and winks.

I didn't always spend money like this. As a child, I hoarded nickels, dimes, and quarters in a huge plastic gin bottle (a promotion that my liquor-salesman grandfather gave to me). This see-through bottle sat in front of the door to my bedroom, half full with silver coins. I did not permit myself to put pennies in the bottle. Instead, I wrapped and rolled them, then hid them in shoe boxes in the back of my closet.

At the time, my family was struggling financially. On the last day of each month, my father would hole up in the basement, trying to figure out which bills were the most important and which ones would wait a few days longer before they were mailed out. Even then, I knew we were living beyond our means. My father kept a little notebook of everybody he owed money to with an amount next to it. When he'd pay the bill, he'd scratch a line through it. His notebook gave me the uncomfortable feeling that we were living on the edge, but it also gave me an odd sense of power. After all, we were getting away with it. We had the finest clothes and ate in the finest restaurants, all on a college professor's salary. It didn't add up.

As a kid, I had various "jobs." These included, but were not limited to, stealing coins from my mother's purse and my father's change tray. I also charged a nickel for a club that I started in elementary school. I'd invite my friends over, serve them milk and cookies, and let them look at porn magazines. I did odd jobs, too, including picking up sticker balls (a penny each) from my lawn, washing cars, recycling newspapers, and doing a paper route.

Back then I hated to spend money. Instead of using my allowance to buy lunch, I starved myself and saved the dollar every day, always converting the bill to change. I never bought anything for myself. The thought of cracking into the gin bottle or opening the shoe boxes was frightening to me. The most important thing was keeping my personal Fort Knox intact; in fact, it seemed critical to my survival. Even the mere suggestion by my parents that I "splurge" and buy myself something "nice" was cause for an angry outburst.

When I celebrated my Bar Mitzvah, I received checks for more than $2,000. I wanted to keep the checks in a special locked box, but my father explained to me that if I were to open a bank account, the bank would actually pay me a percentage to "use" my money. One day my father returned home with coin wrappers for all my nickels, dimes, and quarters. I was indignant, yet curious how much I had saved over the years. I spent days wrapping the coins. I had more than $2,000 worth of change in the gin bottle and almost $1,000 in pennies. Not to mention the checks for my Bar Mitzvah. My father and I packed everything up in shopping bags, jumped into the car, and drove to Hudson City Savings Bank.

There, I opened my first bank account with a middle-aged woman who happened to be the mother of a friend of mine from school. I knew her daughter. I trusted her. She probably wouldn't spend my money frivolously.

It was around this time that my Lotto obsession started. I'd play the scratch-off Lotto and get incredibly excited even if I just won a free ticket. Occasionally, when I was bored during class, I would daydream about winning $50 million and how I'd share it with my family, move to a huge house, and tell my parents that they could stop working. But it was always my dad who bought the tickets for me. I'd never use my own money for this indulgence.

It was college that changed my frugal ways. When I went away to Wesleyan, I wanted my classmates to think that I was one of the "rich kids." All of the money that I had saved for years I started spending on clothing, expensive dinners, and cocaine. I was deeply humiliated by being middle-class and, well, simple in comparison to some of these kids who had gone to private school and whose parents were executives or in the media. I was determined to make money so I could feel more important, more powerful, more in control.

And that's still how I feel today. The desire for money motivates me to work harder, to negotiate harder, and to "win" in business. Money is the payoff for hard work and for outsmarting people. I want to make tons of it and buy huge things, airplanes, yachts, mansions. Lots of money is good, more is better. Over the years, I've made it many ways, overtime at Armani, pimping, stripping, prostitution, public relations. Then I began dealing art and made millions of dollars, most of which I spent in wild shopping sprees. This crazy period ended in 1993 when I was indicted for counterfeiting art. As a result, I faced a sudden fall into poverty, one in which I was forced to think quickly on my feet and figure out a new way to make money. With a close friend, I started an apartment-painting company just to subsist, yet even that business raged out of control. I needed only $500 a week to make ends meet but soon was farming out work and making $10,000. Later, when I was diagnosed with bipolar disorder, I learned that grand entrepreneurial schemes and overspending are common symptoms of the illness.

I don't throw away money like I used to, but I still play the Lotto and daydream about winning $50 million and what I'd do with it. Since I tell myself that I don't have enough money to buy underwear (I have only four pairs, which I make sure are washed regularly), I'd probably buy lots of pairs right away. Not wearing underwear, or socks for that matter, makes me feel like a monk, like I'm living without material possessions. Of course the irony is that even though I know I can't afford "luxury" items like underwear, I have no problem buying costly things like art and jewelry and cars. There's always a conflict between wanting to live like a monk and wanting to live excessively. The kid who saved $3,000 in change and the man who spends $12,000 at Barneys coexist uneasily in me.

Because of this, I have rules about what I can spend money on and what I can't. I won't buy dish-washing liquid in one store if I know I can buy it for sixty cents less at a store a few miles away. I won't call 411. I won't buy gasoline for $2.59 a gallon if I know I can drive a mile farther and find it for $2.29 a gallon. I can take hours comparison shopping at the supermarket, not to mention "tasting" their wares for free, a remnant of my old bipolar sense of entitlement. After all I've suffered over the last ten years, aren't I owed some yogurt-covered pretzels?

I still cannot leave a hotel room without taking all the toiletries. I always think that the seventy-nine cents I save by stealing the toilet paper might be needed to purchase something critical on a rainy day. And yet oddly, I'll drop wads of cash without a thought on luxury items like massages, haircuts, and personal training, and every so often I'll throw out (donate to charity) piles of T-shirts, socks, shoes, and household objects that aren't worn out yet, then go and spend ridiculous amounts of money replacing them. Afterward, I'll buy huge quantities of soap, shampoo, and cleaning supplies because hoarding them makes me feel safe.

During that crazy period in the 1980s when I spent money in a frenzy, I remember thinking that if I ever accumulated $50 million in the bank, I could die happily with no material possessions. I imagined being buried in just a pair of jeans and a T-shirt, all of my things sold at auction for a charity, the art I've collected donated to museums. What a wonderful gift it would be to die like that after all those years of obsessing about having and not having it.

But the fear of being broke still drives me. What if one day I don't have any money in the bank, no money in my wallet, no money in the freezer even? Would I panic? No, I'd probably just create a line of aromatherapy products for pampered dogs or design 24-carat gem-encrusted LEGO sets for the toddlers of the rich and famous. I bet I'd make more money from those two ideas combined than by hitting the Lotto jackpot.

This Way Out

Jill McCorkle

I have heard it said that marriage is about love and that divorce is about money, and I agree. Even those who later confess to saying "I do" when they shouldn't have weren't really thinking about divorce. They were hoping for something good.

For me, marriage was about love and commitment and an orderly life that would allow me to embrace my first real love— writing, that part of me that I had always stayed true to regardless of where I was or whom I was with. In the beginning, I found it comforting that I was marrying someone who was as absorbed in thinking about his work as I was in mine. He was doing his residency in medicine, and so I envisioned myself safely hidden behind a secure and sturdy domestic facade. I could be like the mothers of all those kids I envied growing up. The stay-at-home mom in a paneled station wagon on her way to and from golf or tennis, summers at the beach, no worries beyond tending children and what to fix for supper. But of course I was going to do it all one step better.

The All-American Mom who also is churning out novels and stories and the occasional poem. Two separate orbits spinning. My royalties varied drastically over the years, but I always had the security of at least one teaching job. Though everyone assumes all doctors make huge amounts of money, it isn't true in academic medicine, especially when living in an expensive area of the country. Still, I thought I would get the occasional semester off to write. I thought there would be the standard family vacations and a slow and steady build of nicer furniture replacing knockdowns I had carried around since college. I had the picket-fence fantasy. I'll admit I watched way too much television growing up and believed in the possibilities of "Hi, honey, I'm home." "How was your day, dear?"

When we moved away from North Carolina, where I had a job I loved and a lot of close friends, not to mention my family, we made a deal that I could always go home whenever I needed or wanted to. The forces seemed to be with me when I got a five-year job at Harvard that paid more per year than I had ever made as a teacher *and* I had a book coming out with another close on its heels. I interviewed for that job with my two-week-old son sleeping in an office next door. I was doing it all—parenting, working, writing, gardening, cleaning the house, paying the bills, holding up my end just fine. I wasn't in my first-choice town and I wasn't in my first-choice house and I didn't have a dog, but I was hopeful. I really believed that I could do it all and, further, that when I couldn't do it, my husband would do it for me.

What we couldn't have known was that within that first year my dad would be diagnosed with terminal cancer. Amazing how quickly money can disappear when you need to go home as often as possible—usually every weekend—for three months, with babysitters hired to do all I would normally be doing at home. The whole sad time pulled a plug on a kind of hopefulness I had felt, and suddenly, instead of working to save money for something I was looking forward to, I was working to earn money to pay for time that was behind me, a choice, I might add, that I would make each and every time. Still, it changed me. I no longer wanted the same things. I wanted something closer to what I had always known. I was homesick. I wanted a dog. I wanted more quiet time to feed what should have been the next book.

You can talk about all the different reasons marriages end—no two exactly alike—but the image I am left picturing is of those big metal spikes in the driveways of rental car lots: You can go forward, but you can't back up. Once your tires have crossed the jaws-of-death threshold, you are committed to coming on in. Even if you know that you have made a wrong turn, or perhaps you've changed your mind about that fuchsia Neon you rented, you have no choice but to drive on around the lot, weaving in this lane and that, stopping for this pedestrian then that one, rough terrain, sharp turns, until finally you find an exit sign. In other words, it's a whole lot easier to get into a marriage than it is to get *out* of one. It's also a lot more fun, what with presents and parties instead of taking out loans and getting looks of pity when people hear your news.

It turned out a lot of other people were driving around aimlessly, too. So where is the exit? they asked. They'd been watching me searching the maze for a way out. It began as soon as word hit the street that I was separated. "You're doing what I'm going to do when I can," or, "That's where I ought to be," people said. I often heard this from women I only knew from my children's school events and by their children's names. Out of the woodwork there was Hayley's mom suddenly gripping my arm in the grocery store parking lot and pulling me off to one side. "I'm so sorry," she said and leaned in way too close asking questions in rapid fire. "When did you first know this was going to happen? Did you try marriage counseling? How will you manage? Do you get to keep the house?"

My question for her was, Who can have all that makeup on and hair just so at eight in the morning and what in the hell made her think that she could ask me such things? The only attention she had ever paid me before was once to say, "Oh yeah, I hear you write little articles," and once to invite me, "since you don't really have a job," to do a head lice check at the elementary school.

Excuse me? What is it about deciding to divorce that suddenly makes acquaintances sidle up to me and air their dirty laundry? These were people I barely knew, and yet suddenly the boundaries were swept away; I had driven off down the lonesome highway without a map, and everyone wanted to see where I'd end up. It was clear that I held valuable information—I had a lawyer, I'd filed papers, I'd even taken the state-mandated parenting course that every divorced citizen must take (a very good thing by the way; every state should have one). These women assumed I must have the answers up my sleeve for the taking. How to let go of something that has run its course? How to find a new road to travel? Some of these women seemed wistful and filled with longing. Others were judgmental, quick to imply I must not have worked hard enough, and yet they seemed envious as well. When I finally got around to posing the question (and I learned very quickly not to ask it, as it is akin to asking a hypochondriac how she feels today) "So why don't you get a divorce?" "Well ... I can't do that," they said. "I have children." (So do I.) "How would I ever pay for X and Y and Z?" (Often private schools and summer camps and expensive cars.) And it wasn't long before I realized something. Most unhappily married people who choose to stay together do so because of money and all that it represents: the neighborhood, the trips, the security that a major plumbing or car problem won't force you to go broke. If I had ever had the luxury of writing full-time without any financial worries, would I have felt differently? Maybe, or even if I hadn't felt differently, it would have made for a comfortable nest that might have been difficult to leave. By then, I was so aware of our differences. It wasn't right versus wrong or good versus evil. It was two different people on different tracks who happened to share a primary focus, which was our children.

What I had become during my years in white-bread suburbia was disillusioned and tired of working more than one job when all I really wanted to do—all I had ever wanted to do—was write. I had become a watered-down version of everything I had ever wanted to be—tired of compromise, tired of second choices, tired of feeling homesick. It sounds so ridiculous to name those trite differences, and yet there you have it: You have lake people and you have ocean people. Those who love dogs and those who don't. Those who celebrate holidays big and those who don't. When my dad died, I went out and bought a dog. It was spontaneous and thrilling, and I thought surely there was no harm done. I worked very hard after all. I more than pulled my share of the weight.

A six-pound Yorkie flipped the switch, and the track of this roller coaster we were on sent us off on a new course that was all about our differences and how difficult it was to compromise. It was a bumpy ride and one you wish on no one, and yet it seems so inevitable. When the Yorkie proved to be a child-biter, I jealously found him a home in the Carolinas, and we got a Labrador retriever, a sweet, family-friendly dog. And she is wonderful, but it wasn't what my husband had wanted in a dog, so then we added a sheltie. It was not unlike the compromise that happened when I wanted the occasional trip to the Unitarian church but wound up with years in a synagogue instead.

This is the story of money and what happens when you divorce. I have enormous sympathy for those who are genuinely trapped. I've been told that women usually go down a rank in income and men go up. I don't know if that is accurate. In our case we have both taken a plunge, when factoring in all the legal expenses on top of two households operating on the same amount of income that once fed one. As time passes, that will change, and had I not gotten a full-time job, we *would* accurately have fit that profile. I am fortunate to have the earning potential I do, because I know that our system is not a perfect one and that there are women who have never worked outside the home terrified at the prospect, especially at a more advanced age. And there are men who feed and stoke those fears.

But there are also those who would have no problem surviving on half of the split but want more than the split offers. They will grip your arm with heavy bejeweled hands and say how brave you are to live without before hopping in the BMW and driving to the beach house.

But without what? I always wanted to ask. Without the kind of tension that breeds and grows when in a situation where neither person is happy? Without the kind of hopelessness that sets in when you know you're in the wrong place? It's not like we didn't try, after all. The *third* dog came as a birthday present to me, a kind of peace token from my husband, and though this ten-pound dust ball could not save the situation, I truly did appreciate the gesture.

But it was not enough. I see now that it was already too late for us. Still, it shocked a lot of people when we announced our separation. Why is it so hard to believe that two good and decent humans could look up and not recognize the place they inhabit? That one wants to go over there and ride the Ferris wheel, look at the lights, ponder the fate of the universe, and the other one wants to spin on the Tilt-A-Whirl till he pukes and then go right back for more. A split in desire like that can't be rectified. It is infuriating and is the kind of difference that can throw a divorce into motion. You feel anger and sadness; you cycle through the whole grief process again and again until you come clean enough to put your children first, which means a civilized relationship respectful of their other parent.

Except of course the money thing. That is the last hurdle. People hold tight to money and what it represents the way they *should* hold on to people and ideas. It's all representative. And it all has to be dealt with and solved before you are able to wish your ex happiness and fulfillment. No one wants to leave the fair, but sometimes you have to because you know you can't just sit there belted together for all of eternity when one wants to sway quietly in the night air and the other wants to spin. When one can't get enough of the freak show and the other likes talking to the 4-H students about the diet of your average pig.

I desired such a peaceful path from the moment of separation—truly I did!—but still found myself in there running around frantically like all the other divorcing mice, bumping into glass and wanting my share of the cheese. I wanted my fair share. I deserved it. I had spent years working, and not just outside the home but in the home, all those jobs you can't put a price on, though I once did, itemizing fifteen years of child care and household cleaning and cooking and lawn service. I was worth so much money I couldn't even believe it. And if in fact my time and sweat equity actually counted for anything, it would have been a much easier process, I'm sure. I mean, look how easy it is out there in fan-tasyland. Jen and Brad got divorced so fast. Why, Britney got an-nulled overnight. But they didn't have kids, *and* they had a lot of money, two big factors in getting things done quickly and easily.

But good and easy exit scenes don't come cheap. They are well rehearsed and expensive. *Stella! Rosebud! I'm ready for my close-up. Frankly, my dear, I don't give a damn.* Pick your favorite. A good ending is hard to find.

Do you want dramatic?

After all, tomorrow is another day.

Sarcastic?

Don't go away mad, just go away!

Enlightened?

Que será, será.

And of course this is (in my opinion) the best choice: *Let it go.*

Put it down and let it go. It's what many people end up doing in divorce, though unfortunately it's not the result of spiritual lofti-ness so much as being tired as hell and smoked out of your trench. That was me. I had lots of well-meaning friends telling me what I *really* deserved—back pay for one thing—the house profit all to myself. They told me that I shouldn't finish a book or get a job un-til the divorce was over. "Make him pay," they said, "you deserve better." You gotta love your friends. You need their love. You need their support, but the truth was I wanted a divorce and I wanted it to be as civil and peaceful as possible. I wanted my share, yes. But not as much as I wanted our kids to be okay. I wanted my half. I gave him the china and half the silver. I took the dogs (no argu-ment there).

And I did search for and get a new job, which meant that I would not get alimony, and if there had been any way humanly possible to finish my book, I would have done that, too. The desire to stay in and fight can become a series of warped and false exit signs. It might be right to hang in there and duke it out for some, but it wasn't right for me. I have a sign over my desk that says, WHEN THE HORSE IS DEAD, GET OFF IT. It is a sentiment for stories gone awry—dead-end ideas and half-baked characters. But there are many times in life when I think quitting is the right, best, and only thing to do. There are many who have told me I should have done better, could have done better, and maybe that's true. I have debts that, if I really allow myself to think about it, I shouldn't have. And yet I also have closure, which is worth a lot. I have to factor in there the price of emotional health (not to mention legal bills) and what dragging it all out another year or so would have meant. For me it was time to leave the fair and not look back.

In an ideal world, you would just agree to disagree and split everything fairly and move on. So simple. So what happens? Money happens. It's what makes us want to fight or stall, to employ war tactics and smoke each other out.

The first time I went to court was to discuss money and what I might be entitled to per month. I had come up with a figure I thought was fair, but it had been an arduous process. Two weeks before, my husband's lawyer had sent a subpoena requesting that I show everything I had earned over the past five years and what I anticipated earning in the next two. I asked him if I could also present what money I had spent and owed and what I anticipated spending and owing over the next two years. I still don't understand why I didn't just get a phone call from his lawyer asking me to give this information but instead opened the door to a deputy who wished me a merry Christmas and gave me a check for $14 for accepting the papers. Why I got paid to accept a legal document that was going to make my life miserable or what happens if you refuse that squat sum for making a cameo appearance on *Divorce Court*, I'll never know, but the deputy said serving a subpoena is no big deal, that it happens all the time. "I make a business out of doing this," he said.

"Well," I said, looking at the check. "What on earth will I do with this bit of mad money?" He registered little response. "Why, I can buy a large pizza with more than one topping!" I said and clapped my hands. "Or I could buy shampoo and deodorant. Toothpaste and toilet paper and an economy box of Tide!" This little run-in ended with my letting my three dogs—most notably a jumping and already muddy Labrador retriever—out to follow him to his car. And I think this was preferable to what I was thinking, which was to say, "Fuck you very much," *the* famous line of polite waitresses who are left measly tips by people who expect them to bow and be grateful.

Tuesday was divorce day at the courthouse. I walked in seeing all the others whose marriages had failed or come unglued or been ripped apart. This was it. Like me, they all had dollar signs in their eyes. What were they suing for? Psychic pain, cruel and unusual treatment, child support? Or maybe just good old-fashioned alimony, a small payback for years of being overlooked and undervalued?

Call it what you will. I could see the need and pain in these people's eyes, each one wondering what their love had been worth.

I stood in line that first day between two young lawyers who were all dressed up and talking about how bored they were handling divorce cases. Without a beat they shifted over to a colleague of theirs who had just gotten engaged. "Did you see her ring?"

"Oh my gosh, like huge." Giggle giggle. "And did she tell you about the house they're buying?"

"And the honeymoon?"

I was distracted by their squeals and squawks while I—and about twenty other men and women—waited to hear some judgment from some human with power about money and entitlement and equal distribution. One woman and I spent about an hour talking. We were both wearing pink. I had been told by a dear, concerned student who had a lot of legal knowledge to wear navy, that people who wear navy keep both hands on the steering wheel and balance their checkbooks. It was then I realized I did not own one thing navy and never have. So I wore pink, as did the woman who had been working on her divorce for years and years. It all sounded so complicated and hideous that when I got up to go meet with my lawyer I did so thinking how horrible it would be to have all that money to deal with, those houses and cars and accounts. I thought I would throw up, and the feeling lingered as we sat there going over what I was worth. A lot of cases get worked out there in the lobby on crowded benches, lawyers hammering it out just minutes before they would have appeared before the judge. This saves a lot of money, I'm told, though it still ain't what you'd call a bargain. That day I was given a set monthly amount, which exceeded what I had been getting for a year. It felt like a small step in the right direction, but there were still all the other issues to divide, and like any good soap opera, it couldn't happen right that minute but had to go through several more discussions and rewrites and who knows what.

Two months before my next court date, presumably the one that would grant the divorce, my sheltie, Daisy, rolled over in submission mode—a rare position for her, which I admire tremendously, and I noticed a lump. It proved to be a bad thing. I could agree to the surgery and treatment, or she would be gone in about three months. All I could think at that moment was that I was not ready to lose her. I was not ready for my children to lose her. She is only eight and the best babysitter I have ever had. She doesn't close her eyes until everyone is in and settled for the night, and even then I hear her tippy-toeing around last thing at night to make sure we are all where we're supposed to be. She sleeps at the foot of the stairs once the kids are up in their rooms, within eyeshot of my room and the front door. She is the epitome of faithful and loyal and devoted, all those vows so many take so lightly.

This sad news was delivered to me by the cute boy vet who looked about fourteen. I was told that there were some payment-plan options, so I took a deep breath and asked what kind of money we were talking about. It would with surgery and treatments run anywhere from $5,000 to $6,000, which was about half of what I had paid in legal expenses thus far. By then I was crying—for Daisy and from exhaustion and for sometimes feeling incapable of getting things done, forget doing them well. I was crying for every person and every thing I'd ever lost in my life. And the thought crossed my mind about my financial situation and about the lawyer's bill—many bills—sitting there on my kitchen table. I was in debt with half of a novel and the idea that I should just sit down and try to schlock something out. I had never had that thought before, but there it was. It was right up there with the memory of boys I knew in college who regularly sold plasma and sperm. I have always been rejected when trying to donate blood because my pressure is so low they once called in someone with a stethoscope to make sure I was alive. I of course had no sperm to sell and was pretty sure my eggs would be thought too old to hatch. I would sell the house, which I was going to need to do anyway. I'd have a yard sale. And if worst came to worst, I would approach a friend about a temporary loan.

I announced Daisy's sad news to my ex in hopes that I might get some assistance with this, but that was clearly a turnstile we'd long ago passed through; I did not directly ask for anything, which is where I failed early in the marriage. I should have demanded what I wanted—this town or this house or this religion or this vacation or this time off to write. I actually have always believed the *do unto others* thing and thought it was like a kind of magical incantation that would automatically keep the scales balanced. I am not a litigator. I will work as hard as I can for as long as I can, and then I'm likely to quit unless someone gives me a really good reason not to. Daisy was my dog, the kids' dog. She was *our* dog, our family of three.

I thought of my daughter in the backseat holding Daisy when we went to pick her up and bring her home—a family pet—too large for her breed and thus the one no one wanted, except us. We wanted her. We loved her. We vowed to take good care of her. This is a soul whose whole mission in life is to be loyal and faithful. She is devoted to our safety and well-being. And who could put a price on that?

She sits and waits in the window, watching for my safe return every day of her life. Needless to say, the decision to save her was one I will never regret. I would much rather give all the money I don't have to the extension of the life of this sweet, good creature than to the legal arena, which was starting to feel more like a cockfight—who could throw the most weight and be the most intimidating? Who would call uncle? Cave in to second or third choice. In the great karmic scheme of things, I know it was the right choice, and somehow having made it, having sat there sobbing in a tiny office that smelled like dog pee and alcohol and flea dip, my pants covered in the shed results of Daisy nervously sitting on my lap in the car ride over and then pressed against my legs as I sat, I was able to translate the bigger picture of it all.

How many people did I know who all too recently had gone through the heartache and loss of a loved one? How many people do I currently know completely engaged in courageous battles to save their own lives? I have healthy children, and they have both of their parents. Not together, okay, but they have them, which is a lot more than many can say.

I had once told one of the wishful women that I was the wrong person to talk to about wanting to get divorced unless she meant business, that I would sleep in a tent and piss in the yard before I went back to an unhappy situation. But that of course was not entirely true. Your children come first, and so money is essential. And that's why you do go get a lawyer and answer the door when subpoenaed and sit in a crowded courthouse while waiting your turn like all the other sheep in the chute.

In my particular fantasyland, it's better to have happy and civilized parents on different rides than it is to see them belted in side by side, sick and miserable and begging in weak moments to stop the machinery and let them off. And isn't that a better way to do it? Move along calmly. Locate the exit sign as you might in a theater in case of fire. So you won't be going to Europe or Aruba or even spending a week at the beach. Not this year—but you never did. And you can clip coupons and go places you hate like Sam's Club. Mow your own grass and scrub your own toilets and recycle cans and bottles, agree to teach an extra class here and there—which you always did. And some of that crappy furniture is starting to look real comfortable and will feel even better when you're stretched out on it and have finished paying the legal bills. It's a fantasy. I look forward to sitting on my own stick of furniture and not owing anybody anything.

That final day in court I kept thinking of a band of boys I had admired when I was growing up. They had a signature sign-off that I used to love. When leaving a conflict of some nature, they would just say, "Adios, motherfuckers!" Even now I can see them, the freedom in their legs pumping the pedals of their banana seat bikes, bushy sun-bleached hair blown from their tan young faces. There was something in those jaunty swings onto their bikes, handlebars gripped securely in a way that said *confidence, liberation, freedom.* They had a couple of bucks in their pockets, and that's all they needed. Enough for candy and a Coke, maybe a pack of cigarettes from the machine at the Holiday Inn where we all hung out that summer, sneaking into the pool and taking ice for free. They were twelve-year-old boys with a whole world ahead of them. Open road, clear-eyed, not taking crap from anybody if they could help it. I loved the power of that look. I wanted to feel like that. They were out of there. And when I finally left that courtroom, I was, too.

Stash

Claire Dederer

The stash came into my life a year ago, on a November day full of weather. My father lives on a houseboat, and together we sat at his dining room table by the south-facing window, watching the rain come up the wide gray expanse of Lake Union. After his recent heart attacks, we'd taken to spending time together in this free-form kind of way. The houseboat is a pleasant, oddball place for such hanging out. With its massing of books and art and music, it might be mistaken for bohemia if it weren't so relentlessly tidy.

My father keeps a basket of rocks from places he's hiked. As he and I sat and chatted, my children were dismantling this collection, counting and tossing and rolling. We were discussing plans for the upcoming winter when, in his diffident manner, my father offered me a sum of money.

I said yes. Who wouldn't? Even as I said it, though, a strange knot formed in my stomach. I'm not used to taking money from my father. My husband and I have supported ourselves as writers for many years. We've gotten along fine, especially considering how expensive Seattle has become, but we've dreamed of a bigger house, with a bedroom for each kid, and the sum would just about get us there. In the microsecond that it took me to answer, I weighed our financial independence against the notion of living more comfortably. I said yes. And thank you. Very much.

My comfortably off father, who likes to spend his money on pretty much nothing except skis and backpacks and books, said I was welcome. My father is a tall, long-faced man with a nimbus of gray hair that looks as though it's trying to fly off his head. What with the height and the nimbus, he has a kind of regal quality, and that's just right, because despite his frugality, my father possesses the soul of a monarch. His kingdom is one person: himself. He does what he wants, almost all the time, and he believes you should, too. He lives his life with a Gallic shrug: Suit yourself. He is entirely without agenda.

Maybe this is why he and my mom split up, but I don't know for sure. That's their mystery, not mine. All I know is that I like being around my dad. He doesn't talk a lot, and he always says what he means. It's quite restful to be around. He offered the money, I said thank you, and that was that. Or so I told myself.

My father, when he was a young man, also made his way largely by writing. This is not what he was raised to do. My dad's dad began life in the fur business in Montana. He came to Seattle in the 1920s and worked from the very bottom to the very top of a long-established fur company. My dad could have gone into his father's business and done very nicely. But instead he studied journalism and helped launch two public relations firms. He made a success of himself. I don't know if he felt a furious desire to prove himself, to show he could do it on his own. I know I did. I still do.

Having made its way up the lake, the rain began to fall on the houseboat. The drops hit the lake with plopping, circular precision. My father handed me a check, already made out, as though he'd known ahead of time what my answer would be. Though my husband usually did the banking, I deposited the check in our savings account on my way home. I used the drive-through. The kids squirmed in the backseat, demanding a treat.

Back at home, my husband came out to the porch to greet us. We got no farther than the door before I told him my news. "You're kidding," he said, with a big grin.

"Nope," I said. "You don't mind, do you?"

"Mind? Why would I mind?"

"Money from your father-in-law. It's not weird for you?"

"Believe me, I'm fine with it."

And then we wrote a thank-you note. Or at least I devoutly hope we did.

Upon further discussion that evening, we agreed that the money was to be spent on a new house and was therefore untouchable until we found something we liked. We also agreed we were too busy to house hunt right now, and so it would be a while before we used the money. Meanwhile, we swore to keep it intact. I suppose that was how it became the stash. Otherwise, it would've been plain old money.

The stash made me look at the world a little differently. For starters, it made me wonder who else had one. Our part of Seattle is filled with people leading unlikely lives: Fancily dressed people who hang about the café, drinking endless cups of coffee. People who play in rock bands and can't hold a job because they might have to go on tour. People who spend the day mulching. Clearly stash-holders all.

Dropping my daughter off at school, I looked with new eyes at the other parents. My daughter goes to a cooperative elementary school where the parents help in the classroom and do all the administrative, janitorial, and fund-raising work. Little in the school is store-bought. We parents knit, weave, cook, and build the materials the kids use in their lessons. It's like colonial fucking Williamsburg in that place.

No one at the school has a ton of money, or at least no one cares to look as if they have a ton of money. Rusting Subarus and old VW vans are much in evidence. Dressing up for the annual auction involves a lot of ironic thrift-shop finery. Our chosen luxury is time. We lead lives of enormous flexibility. Many of us are artists and musicians and writers. We work late from home so we can spend the day in the classroom pressing cider. Which of us, I wondered, had secret money?

One day I was babysitting for a friend, another parent at the school, who is the most frugal, simple-living recycler I know. He only shops at garage sales and thrift stores (though his wife occasionally sneaks out to IKEA). While the baby slept, I leafed through a photo album from my friend's childhood. It was like looking at photos from a Bouvier biography. There he was, about four years old, in English riding gear on a pony in front of his parents' mansion. There he was in prep school tie and blazer standing in front of a giant shingled "cottage." There he was with his Izod-clad parents.

Stash, I thought. But why did it feel like an indictment? Not just of my friend, but of myself?

Although it filled me with a vague sense of guilt, I liked to think about the money my father had given us. I lingered on it.

It seemed a naturally private thing, something that would not hold up well to the light of day or the rigors of general conversation. I worried what the other parents would think if they knew about it—somehow it felt like a secret advantage, as though I were taking steroids. The obscure sense of shame only made it all the more delicious. I even liked the name we'd given it: stash. It sounded like drugs. Good drugs, the kind you kept hidden away in an old Moroccan box at the back of your closet.

I wanted to take the money out of the bank and have a look at it, but my husband said no. He said, "Who are you? Scrooge Mc-Duck?"

In fact, the domestic sphere was growing a little fraught. Bruce was at work on a book, so we were living on a fixed income. Like old-age pensioners, but—clever us!—with dependents at home. We both seemed to work incessantly, but still money flowed out just as quickly as it came in, like a tide that never went entirely in or out but moved back and forth in a nervous-making, barely achieved stasis. The checks came in: big ones from magazines, smaller ones from newspapers, tiny ones from royalties and reprints. And the money went right back out, spent on the almost invisible expenses of family life: shock absorbers, swim lessons, doctor co-pays.

Maybe my dad sensed our straitened circumstances, I don't know. Once it came into our lives, though, the money he gave to us sat like a wet black solid rock underneath the flow. We didn't talk about it, but it was there, waiting. We tried to act like it didn't exist. We tried to pretend we didn't need it. But it sat there, and as our own money dwindled, the stash became almost a threat: What would happen if we withdrew some of it to pay the babysitter? Would it be like touching the third rail? It was one thing to get the stash and invest it in a house. It was another thing to simply spend it. If it got frittered away, we would be naked, exposed as spendthrifts.

One night I was out running errands while Bruce was paying the bills. When I came in the door and looked from his stricken face to the pile of bills sitting on the table, I felt as though I'd been out dancing, or smoking crack, or having an affair with a Spaniard. The checkbook dangled from his hand in a gesture that semaphored defeat. I suddenly felt guilty for all those expensive boxes of See's Candies I'd been buying. My husband went to the kitchen. He poured himself the grimmest bowl of cereal ever poured. He hunched over it, his beautiful long spine bent almost to an inverted U, and said, "I just have to say this. Our savings account is almost gone."

I tried to match my manner and my face to his, to look as though I, too, were very, very worried about this terrible spending of our savings. I vowed to curtail our budget. I constructed wild plans involving consignment shops. I vowed to seek more freelance work and cradled Bruce's rough head in my arms. I wasn't really worried, though—I had confidence in the stash. I could feel it underneath us, holding us up, in a way he could not. It somehow had become my personal property, a fabulous accessory not suitable for Bruce to wear.

And yet at the same time I felt obscurely that he with his persistent money worries was better than I.

I grew up in a leafy Seattle neighborhood and went to a fancy private school. Like many children who read a lot, I was full of angst about this situation and expressed it in the usual ways. In my teenage years my friends and I frequented the scuzzy, vaguely European coffeehouses of the University District, where I turned out to be highly susceptible to the angry, leather-jacketed men who hung around such establishments. They would tell me I was a spoiled trust fund baby, and I would give them my phone number.

The men were mad at me for having money, and I was mad at me for having money. Rage is the emotion of the powerless. To be a child is to experience rage. Certainly children of poverty are entitled to an infinitely vaster, more profound rage than the rest of us. But we all have reasons to feel powerless. To a child trying to break free from her parents, money feels like control. Even money that is freely given, with love and respect.

So I railed against my burgher family and wore shoes with holes in them. I volunteered at a radical collective bookstore and made my poor mom park the Volvo around the corner when she picked me up. Like some kind of beret-wearing robot, after senior year I trundled off to an expensive artsy college. Every student there had been the weirdest person in his or her high school senior class and intended to continue in that vein. The postcollege lives we envisioned for ourselves would be devoted to important work like smashing imperialism and going to punk rock shows. Money wasn't something we really talked about. Money would work itself out. The important thing was expressing yourself, and smoking. We might as well have been wearing velvet pouches filled with doubloons. Many of us, to be fair, have used our private, never-mentioned money well, becoming social workers and teachers. An inordinate number have pursued careers in modern dance.

The problem with having a stash—and believe me, no one who has a stash is about to give it up—is the sense of inauthenticity it confers. Your financial worth is unmoored from your actual achievement. I had felt this way as a young person. And so, unlike my husband, I knew just how to feel when my father gave us money. Entitled, and pissed off. Gratitude was in there, too, a hard, solid nut at the center.

When I first met my husband, we were both working as critics at an alternative weekly. I was movies and he was books, so he had the moral advantage right from the get-go. He stalked around the office with a fierce look on his face, daring anyone to talk to him. When you cornered him in his cubicle, he turned out to be a giggler. I liked the way he wrote, and I liked the way he admitted to wearing clothes his mother picked out for him. He had an air of self-contained riches, like if you stuck a shunt into him out would pour everything you ever needed. He was an extremely fast typist. I liked to watch his long wrists and big spatulate hands as he typed, typed, typed away.

One day we were sitting in the filthy armchairs in the editorial department, having one of those interesting-young-person conversations about what we dreamed of doing with our lives. I was excited, sitting across from this tall, serious person. I wanted very much to impress him. I went on and on about wanting to write an important literary novel (which, as we know, has never come to pass). When I was finally done, Bruce said, "I'd love to just make a living as a writer for the rest of my life."

Bruce didn't come from money. He came from a middle-class family—station wagon, ranch house, dog—with enough to get along but not enough to spend on young people going around acting silly. Meeting him was a shock. I'd never met anyone before who combined a serious work ethic and talent. Suddenly I saw I could be a writer without being a slacker, dilettante, or shirker. Before, being a writer had meant being a trust fund kid. Once I met Bruce, I saw it could mean supporting yourself and working hard.

I threw in my lot with him. I worked alongside Bruce for the next ten years or so, often literally side by side in our little backyard office. We bought a house, had kids (no joke with C-sections at $30,000 a pop), cared for them, even paid the heating bill, even socked some savings away—all with money we made ourselves. No help. No stash.

When we are children, we have the luxury of raging against all the stuff our parents give us. And then we grow up. In the spring, a few months after that stormy day on the houseboat, my father had a series of seizures. These were different from the heart attacks he'd been having for the past few years. During the seizures he would experience what he described as "20 percent loss of power," and then black out.

One sunny Monday morning, he went to see the neurologist. My three-year-old son, Willie, and I picked him up from the doctor. As we walked through the untrustworthy April sunshine to my car, my father told me that he'd been diagnosed with adult-onset epilepsy. The outlook was promising; there was an antiseizure medication for which he was an excellent candidate.

Our mood was good. After my family had endured years of his heart attacks, which were unpredictable and basically untreatable, here was something that could be controlled. We decided to go by his houseboat to pick up a snack, and then take Willie to the park since it was turning into such a pleasant day.

When we got to the houseboat, Willie asked his grandfather for something to drink, and we all three crowded into the tiny kitchen. Willie, who has a voice that might kindly be described as penetrating, insisted on his drink. My father closed his eyes in what I thought was a gesture of patience. He licked his lips, his tongue hanging out of his mouth a bit. He licked again, and once more. He began to pitch forward, right into my arms.

We stood there a moment, me and this person who suddenly wasn't my father. Mostly, I felt surprised—this just didn't seem like something my dad would do. He would never willingly surrender control of himself to another person, and he certainly wouldn't visit his weight upon his child. Then he began to slip from me.

Grappling with him like he was a gigantic baby I was about to diaper, one hand along his hips and one against his neck, I tried to lay him flat on his back. He's not a heavy man, but he's six foot two, and his head got away from me, smacking the floor with a sickening, hollow sound. I called 911 and heard the hysterical note in my own voice.

Time blinked, and the medics were there. Willie introduced himself to them. I located the medical notebook my father kept and gave it to the medics, and they took him away.

I don't know if I saved my father's life. Would he have cracked his head on the counter as he went down? Would he have woken up on his own? I don't know. But I do know that he, the king, would not want to deposit his life into anyone's hands, especially his daughter's. I know that he, a person whose idea of perfect happiness is to walk alone into the mountains, doesn't want that kind of help. And yet he took my gift of help with grace. He called me up a week after I caught him and told me that if there were a grocery store for daughters, he would pick me off the shelf. Coming from my father, this was a wildly emotional admission.

I never realized how uncomfortable—how angry—I was about my father's gift until the day I caught him in my arms. Even though he had been as clean and straight and agenda-free as possible about the money he gave me, I had still acted like a child. I thought his gift meant something—something parental. I thought it meant that he saw me and Bruce as failures. I never stopped to think that this might be merely my own perception, not his.

Now I realize that the least I could do was accept his gift with grace, the way he had accepted mine. Believe me, you never know how much you love your father—his wolfish shock of hair, his legs nearly as skinny as his arms, his rare smile—until you've held his dead weight in your arms. I'm his daughter; he's my father. We give each other what we can afford.

Not long after my father's fall, Bruce and I made some changes. After too many evenings of watching him grow despondent over the bills, I took over our finances. Now I organize the bills and make the financial decisions and set the budget, which under my regime allows for a lot of visits to See's Candies. And when I've toted up the balance sheets, I literally hide them from Bruce. He has no idea whether or not our savings are gone, or if there's any stash left, or if we're all headed for financial hell in a chocolate-laden handbasket.

Bruce, the most responsible man on earth, the smartest guy in the room, has become my princess, my teenage daughter, my darling ignoramus. Finally I'm the grown-up, and he gets to be the kid for a while. I don't think Bruce will ever feel the stash the way I do. I don't think he'll have that resentful, velvet feeling of excess, that feeling of not quite deserving what you have. I think you have to grow up with money to know that feeling.

The important thing is, at some point, just to get over it.

Money is neither morally good nor morally bad. It just is, and when you're lucky enough to have some, you ought to have the grace to be grateful. It took me a year of my life to learn this, a year when I lived with a stash in the bank. The money sat there untouched, like an ogre in a dungeon or a maiden in a tower. It might sit there still. It might not. No one knows except me.

The Perilous Dune

Jeanne McCulloch

When I was young, before I was old enough to lie about where I'd been the night before and how late I'd come home, the thing I lied about with frequency was my address. Not egregiously, but artfully. I would say very precisely, when asked, that I lived between Madison and Park avenues on Seventy-third Street in Manhattan, which, if I had been living in the courtyard of our apartment building on the Upper East Side, would have been correct. Certainly our kitchen, eighteen stories up, overlooked the courtyard, so why not claim it as my address? Nothing could have gotten me to admit to a stranger that in fact the entrance to the building was around the corner on Park Avenue, and that my family resided for twenty-five years in the duplex at the top. I was too afraid of what the immediate equation would be. Money. That inherited wealth could be a birthright, a genetic twist of fate as random as, say, long legs or big eyes, was a notion I distrusted. How much was real, and how much was illusion, and how might the perception of money make me different from anyone else? These were questions I considered uneasily as I lied about my address.

The unlikely source of my family's financial well-being was my father, whose day-to-day reality was to sit around our living room with his nose in a book and stacks of index cards in piles by his feet, studying foreign languages. By his death in 1983, he spoke as many as fourteen and had spent much of the time he wasn't in our living room traveling to use these languages in their native context. He was a quiet, patient man from Missouri whose grandfather had been in the right place at the right time and had become a multimillionaire utilities magnate in the early twentieth century. This was all lore by the time it was handed down to us, but for my father, already an older man when I came along, there was no shame that required lying about one's address, nor, for some reason, was there any shame in not making a salary. He happily settled back into the world of his words and ideas and index cards and gamely donned his tuxedo whenever my mother declared it was time for the next party.

Which, very often, she did. Early on I recognized that the smell of Chanel perfume in the hallway leading to the master bedroom meant a night on the town. I would tie my father's bow tie and help push the ebony studs into his dress shirt. He would pat a cigar into the pocket of his coat. My mother wore long, feathered ball gowns with a string of emeralds around her neck, and after she left, my sisters and I would collect the stray feathers that had fallen on the rug. It was all so grand, I thought. Sometimes as I fell asleep, I'd picture my parents waltzing, moving together with such grace and synchronicity it seemed they'd been dancing together forever.

This was in the late 1960s and early 1970s, when on the left-leaning side of Manhattan the sociopolitical maelstrom gave birth

to the limousine liberal, a breed of which my mother was a char-
ter member. By night, she may have been high-stepping it at the
Waldorf or the Colony Club in her ostrich-feather gown; when I
think of her by day in that era, she is disappearing into a hired
black limousine, her Hermès scarf tied neatly over her head, off to
Harlem to tutor young children at a neighborhood storefront twice
a week. In our family, as in many families then, we put on black
armbands and marched to save the planet, end the war, end poverty;
we marched for civil rights and women's rights, leafleted, picketed,
rode buses to Washington, D.C., to scream our heads off, yet no one
called attention to the fact that when all was said and done, and
everyone was off the bus, back in the gilded ballrooms of Manhattan, in true Gatsbyesque fashion, despite the times, the band
played on . . .

Not long after I was born, my father bought a long gray
shingled house on the beach on Long Island that stretched along
the sand dunes like a giant sleeping cat. He bought it so that despite
his endless pilgrimages in search of, say, a Masai warrior to practice
his Swahili with, or a Yugoslavian bartender with whom, over a few
drinks, he could hone his Serbo-Croatian, we would always have a
family home. So that by shaping sand into castles, spitting watermelon seeds down each other's shirts, and surf casting for bluefish
every Labor Day, we might grow roots. My mother named the
house after the street sign she erected in the driveway that first
summer, CHILDREN AT PLAY. Every August, when my four half siblings from my father's first marriage arrived with their children, it
was a giant slumber party in the house by the sea. We'd fall asleep
against a tumble of cousins in quilts to the steady refrain of waves
gliding along the shore, the adults at the dinner table downstairs

laughing, my father telling some off-color story, the moonlight out-side our bedroom spackling a silver route to the horizon. The last night of every summer, when we younger ones were allowed to eat with the adults, my mother would always make a toast to the "clan," as she called us, and from her seat at the head of the table she'd hurl her wineglass over her shoulder so it shattered against the mantel in infinitesimal slivers of crystal, always just narrowly missing the painting of the nude woman above. It was a violent, passionate act that made me convinced that amid the finger bowls, the candlelight, against the sound track of crashing waves, and in the tolerant, bemused presence of a uniformed butler named Fred, perhaps we were all slightly if not totally mad, and perhaps money, or more particularly the cushion that wealth provided, had made us so.

"We live on such a perilous dune," my mother would al-ways say as the August storm season approached. She would sit reading *The New York Times* on her end of the couch, her half-glasses in a slow slide down her nose, scrutinizing the weather re-port as the wind blew in audible moans and the sea bounded up toward our deck. She was a Florida girl, my mother, and to her hur-ricanes meant you filled all the bathtubs with water, put batteries in the radio and the flashlights, lit candles, opened wine, and ate everything in the freezer. "We live on such a perilous dune," she'd say, "this could all go"—and she'd snap her fingers—"like that."

I think now that she was speaking less on behalf of the weatherman and more in terms of the perils of fortune. In my mind I pictured us all: a giant ark, a floating mansion, drifting helplessly out to sea, scrambling for something to save. It ended up a perilous dune indeed, but not by any ministrations of nature, unless one counts the IRS as a natural disaster. After my mother died three years ago, taxes made it impossible for my sisters and I to keep the house by the sea. As fate would have it, the *l* fell off the street sign that very summer my mother died, and CHILDREN AT PLAY suddenly became what it suddenly was: CHILDREN AT PAY. As my father should have known, you can't sink roots in sand, that the family home he provided for his daughters would inevitably be washed away by the vicissitudes of inherited wealth. Only my mother, raised in hurricanes, foresaw the perilous *après-moi* truth.

The last summer, as we were packing up, we found my mother's ball gowns in a row of dusty garment boxes in one quiet corner of the attic. They were encased in thick plastic bags, the feathers flat, matted down over the years. The boxes smelled of mothballs. Late one night, braced by the spirit of nostalgia and red wine, my two sisters and I trudged up to the attic and bumped the boxes down two flights of stairs. Things forgotten came back: the black velvet with white ostrich around the neck was her favorite. Another was navy blue organdy with dyed blue feathers ringed at the wrists like muffs. What resulted from the sudden discovery was a spontaneous fashion show for our husbands, each of us taking turns doing exaggerated catwalk steps around the couches, littering feathers along the pale green carpet in our wake. In a video taken that night, the men are smoking cigars while my sisters and I, flushed and giddy, segue from one costume change to the next. Yet the mirth had a disdain to it that was at once murky and palpable, that such a costume would have been so much a part of the accepted pattern of our life, and that that life—the sheen, the glow, the mythic glamour—could pass from our hands so easily and definitively, and all we could do was watch. But what was it, really, that was passing? In truth, wearing a feathered ball gown, I discovered that night, is an uncomfortable sensation. The gown hangs heavily on the shoulders and makes a discordant swish as you labor the fabric across the room. Furthermore, the feathers tickle the cheeks. Simply putting on my mother's costume, smelling, vaguely, the stale whisper of her Chanel perfume, I calculated that this outfit, plus the teetering on high heels for an entire evening, could not have been as glamorous or regal as it was painful and tedious. On some of the white feathers, there were faint stains of her bright red lipstick. My mother always wore very, very red lipstick.

By the end of the night, the entire collection of dresses lay abandoned, collapsed like overspent party girls in a pile on the couch as we drank one more toast to the passing of time, and in the end I think my cousin's daughters, both in their early twenties, took a few back to college with them. "Good for a party maybe, get a laugh," one of them said, shrugging. The rest we took the next day to the local thrift store in exchange for a straightforward tax deduction. "Take it where you can get it," my youngest sister joked, loading the feathered gowns and my mother's entire prized Lilly Pulitzer collection into the back of her Jeep in a clump.

So money, what of it? There were beautiful times and there were terrible times, just as in any family. Does the beauty of a long gray shingled house by the sea, the bonfire lighting up the night sky on the beach every Fourth of July, the softly lit white tents where the grown-ups danced in midsummer, does the suggested postcard beauty of these scenes suggest the beautiful times were more beautiful for my family than for others, or the terrible times more terrible? One of my earliest memories is of when our neighbor, drunk, left his own beautiful house and swam into the sea because he didn't love his life despite his beautiful wife and beautiful kids and beautiful bank account. As the Coast Guard dragged his body out of the surf in front of our eyes, he wept that he had been saved, then swam out again and again until later that summer he finally swam out for keeps. Early on I understood that a mansion by the sea can just as easily be a jail cell as a dreamscape.

"The houses are all gone under the sea," T. S. Eliot wrote in one of the songs in *Four Quartets*. I thought of that line as we packed up that last summer, and of another of Eliot's, from *The Waste Land*: "These fragments I have shored against my ruins." The images of the house by the sea, the images of three young girls in matching dresses following their parents through a privileged childhood they could neither accurately explain nor accurately apologize for. "This was an amazing place to be a kid," I said aloud to my husband that last day.

"Amaze": "to fill with wonder." Also: "to bewilder." Beyond the sweet, gentle smell of the honeysuckle in the driveway, the high two-toned trill of the morning bobwhite, the cold watermelon seed shooting down a shirt, gleefully spit by a boy cousin all the girls in town admired, beyond all this inevitably there are other, darker memories: of my father leaving this house for the last time strapped to an ambulance stretcher following a fatal stroke, the strap a thin, final harness to our life; of my mother living on for twenty years in a grief that became a rage, her last summers spent alone in the house by the sea in a wheelchair, accompanied by a nurse, by occasional family and friends she no longer recognized but reflexively cursed, by the endless beat of the waves that just keep coming and coming.

"Don't talk about money," my mother had always warned. By which she meant: Don't ever talk about our money, the fact that we have money. Don't ever talk about it, because people may try to take advantage of you. Subtext: they won't see you for who you are, only for what you have.

This past summer I took my son, Sam, to a beach a few towns down from the house where I had grown up so he could Boogie-board. It was a late August day, the water warm, the sky dark blue in anticipation of autumn. The corn was lush and tall in every field we passed as we headed toward the public beach parking lot. For a while Sam flung himself through the surf, a buoyant puppy; then, when he was exhausted, he dragged his board out, and we stood together at the shore looking out at the view I had watched my whole life from the quilted bedroom at the top of the stairs in the house by the sea. The waves that just keep coming and coming and coming. Sam stared quietly for a while at the horizon as he caught his breath, then he turned to me with his gap-toothed smile, his eyes full of the sheer exuberance of wonder, and said, "Think about it, Mom. Infinity. Come on. I mean, you gotta love it."

Being almost nine, Sam likes to boggle his brain with big concepts like that. And I thought, So there it is. His legacy isn't about any cushion of wealth that's going to soften his ride. His legacy is infinity, the sense of infinite possibility. His possibilities, no less than mine, are as endless as the waves. They just keep coming and coming and coming. That is his ticket to ride.

Preexisting Condition

Jonathan Dee

I had a problem with my shoulder. It would pop out of its socket with little provocation—when I was taking off my shirt, say, or rolling over in bed—but within a few seconds I could coax the joint back together again, and with the help of a couple of aspirin everything went back to seeming as it should. If it happened in someone else's presence, I'd agree afterward that it was something I really ought to have taken care of; but since the ways in which such a thing might be taken care of were liable to be inconvenient and scary, I put it off.

Then one autumn evening in Central Park, while I was playing first base in a softball game, my shoulder dislocated in such a way that I couldn't get it back in quickly, or indeed at all, bringing everyone's enjoyment of the game to a terrible halt; when I started exhibiting signs of shock, a teammate flagged down a sympathetic guy in a Jeep who drove across the field to take me to the emergency room. On our way back to the pavement, he hit a deep rut in the field, which induced the bone to pop back into the socket, though not without a certain amount of screaming on my part.

So much for putting things off. I saw a doctor and described my symptoms. I expected lots of X-rays and MRIs to ensue, but instead he put his left palm flat on the back of his head, so that his elbow stuck out to the side, and said, "Do this." I gave him a look suggesting we both knew what would happen if I tried to do that. He nodded and scheduled my surgery for the following week.

At that point, I was working irregularly as a magazine freelancer. The insecurity of this life was mitigated by the fact that I had recently moved in with my girlfriend, who had a real job— "real" in the sense that she got a paycheck every two weeks, with taxes taken out of it, just like a regular grown-up. So if a month went by in which I made no money at all, we were safe, though not by much. As for health insurance, upon leaving my full-time job a year or so earlier, I had taken out a policy with some fly-by-night outfit in Chicago—one I'd never even heard of before I signed up, but when you're looking for coverage as a self-employed individual, you have little choice but to take what you can afford. I checked their list of authorized procedures, and this one (my surgeon had told me it was called an inferior capsular shift) was on it. Even so, out of pure paranoia, I called the HMO a few days before the surgery; I described the procedure to whoever answered the phone, and he reassured me that I was covered.

My shoulder was cut open, and the loose rotator cuff severed, tightened, and reattached. Three days in the hospital, another week or two in a Vicodin haze, six weeks total in a sling, three months of physical therapy. A cool scar. Then one day the following spring, while my girlfriend was at work, I picked up the mail downstairs; in it was a registered letter from my HMO informing me that after further review, they had reversed their earlier decision to pay the cost of my surgery. I had told my doctor that I had first noticed the weakness in my shoulder six months earlier (a lie, in fact; I had noticed it much longer ago than that). But sometime within those six months, I had been late with one of my insurance payments by more than the allotted ten days—which, according to my policy, restarted the clock in terms of what constituted a preexisting condition, for which they were not responsible.

The bill for the surgery was $14,000. There was a phone number at the bottom of the letter, which I called, but that devolved quickly into my shouting obscenities at the woman at the other end of the line, who hung up on me. Screaming at functionaries can be cathartic, but not this time. Red-faced, breathing too fast, I sat on the couch in my living room—a couch that my father and stepmother had given to me in lieu of throwing it out, a couch that, like almost all our furniture, was itself an emblem of the fundamental provisionality of my adulthood—stared out the open window, and allowed the gravity of what was happening to bear down on me.

Each one of my girlfriend's paychecks was like a trapeze—our safety depended on its appearance at the precise moment we reached out for it—but still, stressful as those days were, they had seemed like the beginning of something. We had joined our bank accounts at her suggestion. That she had to talk me into it wasn't a matter of my own bitter experience but just the opposite: after a decade of half commitments, one-timers, bad behavior, and a tendency to pine for the unavailable, this was the first serious relationship I had ever been in. Now she would be home from work in another four hours or so. I won't forget those four hours as long as I live.

Because it was the end of everything. We couldn't even begin to deal with a debt of those proportions, and it was my fault; knowing all the bullshit rules of an insurance policy was just another of those adult responsibilities to which I had proved unequal. It was a relief, in a way, to think that she would leave me, because at least that way the various practical hardships, and the consequent shame, wouldn't fall on her too. She wouldn't have to share my reduced circumstances, and I wouldn't have to bear her resenting me for them. I couldn't bring myself to call her at work and tell her what had happened, because at least this way we would be together, so to speak, for a little while longer. I dreaded her coming home that evening as I hadn't dreaded anything in my life since childhood. I felt so stupid for having been caught believing that adult life was characterized by progress rather than decay, when I didn't have to look any further than my own biography to know that wasn't true; and it was in line with everything I had ever learned that money was to be both the symptom and the instrument of my ruin, the Shiva of relationships, the destroyer of affections. Our apartment wasn't huge, but it was certainly the biggest one I'd ever paid rent on. It looked like a stage set to me now; I sat in it and waited for her to come home and learn what I knew.

My parents met while working at Time Inc. in the 1950s. My father was an advertising executive there, my mother a secretary. He had come to Time Inc. by way of a large Catholic family outside Boston, a stint in the Army in World War II, and Brown University. My mother arrived there via a childhood so byzantine and abusive that it would take another essay to describe it. Perhaps it will suffice to say that I was in my thirties before I learned that she was lying about being an only child. She had—may still have, for all she or I know—a brother and a sister, but such was her past that she could not move forward in life without cutting herself off that ruthlessly from every vestige of it.

Denial on that kind of epic scale works pretty well in the short term but rarely in the long. Soon after I was born, my mother was committed to a psychiatric hospital. (Years later, when I was about eleven, she and I went to see *One Flew over the Cuckoo's Nest* together; the scenes of Jack Nicholson receiving electroshock therapy sent my mother crying to the exit. I had no idea why, and she couldn't tell me.) She wasn't there for long, and under the care, as it happens, of the same Manhattan psychiatrist who was later revealed to be secretly treating Richard Nixon, she returned home to what was, economically speaking, a pretty bullish upper-middle-class life. My father made good money and was moving up in a rock-solid organization. He drank a lot, but in those days, and in that particular business culture, he would have called more attention to himself by being unwilling or unable to drink a lot. We even had a little weekend house in Connecticut, a brick two-bedroom cottage referred to by the locals as the potting shed because that was its original use back when most of the town had been one massive family estate. The small house and its large grounds, which still held the brick footprint of a huge dismantled greenhouse, had a calming effect on my mother, as they would have had on anyone, really; the flip side of this calm, though, was the anxiety that built in her every Sunday evening when the time came to leave the house behind and return to our apartment in the city. Finally she let it be known that she would prefer to live in the country full-time. My father, who was in over his head when it came to my mother's troubles and understandably anxious to do anything he could to avoid a collapse as bad as or worse than the last one, consented. This was in 1967, when I was five years old.

It was the beginning of the end for my family, but that wasn't immediately apparent—in fact, things got better for a while before they got worse. The potting shed was inadequate to the full-time needs of a family of four, so a new, much more modern wing was added to it. We were almost three hours from Manhattan, too far to commute every day, so my father took the train to the city every Monday morning and returned every Friday night; few of my childhood memories are as visually distinct as that of waiting in the station parking lot, in the warmth of our car, and staring into the pitch darkness, waiting for the train's headlight to emerge. He kept a pied-à-terre in the city, which my mother claims he used to conduct a long series of affairs. (She may be right about that; I'll never have any idea.) At some point he started coming home on Thursday nights instead of Fridays, which thrilled me. Then he started going in on Tuesday mornings. Then he set up an Olivetti typewriter on a desk in my parents' bedroom, and the whole rhythm of his weekday presence or absence became more improvisatory.

One night I had my best friend at the house for a sleepover. We were already in bed when my father came in to say good night to us. When the door closed behind him, my friend whispered to me excitedly, "He's drunk."

"No, he's not," I said. I wasn't trying to deny something I was ashamed of; I genuinely had no idea what he was talking about. Of course that's because I had no paternal good nights other than my own as a frame of reference; and he was drunk every night. Never abusive—in fact, if anything, I think it made him more openly affectionate—but the next morning he would frequently be described to me as "sick," and I'd be advised not to disturb him until later in the day when he felt better.

He was quietly fired from a series of jobs. Friends would try to throw some freelance work his way; the pied-à-terre gave way to the spare bedroom in a friend's house in Westchester. My mother, still a somewhat fragile character, went back to work as a secretary, first part-time and then full-time, though opportunities for secretarial work were sharply limited in an area rural enough that many of my schoolmates were farm kids. At one point she worked in the home of a local writer who was researching a gigantic tome about drugs. I remember her taking me there on days when I was too sick to go to school and she had no one else to leave me with; I would wander feverishly around this old man's home, his own children grown and gone, looking at the shelves full of mysterious books and government reports, the only sound in the house that of my mother's phenomenally speedy typing.

The situation at home wasn't great. But I honestly think my parents would have been willing to go on living that way indefinitely. They were no longer in love with each other; in fact they spent very little time together, but they would faithfully go to parties and other sorts of events at which they were expected to be present as a couple. Their marriage, for all its deficiencies, had turned as so many marriages do into the type of convenient, high-functioning partnership a friend of mine calls "running the family business." The real agent of decay in our lives was always, and unmistakably, money. It did the one thing it knew how to do—it ran out—and with it, gradually, went our ability to stand being around one another. I don't know which was worse—my mother's complete transparency on the subject or my father's feeling that it was something about which respectable people simply did not speak, which of course gave it an almost supernatural tinge in my eyes and made it seem that much more capricious and unappeasable.

My brother is seven years older than I, which made his lot, as things began to degenerate in a serious way, both easier and harder than mine. When, for example, the checks covering his modest college tuition began to bounce, he was old enough to see what was happening as the result of poor choices made by flawed people. He was able, in other words, to be angry at them, which was no fun for anyone, least of all for him. But I was still too young to connect the ebb of money with the pathologies of my mother and father themselves. In my mind, money was an element. You tracked its threatening movements carefully, but when the storm came, there was nothing you could do about it except brace yourself.

Four years after we moved in to it, we put our house up for sale. It's a measure of how dire things had become, and how quickly, that when it was sold we moved not in to a new home but in to the vacant summer home of friends of ours: that is, we had no plan beyond the next several months. Eventually we found a small rental closer to town, and there it was that my father came home one Friday night and told my mother, as they sat at the kitchen table talking in low voices so I wouldn't overhear them as I watched TV in the next room, that he had been fired again.

"I've had it," she said in a near whisper. "I can't hold everything together by myself anymore. Either you start bringing home more money, or get out."

"Okay," said my father. "I'll get out."

It wasn't the answer she was expecting. Now, with my brother away at college, she and I were officially on our own. It would have been pointless to ask for alimony from my father, but he was ordered by the judge to pay a modest amount of child support. Some months he came up with it, and some months he didn't. My mother did not bother to pretend that Armageddon was not at hand. She talked to me about it openly, and about my father's failings past and present, and while it's easy to say she should not have done that, even at the time I was sympathetic to the fact that she didn't really have anyone else to talk to. I internalized her panic very early. We didn't talk a lot about right and wrong in our house; when my mother told me she had quit her job because she'd discovered that her boss, a beloved, old small-town lawyer, was looting his clients' estates, I'm ashamed to remember how I let her have it for what she'd done to us.

We moved at least once a year for the next five years. Each place was a little smaller (except when we spent winters rent-free in friends' summerhouses—those tended to be pretty nice); each place constricted the area in which my mother and I were locked together. In winter there were discussions about heat and how we could make do with less of it. Items that I tended to run through quickly—sneakers, jeans, eyeglasses (which I had a penchant for breaking)—were replaced with the cheapest possible model. There was something—it's painful to say so—a little vindictive on her part when it came to some of these purchases. I was a twelve-year-old boy, eager to show, through whatever surface representations were available, that I was just like everyone else, but my mother was not about to help me pretend that this was true.

Just a few days ago I received an e-mail from someone I met at a conference last summer. One attendee had taken nine hundred snapshots of the gathering and posted them on the Internet, and this woman asked if I knew that whenever I smile for a camera, I don't open my mouth. I did know that. My teeth are quite crooked, to the point where the way they grew in altered the shape of my face. (When I was in my twenties, an orthodontist once offhandedly told me that my chin and the tip of my nose are too close together, a remark that kept me from asking anyone out on a date for months.) My childhood dentist prescribed braces, but the money wasn't there. It's not something I feel sorry for myself about, though the coda is upsetting; my daughter smiles back at me in the same lips-together fashion, and her teeth are perfect. Still, it's worth considering that money's withdrawal from our lives defined us so comprehensively that it even changed my face.

My father's gross income for the year following the divorce was just over $5,000—slightly less than the sum of his court-ordered child-support payments. An exchange of letters between my parents' lawyers argued the question of whether my mother's threats to sue my father for back child support might be mooted if I moved in with him in his apartment a few hours away, where the public schools were reputedly excellent. I should say that I learned these things by looking through a folder I had discovered my mother kept in a file cabinet in a storage room behind the kitchen. Everything I found in there pained me, but I couldn't stay away from it. A kind of secret dialogue was going on over my head, a dialogue in which my future was being decided, not by me, or even by my parents really, but by money. Its stubborn evanescence brought change, and change, I knew, was never for the better.

By then, my mother and I were getting on each other's nerves in a serious way—I resented her cheapness and her constant agitation, she resented my childish inability not only to see how bad things were but also to blame my father for them—and it came as a relief to both of us, I think, when I was awarded a scholarship to boarding school. I did not write or call home for my first month there, and one night, near the end of my freshman year, I called my home number for the first time in a long while and learned that it had been disconnected because my mother had moved. (I was able to call her at work the next day to find out what had happened and to learn my new address and phone number.) But by then, setbacks like that were starting to lose a little of their power over me. People think of prep schools as an orgy of status display, but in fact the atmosphere is downright socialist compared with the average suburban adolescence: everyone lives in identical dorm rooms, no one is allowed to have a car, everyone observes the social imperative to dress down as sloppily as possible. The strongest hint you got about the social realm a kid might occupy outside of school was his stereo—that was the only item on which people weren't embarrassed to get caught spending lots of money. In short, it was an excellent place to reinvent oneself, even if it was mostly just a matter of maintaining one's privacy. When my father nearly died, he had the courtesy to do so in the summer between my sophomore and junior years; I went back to school in the fall and never told anyone about it.

Boarding school might seem like an odd choice for a family without much money, but it's the richest schools that can offer the most financial aid, and Andover was very generous to me. My first year's tuition there was $500, and in four years it never rose above $1,000; still, my family could not pay it, and at least once the school simply waived the debt midyear rather than send me home. Not that my parents took that obligation lightly—far from it. There was always a heavy premium placed on education in my family, an emphasis on attending the best schools even when our finances suggested a more moderate approach. I used to think that this was a parable about social class—that my family had been founded on a certain premise about itself, about the sort of people we were, and that that premise survived even our obvious disqualification from the group to which we felt we belonged. But I see now that that's not it. My parents couldn't show a good face to the world anymore except through their kids. Elite schools, superior grades, these things didn't speak to the family's future—they were the bricks and mortar of the pretense that things were just fine right now.

I was always pretty complicit in this facade, though once, when I was in seventh grade, it had briefly cracked. On an ordinary Sunday night I had an English paper to write; English was my favorite subject, but for some reason I was blocked—I couldn't write it, and I couldn't write it, and it was due the next day, and when my mother told me it was time to go to bed, I told her that since I didn't have my English paper written, there was no way I could go to school the next day. She didn't take me seriously; why would she? But the next morning I refused to go, and the morning after that, and the next few mornings after that. I think my mother had enough experience with mental illness to have some idea what was going on, and to be scared by it. After a week of this, she took the day off from work and drove me in silence to see a child psychologist. The doctor talked to me alone for an hour, and then alone to my mother for a while after that. On the drive home she told me that the doctor had recommended I continue coming to see him, at least once a week, indefinitely. For once she didn't mention money; instead, she told me that she would leave the decision up to me. But I was old enough to know what was really at stake in a moment like that. It would have finished us. I told her I would be fine, and I returned to school the next day. If you want to think about mental health purely in economic terms, a little therapy back then might actually have saved me some money in the long run. But that's the thing about being poor; after a while, all your choices are short-term ones.

When I was in college, I met a girl who lived on Park Avenue in Manhattan. Her father was an alcoholic who had drunk away his savings, his job, his marriage, his home, but instead of sobering up or dying, he continued to free-fall until he reached the point where he was living on the street. This was when his daughter was a teenager. She would walk to her fancy private school via a number of different routes, but inevitably, every once in a while, her father would intercept her. He would greet her warmly, ask after her mother, and talk would turn to how sorry he was, how he planned to clean up soon. Then he would ask her for money. As a college student, this girl's salient characteristic was that she was one of those straight-A students who, a few days before an exam, would begin to freak out; she thought nothing of staying up three nights in a row, skipping meals in order to study, cutting off contact with her friends, boring her roommates to death with dire predictions of her own failure. Then she would get an A. She was terrorized by the standard of her own success. I haven't seen her in twenty years, and I hope and expect that she's figured out some things about herself, as most of us do when childhood is safely behind us; but at the time, she had no sense at all of the connection between these two phenomena, her groundless yet near-crippling anxiety about her grades and the story of her father. I understood it immediately. With each step up the ladder, the step beneath it disappeared, so that the higher she rose in life, the more vertiginous her position. The fall is incremental, but that doesn't mean it can be arrested. This girl felt in her marrow that she was one B-minus away from losing everything, and in the face of her experience who would be smug enough to tell her she was wrong? Her life was a series of false bottoms; no amount of money would ever be enough to make her feel safe from disaster.

I know how she felt. My relationship to money has been warped forever. I am an unpleasant combination of cheapskate and fatalist; I try my hardest to hold on to every dollar precisely because I feel money's irresistible will is to disappear. The next day's mail can always bring some catastrophe that will sweep it all away, and your closest affections with it.

So ten years later, as I paced through my darkening apartment, I wasn't panicking exactly, because I knew what would happen. I just wanted to get it over with so I could start to deal with whatever was to follow, whatever was beneath the life that was now giving way. The phone rang a few times, but I didn't answer it. Finally my girlfriend came home and found me sitting stricken in our one living room chair.

I told her what had happened. What I didn't say, but what was on the tip of my tongue the whole time, was that she shouldn't worry that I would be surprised or angry if she decided that this was not what she had signed on for. I understood that sometimes your job is to save yourself. She blanched a little when I told her how much money was involved. And I remember that what she said amazed me not because it was especially heroic or forgiving or graceful under pressure but because of the sheer, thrilling, promising *normality* of it:

"God," she said, "from the way you were acting, I thought someone was dead. We'll figure something out. It's just money. If this is the worst thing that ever happens to us, we're going to have a pretty happy life."

Reader, I married her. It took us five years to pay off that debt; the hospital and the anesthesiologist were pretty understanding, though the surgeon, unsurprisingly, was an absolute dick about it, responding to my requests to work out a payment schedule by turning my account over to a collection agency. But my wife was right. Worse things have happened to us.

About the Editors

Jenny Offill is the author of the novel *Last Things*, which was chosen as a notable or best book of the year by *The New York Times*, *The Village Voice*, the *Los Angeles Times*, and *The Guardian* (U.K.). It was also a finalist for the *Los Angeles Times*'s Art Seidenbaum Award for First Fiction in 2000. She is co-editor with Elissa Schappell of the anthology *The Friend Who Got Away*. Her fiction and nonfiction have been published in *Story*, *Epoch*, *Travel and Leisure*, and *The Washington Post*.

Elissa Schappell is the author of *Use Me*, a novel in stories, which was runner-up in 2001 for the Hemingway Foundation/PEN Award; a co-founder of the literary magazine *Tin House*; a contributing editor at *Vanity Fair*; and a frequent contributor to *The New York Times Book Review*. She is co-editor with Jenny Offill of the anthology *The Friend Who Got Away*. Her essays, interviews, and stories have been published in *The Paris Review*, *Spin*, *The "Mrs. Dalloway" Reader*, *Cooking and Stealing*, and *The Bitch in the House*.

Henry Alford has contributed to *The New York Times* and *Vanity Fair* for over a decade and to *The New Yorker* since 1998. He is the author of a humor collection, *Municipal Bondage*, and of an account of his misadventures in the acting trade, *Big Kiss*, which won a Thurber Prize.

Andy Behrman is a Los Angeles–based writer and the author of *Electroboy: A Memoir of Mania*, a chronicle of his battle with bipolar disorder published by Random House in 2002. The book is currently being adapted into a major motion picture. In addition, Behrman is a mental health advocate and speaks about his experiences with bipolar disorder. He has written for *The New York Times Magazine* and *New York* magazine.

Susan Choi is the author of the novels *The Foreign Student* and *American Woman*, which was a finalist for the 2004 Pulitzer Prize.

A sometime instructor of fiction in the creative writing program at Brooklyn College, she lives in Brooklyn with her husband, Pete Wells, and their ingenious son, Dexter.

Charles D'Ambrosio is the author of two collections of short stories, *The Point* and *The Dead Fish Museum*, as well as a book of essays, *Orphans.*

Claire Dederer has written about books and culture for *The New York Times*, *Newsday*, *The Nation*, *New York* magazine, and many other publications. She lives in Seattle with her husband, the writer Bruce Barcott, and their two children.

Jonathan Dee's four novels are *Palladio*, *St. Famous*, *The Liberty Campaign*, and *The Lover of History.* He is a staff writer for *The New York Times Magazine*, a frequent contributor to *Harper's*, and a former senior editor of *The Paris Review.* He teaches in the MFA programs at Columbia University and the New School.

Marian Fontana's book, *A Widow's Walk*, was published by Simon and Schuster in 2005. Her work has appeared in *Vanity Fair*, *The New Yorker*, and *Parenting.* She is currently president of the September 11th Families Association. She is also creating a two-person show for the stage and working on her second novel.

Daniel Handler is the author of the novels *The Basic Eight*, *Watch Your Mouth*, and *Adverbs*, and, as Lemony Snicket, a sequence of novels for children collectively titled A Series of Unfortunate Events. He lives in San Francisco with his wife and child.

Walter Kirn is a critic, journalist, and novelist who lives in Livingston, Montana. His most recent book is *Mission to America*, a novel.

Ruth Konigsberg is a contributing editor to *Glamour* and founder of womentk.com.

Fred Leebron, director of the MFA program in creative writing at Queens University of Charlotte, is a professor of English at Gettysburg College. His novels include *Six Figures*, *In the Middle of All This*, and *Out West*. He has received a Pushcart Prize, a Michener Award, a Stegner Fellowship, and an O. Henry Prize. He is co-editor of *Postmodern American Fiction: A Norton Anthology* and co-author of *Creating Fiction: A Writer's Companion*. His essays have been published in *Parenting*, *More*, and *Redbook*.

Brett Martin's work has appeared in *Vanity Fair*, *The New Yorker*, *Esquire*, *GQ*, *The New York Times*, and many other publications. He is a contributor to NPR's *This American Life*. He lives in Brooklyn.

Jill McCorkle is the author of seven books, five of which have been named a *New York Times* Notable Book of the Year. Winner of the New England Book Award, the John Dos Passos Prize for Literature, and the North Carolina Award for Literature, she has taught writing at the University of North Carolina, Bennington College, Tufts University, and Harvard. She currently teaches at NC State.

Jeanne McCulloch is a former editor of *The Paris Review* and *Tin House* and the founding editorial director of Tin House Books. Her work has appeared in *Vogue, Elle, The Paris Review, Tin House*, and *The New York Times Book Review*, among other publications.

Lydia Millet is the author of five novels, including *My Happy Life*, which won the 2003 PEN USA Award for Fiction, and, most recently, *Oh Pure and Radiant Heart*.

Meera Nair's debut collection, *Video*, received the Asian American Literary Award for Fiction in 2003 and was a *Washington Post* Best Book of the Year. Her work has appeared on NPR's *Selected Shorts*, as well as in *The Threepenny Review, Calyx, The New York Times*, the *National Post*, and the anthology of Asian-American writing *Charlie Chan Is Dead 2*, and on www.beliefnet.com. She is currently at work on her first novel, which will be published by Pantheon.

Chris Offutt is the author of *Kentucky Straight, Out of the Woods, The Good Brother, The Same River Twice*, and *No Heroes*. His stories and essays have been published in *Esquire, GQ, The New York Times, The Best American Short Stories*, and *New Stories from the South*. He is the recipient of a Lannan Literary Award, a Whiting Writers Award, a Guggenheim Fellowship, an NEA grant, and a literature award from the American Academy of Arts and Letters.

Kathryn Rhett is the author of *Near Breathing*, a memoir, and editor of the anthology *Survival Stories: Memoirs of Crisis*. She has published nonfiction and poetry in literary journals such as *Creative Nonfiction*, the *Harvard Review, Michigan Quarterly Review*, and *Ploughshares*, as well as personal essays in magazines such as *Real Simple*. She teaches creative writing at Gettysburg College and in the low-residency MFA program at Queens University of Charlotte.

Steven Rinehart is a software executive and the author of the story collection *Kick in the Head* and the novel *Built in a Day*. His fiction and nonfiction have appeared in *GQ*, *Harper's*, and other magazines and journals. He lives in Harlem, New York.

Isabel Rose is the author of the novel *The J.A.P. Chronicles* and has also written, produced, and starred in a play of the same name. Her debut album is forthcoming.

Tony Serra has been practicing law for over forty years and in 2003 was named Lawyer of the Year by the Criminal Trial Lawyers Association of Northern California. He has spent his life defending society's outcasts, including members of the Black Panthers, the Symbionese Liberation Army, and Earth First! His role in the *Chol Soo Lee* case was depicted in the film *True Believer*.

Felicia Sullivan is a New York–based writer with an MFA from Columbia University. She is a two-time Pushcart Prize nominee, and her work has been published in *Swink*, *Post Road*, *Mississippi Review*, *Pindeldyboz*, and *Publishers Weekly*, among other publications. Her memoir is forthcoming from Algonquin in 2007. She is the founder of the literary journal *Small Spiral Notebook*. Visit her Web site at www.feliciasullivan.com

This book was made possible by the generous
contributions of Rob Spillman, David Hirmes,
and the Brooklyn Writers Space.